The World of the Roosevelts

Published in cooperation with the Franklin and Eleanor Roosevelt Institute
Hyde Park, New York

General Editors:
William E. Leuchtenburg, William vanden Heuvel, and Douglas Brinkley

FDR AND HIS CONTEMPORARIES
Foreign Perceptions of an American President
Edited by Cornelis A. van Minnen and John F. Sears

NATO: THE FOUNDING OF THE ATLANTIC ALLIANCE AND THE INTEGRATION OF EUROPE
Edited by Francis H. Heller and John R. Gillingham

AMERICA UNBOUND
World War II and the Making of a Superpower
Edited by Warren F. Kimball

THE ORIGINS OF U.S. NUCLEAR STRATEGY, 1945–1953
Samuel R. Williamson, Jr. and Steven L. Rearden

AMERICAN DIPLOMATS IN THE NETHERLANDS, 1815–1850
Cornelis A. van Minnen

EISENHOWER, KENNEDY, AND THE UNITED STATES OF EUROPE
Pascaline Winand

ALLIES AT WAR
The Soviet, American, and British Experience, 1939–1945
Edited by David Reynolds, Warren F. Kimball, and A. O. Chubarian

THE ATLANTIC CHARTER
Edited by Douglas Brinkley and David R. Facey-Crowther

PEARL HARBOR REVISITED
Edited by Robert W. Love, Jr.

FDR AND THE HOLOCAUST
Edited by Verne W. Newton

THE UNITED STATES AND THE INTEGRATION OF EUROPE
Legacies of the Postwar Era
Edited by Francis H. Heller and John R. Gillingham

ADENAUER AND KENNEDY
A Study in German-American Relations
Frank A. Mayer

THEODORE ROOSEVELT AND THE BRITISH EMPIRE
A Study in Presidential Statecraft
William N. Tilchin

TARIFFS, TRADE AND EUROPEAN INTEGRATION, 1947–1957
From Study Group to Common Market
Wendy Asbeek Brusse

SUMNER WELLES
FDR's Global Strategist
A Biography by Benjamin Welles

THE NEW DEAL AND PUBLIC POLICY
Edited by Byron W. Daynes, William D. Pederson, and Michael P. Riccards

WORLD WAR II IN EUROPE
Edited by Charles F. Brower

FDR AND THE U.S. NAVY
Edward J. Marolda

THE SECOND QUEBEC CONFERENCE REVISITED
Edited by David B. Woolner

THEODORE ROOSEVELT, THE U.S. NAVY, AND THE SPANISH-AMERICAN WAR
Edited by Edward J. Marolda

FDR AND CIVIL AVIATION

FLYING STRONG, FLYING FREE

ALAN P. DOBSON

FDR AND CIVIL AVIATION
Copyright © Alan P. Dobson, 2011.

First published in 2011 by
PALGRAVE MACMILLAN®
in the United States—a division of St. Martin's Press LLC,
175 Fifth Avenue, New York, NY 10010.

Where this book is distributed in the UK, Europe and the rest of the world,
this is by Palgrave Macmillan, a division of Macmillan Publishers Limited,
registered in England, company number 785998, of Houndmills,
Basingstoke, Hampshire RG21 6XS.

Palgrave Macmillan is the global academic imprint of the above companies
and has companies and representatives throughout the world.

Palgrave® and Macmillan® are registered trademarks in the United States,
the United Kingdom, Europe and other countries.

ISBN: 978–0–230–10666–6

Library of Congress Cataloging-in-Publication Data

Dobson, Alan P.
    FDR and civil aviation : flying strong, flying free / Alan P. Dobson.
        p. cm.—(The world of the Roosevelts series)
    Includes bibliographical references.
    ISBN 978–0–230–10666–6
        1. Aeronautics and state—United States—History—20th century.
    2. Aeronautics, Commercial—Law and legislation—United States—
    History—20th century. 3. United States—Politics and government—
    1933–1945. 4. United States. Civil Aeronautics Administration—History.
    5. Roosevelt, Franklin D. (Franklin Delano), 1882–1945—Political and
    social views. I. Title. II. Series.

HE9803.A3D63 2011
387.70973′09043—dc22   2011012636

A catalogue record of the book is available from the British Library.

Design by Newgen Imaging Systems (P) Ltd., Chennai, India.

First edition: July 2011

10 9 8 7 6 5 4 3 2 1

Printed in the United States of America.

Contents

Preface

Dumas Malone wrote in his biography of Thomas Jefferson that "like Nebuchadnezzar, Jefferson never saw anything faster than a horse." For the 2,400 years between those two men, humans traveled by horse and sailing vessels—nothing faster. Today we fly all round the world at speeds approaching and exceeding that of sound without giving it a second thought, beyond schedules and rising airfares. Air cargo has revolutionized commerce, and air warfare has revolutionized battle, all within the one hundred years since the Wright brothers made their flight. The nineteenth-century communications revolution that moved people, goods, and ideas at the speed of steam gave way to radio waves and combustion engines. Then pistons gave way to jets, and the world got amazingly smaller. Comparing the significance of historical events is always apples and oranges, but surely the impact of the development of commercial aviation during the twentieth century is as great, perhaps greater, than dropping atomic bombs or the Yalta agreements.

High politics fascinates us all. The dramatic interplay of great leaders, conflicts of ideologies, the wars and confrontations of the twentieth century all sell books and capture the public imagination. And well they should. Somehow, commercial aviation—arguably more important than military aviation, though they are hard to separate—gets lost in a slot labeled history of technology or business. It is the ignored revolution in a world transfixed by revolution.

Much of the world we know in the early twenty-first century took initial shape during the disruptive Second World War. Institutions such as the United Nations Organization, the European Union, the World Bank, and the IMF all developed during and/or immediately after the war. The Great Depression that melded into war brought new energy to attempts by national governments, great and small, to regulate matters that affected a nation's well-being, particularly, the economy. Commercial aviation was no exception.

At war's end only two nations had the equipment and experience on hand to expand their investment in and concern for commercial aviation. Great Britain had its far-flung empire of commerce, a stronger (and, time would demonstrate, longer-lasting) empire than the one held together by politics and power. But it had no cash. The United States not only had the cash but, with Franklin Roosevelt as president, had a leadership committed to internationalism, in commerce as well as politics. Moreover, it had a history of collaboration between the national government and the private sector, today's populist conservative rhetoric to the contrary notwithstanding. However much capitalization of U.S. civil aviation came from the private sector, the federal government's promotion of civil aviation played a crucial role.

There is no better example of the internationalization of the New Deal than the commercial aviation agreements (and nonagreements). Sometimes Roosevelt's spoor is hard to find. Confronted by insularity, by protectionism, and by nationalism, he managed—sometimes indirectly—the creation of an amazing world that allows us to have breakfast at Brennan's in New Orleans and dinner at the Atrium in New Delhi the same day. More importantly, it allows entrepreneurs to conduct face-to-face business on the same schedule. But it was high politics that allowed the commercial air revolution to take place.

From the outset of his presidency, FDR sought to free up commercial aviation from the barriers to travel and trade that choked off communications. He spoke of free ports, both for information and for trade. He supported the American airline industry in general and Juan Trippe and Pan American Airways in particular. That airline became the "chosen instrument" for the expansion of U.S. prestige and interests into South America and the Caribbean. But FDR never forgot his classic internationalist economic liberalism. Whatever the short-term requirements of depression, war, and politics, he consistently returned to the classic American form of resupinate mercantilism. In good part, that stemmed from American tradition going back to the founding of the nation.

The English colonies in America had been developed, for the most part, as trading enterprises. Commerce in agricultural produce and raw materials allowed the colonials to buy manufactured goods and to prosper. When England tried to restrict that commerce so as to maximize profits for its merchants (and taxes for the Crown), American colonials responded angrily. Whatever the myriad causes of the American Revolution, "restraint of trade" was key. In order to survive and prosper, the new nation, with a relatively small population compared with the European states, had to construct a combination of beliefs and strategies that legitimized international trade in a world of empires where foreign trade was restricted. After all, the argument went among Europeans, one could not *create* wealth, so long-term prosperity called for all the wealth to be kept within the empire. The American founders stood that argument on its head, claiming that the entire world was legitimately the nation's trading partner. To close off international trade was immoral. That doctrine, call it palindromic or resupinate (both more elegant than ass-over-teacups) mercantilism, was not always followed as the United States went from a precarious existence in 1783 to superpower status two centuries later, but it became and remained an embedded national tenet, an unquestioned premise, however inconvenient.[1]

But even a century and one-half later, as the Second World War was ending, those concepts ran into entrenched opposition from the British government, which feared the loss of control and profits if it had to compete directly with the more powerful Americans. As Winston Churchill put it to Roosevelt during the civil aviation negotiations: "I have never advocated competitive 'bigness'...between our two countries in their present state of development. You will have the greatest navy in the world. You will have, I hope, the greatest air force. You will have the greatest trade. You have all the gold."[2]

Americans, caught up today in the either-or polemics of free markets versus government regulation for progressive as well as economic reasons, may find in commercial aviation an example of the benefits of compromise over what advocates claim are principles but often seem simply political. The British, currently walking a tightrope between Europe and Atlanticism, may find a different lesson: Are the benefits of freedom of the seas (and the airways) greater or less than the benefits of the new European nationalism?

WARREN F. KIMBALL
Rutgers University (emeritus)

ACKNOWLEDGMENTS

I WOULD LIKE TO RECORD MY GRATITUDE TO THE CARNEGIE FOUNDATION, Scotland, the Franklin and Eleanor Roosevelt Institute, and the British Academy for travel and subsistence grants that made the research for this book possible and to the University of Dundee for sabbatical leave in 2009, which enabled much of the book to be written.

CHAPTER 1

INTRODUCTION: TWO CHALLENGES— ROOSEVELT AND CIVIL AVIATION

> But the airplane flies over national boundaries and from one country into the heart of another. Thus the development of the skyways of the world has created a new international problem, that of the freedom of the air.
>
> Sir Frederick Handley Page[1]

THE TWENTIETH CENTURY WILL BE REMEMBERED AS THE AMERICAN Century and as the age of manned flight, among other things: in no other human endeavor was more progress made than in conquering the skies.[2] This was not just about technological successes; it was also about harnessing them for commercial purposes. The world was transformed between December 17, 1903, when the Wright brothers made the breakthrough in powered flight, and the end of the twentieth century, when over four million passengers a year crossed the Atlantic: quite a change, quite an achievement. It is in the consummation of civil aviation's triumph that the American Century and the age of manned flight merge, because no other nation has been as dominant in civil aviation as the United States, and the president that made much of that possible was Franklin Delano Roosevelt.

Roosevelt presided over America's emerging dominance in civil aviation and consolidated its position, guaranteeing its supremacy for over half a century. Whether it was the kind of supremacy he imagined, however, is something that needs more interrogating than has hitherto happened. In the 1930s he helped mobilize the reform of the regulatory framework of the U.S. domestic airline system, and he strove to create a new and liberal multilateral international civil aviation regime for the postwar world. In 1944, when most of the nations of the world assembled to address the problem of international aviation, his multilateral vision was only partially realized, but his ideas continued to resonate, U.S. airlines flourished after the war, and the world was transformed. In 1946, American and British airlines were only allowed two round-trip flights a week. And the planes that they flew were not jumbo jets. But, as ideas championed by Roosevelt gained currency and effect, British and American and other countries' airlines crisscrossed the oceans much more frequently. By the end of the century there were hordes of passengers crossing the Atlantic crammed into jumbo jets, and in March 2007, the European Union and the United States reached an agreement on the first stage of an Open Aviation Area that aims to deliver a common airline market for the North Atlantic region. This would allow airlines to operate largely free from politically required regulation and become just like any other commercial enterprise and that certainly reflects many of Roosevelt's ideas. According to one expert assessment, this could increase annual transatlantic passenger numbers from four million to eleven million: something of a contrast with the state of civil aviation affairs in 1946 and an even starker contrast with 1903, when man first began successful powered flight.[3] Evidence of just how important Roosevelt's legacy was in this transformation will be considered in due course.

   Throughout, this study addresses three problem clusters. The first concerns Roosevelt himself. What understanding did he have and how did his ideas develop about civil aviation? What exactly were his ambitions and which policies did he promote in order to try to achieve them? How deep was his interest and actual commitment? An anecdotal response to the last question might be to point out that throughout the Second World War there was no more abrasive and ill-tempered exchange between Roosevelt and British Prime Minister Winston Churchill than those concerning the postwar international aviation regime, but generally speaking, answering these questions more substantially will not be easy.[4] Part of the difficulty arises because Roosevelt and his policies are notoriously difficult to pin down. Not only did he refuse to keep an official record of his deliberations, but he had an almost limitless ability to reinvent progressive policies, shift their trajectory, and change their emphasis. In this, he was an archetypical Liberal.[5] The second problem cluster concerns the domestic U.S. civil aviation industry. What was it actually like in 1933? How did Roosevelt see it and what were the domestic factors with which he had to contend in order to shape successful and politically acceptable policies? The third concerns the international civil aviation regime. How was it configured when he came into office? What problems did it pose? How did they interweave with U.S. domestic factors, and how and why did Roosevelt attempt to transform it?

Ultimately, the argument developed here is that Franklin Roosevelt was a decisive actor in the development of both U.S. domestic and international civil aviation and that in the specific policies that he failed to achieve in the international realm he nevertheless bequeathed an important legacy for the future. Over the years he developed a sophisticated understanding of the industry's needs and crafted policies that would meet them in a way that promoted freedom in the global marketplace in a manner compatible with his enlightened view of American commercial and national defense interests. However, his early interventions in the industry were controversial, at times ill-judged and complicated, because they were interwoven with broader issues to do with administrative reform. Furthermore, like everyone else, he confronted challenges of an entirely new industry with its unique needs and problems. No one had automatic answers or ready policies and Roosevelt too had to feel his way. The result of all this is that only a rather opaque picture has emerged of Roosevelt's part in the development of civil aviation. His role in designing policy has been generally overlooked or, when it has received attention, misunderstood. Lloyd Welch Pogue, Roosevelt's chairman of the U.S. Civil Aeronautics Board (CAB) 1942–46, remarked in an interview in 2000: "Well, the trouble with Roosevelt on aviation was he just didn't know what he was doing."[6] As Pogue was highly knowledgeable about aviation and an extremely able administrator and policy-maker, his judgment is not a good augury for someone with the ambition to write a book premised on the idea that Roosevelt was singularly important in developing U.S. domestic and international aviation regimes. However, as the narrative unfolds, evidence will emerge that challenges and indeed overturns Pogue's judgment. Even so, the very fact that such an astute man as Pogue misread Roosevelt directs us toward a significant and broader problem. When trying to explain any facet of Roosevelt's wonderfully rich and expansive political career, puzzles, enigmas, and their wrapping together come to mind. The fact is that it was quite common for even Roosevelt's closest advisers to be puzzled by precisely what the president was after and what his main strategy for achieving it might be.[7] The main challenge here is not to unravel the large-scale puzzles and enigmas that were Franklin Roosevelt, but to focus on discovering what he thought about civil aviation policy and what he did to nurture and expand it, first at home and then abroad. In doing that some modest contribution might be made to clarifying the broader picture.

Roosevelt contributed crucially to civil aviation policies during a period of domestic reform between 1933 and 1941 and then during planning for a postwar international regime between 1941 and 1945. He undoubtedly drew on a rich store of experience and ideas when developing his thoughts about this complex industry. However, there are three sources that seem particularly significant: naval strategic doctrine, freedom as a likely model for commercial practice, and his ability to grasp spatial dimensions. His strategic considerations owed much to the writings of Alfred Thayer Mahan, the great naval strategist. According to his mother, he pored over Mahan's *History of Sea Power* to the point that he knew it by heart and he told his wife, Eleanor, that it was "most illuminating."[8] Other things contributed to how Roosevelt grasped the world geopolitically, but Mahan was undoubtedly a key influence, and this is important as Roosevelt always saw civil aviation bedded in the wider context of America's strategic defense needs. Working in tandem with his strategic appreciation, Roosevelt was guided in his broad commercial vision by Grotius's ideas about freedom of the seas, and he hoped to transpose that doctrine into the field of air communication.[9] Just as freedom of the seas for commercial enterprise had developed within the context of Grotius's legal principles in the nineteenth century, so would commercial civil aviation in the twentieth. Freedom was a rare constant in Roosevelt's often inscrutable thinking. He dramatically laid out his famous four freedoms in his annual message to Congress on January 6, 1941: the freedoms of expression and religion and freedoms from want and fear. With British prime minister Winston Churchill at Placentia Bay, Newfoundland, in August 1941, he affirmed similar principles in the Atlantic Charter, which specifically called for freedom of the seas and nondiscriminatory access to trade and commerce. Time and again Roosevelt favored freedom. He successively supported Secretary of State Cordell Hull's Reciprocal Trade Agreements' program and wartime plans for an International Trade Organization for the progressive reduction of tariffs and an end to discrimination; the designs of Treasury Secretary Henry Morgenthau and his adviser Harry Dexter White for freely convertible currencies stabilized through the International Monetary Fund; and freedom of information. In preparatory talks for meetings with British foreign secretary Anthony Eden in March 1943, Roosevelt "talked a great deal on [the]...subject of a United Nations news service. He believed that there should be what he called 'Free Ports of Information' established at strategic points around the world, so that there would be no area wherein the people could be denied access by totalitarian censorship to the same news that was available to all other people."[10] Freedom was unquestionably a leitmotif in his thinking.

The third signpost to his thinking about commercial aviation is his startling ability to grasp and remember spatial dimensions. Roosevelt had a wonderfully detailed knowledge and love of the world's geography, witnessed to by the huge fifty-inch globe he kept in his office, and he thought in truly global terms.

> His was not just a situational awareness, a feeling for local conditions. It was a spatial imagination on a grand scale, an ability to conceive of the larger

dynamics of things and to anticipate their movement, nearby and also far away. His was truly a kind of projective-imaginative genius.[11]

This extraordinary global perspective along with strategic thinking derived from Mahan and his commitment to commercial freedom informed his vision of the future of aviation.

Roosevelt abided by general principles but often changed his ideas on specific policies to deal with difficult contingencies.[12] He was preeminently a practical man.[13] He thus changed his views in adapting to specific circumstances on some aviation issues, for example on administrative reform of the industry and on government part-ownership of airlines, but somewhat surprisingly, given rapid developments and powerful competing priorities, he was fairly consistent in both the general and particular of policy matters. This was not easy, as he juggled with competing interests and advice both at home and later abroad that invoked issues of fair competition and the benefits of chosen instruments (government-favored companies), the needs of safety, obligations to protect vested interests, the need for appropriate means of governance, imperatives of national security, and the dictates of national pride. Indeed, much of this book will interrogate how these priorities jostled for place in aviation policy.

Any signposts indicating how Roosevelt thought about and devised policies are welcome tools when trying to make sense of this complex man, but they are doubly welcome when dealing with such a difficult area as civil aviation: it is one of the most complicated of all commercial activities. As the twentieth century progressed, it became clear that aviation had the potential to "shrink the world," opening up new possibilities, not only for commercial and military strategies, but also for the spread of culture, ideas, and freedoms. But, before it could do any of those things, civil aviation confronted a series of problems, novel for a commercial enterprise, which had to be overcome before it could expand. If anyone for a moment doubts the claim that civil aviation had unique problems then one illustration might suffice to convince them. A recent study posed the question: *Who Owns the Sky?* This is not a fatuous query, and some kind of answer had to be given before commercial operations could be confidently embarked upon. At the start of the twentieth century the prevailing legal view was *cujus est solum ejus est usque ad coleum*: he who owns the soil owns up to the sky. It was because of this and the possibility of trespass that some thought that the "promise of air travel might never be realized because pilots would have to pay for the privilege of using the airspace of all the landowners below."[14] This was a problem and a unique one, but it gave way to common sense and the pressure of commerce. In a benchmark case before the Supreme Court of the United States in 1946, the court effectively decided that airplanes could freely overfly land, but not at the expense of inflicting direct damage on landowners below.[15] People did not want their safety, peace, and quiet to be overly challenged from the air. Neither did people want cutthroat competition that could both commercially undermine an industry so dependent upon capital investment and compromise safety standards that might endanger passengers in the air and the general public below. On all these counts government would be required to intervene to establish infrastructure and a workable form of regulation for the industry, and once airlines sought foreign markets, further needs and complications arose.

Civil aviation has operated at the interface of economics and politics ever since the formal establishment of national sovereignty over airspace in 1919.[16] This dictated that the operation of any international route between two states had to be agreed upon between the parties involved in what was usually a complex exchange of politically determined commercial rights.[17] With commercial aviation compromised by aspects of security, national prestige, and safety and public service factors, the result was a plethora of government regulations that controlled prices; imposed cabotage (the reservation of domestic flights for a state's own national airlines); restricted market entry, frequency, and capacity of flights; and insisted on national ownership and control of airlines. At issue, particularly for international services, was how to cut or, at least, loosen the Gordian knot that tied sovereignty to the airline industry. Until that was done, the marketplace would remain fragmented and the playing field competitively uneven as governments supported and subsidized national airlines and restricted the operation of foreign companies. Furthermore, strategic and defense considerations were always important when addressing the health and welfare of a country's civilian airline industry and this was no different in the United States. But while civilian and military aviation generally fed off each other—for example in research and development—and were seen as inextricably entwined in national security, at the same time their requirements also often conflicted (for airspace or for routes over sensitive military areas). All these issues posed intractable problems for policy-makers in their attempts to create an efficient commercial airline system that also met noncommercial imperatives dictated by strategic defense needs, safety standards, and the changing vagaries of political fashion.

Such complexities impacted on policy-makers, including Roosevelt, and forced compromises and accommodations. His commitment to the principle of freedom thankfully provides us with a valuable signpost for the direction in which his policies were to lead the civil aviation industry, and where possible he believed it should indeed be followed, but abuses of the marketplace and national security would also have to be pragmatically taken into account. His natural inclination was curbed by the need to nurture a viable, coherent, and safe industry that would service national transportation requirements of the traveling public and bolster defense needs. The regime, which emerged under the aegis of the CAB in 1940, was tightly regulated, but Roosevelt's default position was always to favor a freer and more open system. In the international sphere he sought a freedom that would allow the development of international routes and enable U.S. airlines to compete with their foreign counterparts, which meant formulating new policies. Not only was the international system more of a challenge than the domestic because of the sovereign airspace of others, American policy-makers would have to work out just how open and competitive they wanted the system to be and how far they could go in persuading other nations, and particularly the British who controlled vast swathes of airspace because of their empire, commonwealth, and client states, into accepting their proposals. Americans could not play this game alone. How Roosevelt perceived of these problems and what he proposed as solutions are central themes of this study.

It is widely and well known that the United States led the way in powered flight. On December 17, 1903, Wilbur and Orville Wright were the first to fly a man-carrying powered airplane in sustained flight, and by January 1914 the first scheduled air service in the world began between Tampa and St. Petersburg in Florida. But then, something happened that is not widely recognized: the United States ceased to be the world's aviation pioneer and became an onlooker and a would-be emulator. Americans still notched up some firsts: on May 15, 1918, the first regular airmail service began between Washington and New York, and on March 3, 1919, William E. Boeing and Edward Hubbard flew the first international airmail route between Seattle and Vancouver.[18] Notwithstanding these successes, the First World War had by then snatched away America's early civil aviation lead as production in Europe was fuelled by a war urgency that led to remarkable advances in airplane technology. Nothing illustrates this better than the facts that after the United States entered the war in 1917, the first combat plane to enter production and the only one to be mass produced by American industry was the British de Havilland DH 4. It was also the only American-built plane to operate over enemy territory during the war. After 1918 the situation deteriorated even more with the United States slipping further behind its European counterparts.

Up to 1927, although hundreds of thousands of Europeans had done so, practically nobody in the United States had traveled by air. In all the country there were but thirty airliners, all together holding seats for no more than two hundred passengers. Despite expectations, there had been no aviation boom in the land of the Wright brothers after World War I.[19]

"It was by...—borrowing from others already well advanced in aeronautics—that American aviation technology 'caught up' with the rest of the world after a decade of under-funded neglect."[20] In fact this borrowing was by no means the only factor that helped propel the United States back into the lead in civil aviation.

After the end of the war the United States lagged behind its European counterparts, and a particular constellation of factors helped perpetuate that state of affairs for nigh on a decade. The U.S. Army Air Service shrank from 190,000 enlisted officers and men in 1918 to 27,000 by June 1919 as the country was sucked back into Isolationism. What might have provided a dynamic for change and development was not to be.[21] In the civilian arena, unlike in continental Europe, the United States' railway system remained intact, which did not encourage the development of a new and still risky form of transport. Neither did the United States have a vast empire which needed tying closer together by the development of fast air routes. And finally, capitalist orthodoxy and a desire for "normalcy" prejudiced the chances of government subsidies for a new industry. The result was that by the mid-twenties the United States lacked both military airpower and significant commercial capability.[22] U.S. airlines in total were carrying less than 6,000 passengers a year. Then, after 1925, things changed dramatically. Government awoke to the needs of the airlines. Between May 1927 and October 1929 nearly $1 billion flooded into the industry. By 1929 the United States had overtaken Germany, the European leader in air passenger traffic. In 1930 U.S. airlines carried more passengers than the rest of the world put together, and by 1933, the year Franklin Roosevelt entered the White House, U.S. airlines carried 550,000 passengers, just short of a hundred times more than they had barely eight years earlier.[23] Not just America, but the world was on the cusp of a massive qualitative change in the commercial airline business, but before examining what Roosevelt made of all this and how he responded to the situation, we must first explore in more detail how the remarkable changes came about in the U.S. civil aviation industry that he inherited.

CHAPTER 2

ROOSEVELT'S INHERITANCE

"...incompetent, criminally negligent and almost treasonable."[1]
Brigadier General Billy Mitchell on government and
air defense shortcomings: September 1925.

U.S. CIVIL AVIATION EMERGED IN THE SECOND HALF OF THE 1920S from the doldrums that it had settled in after the First World War. It then soon recaptured world leadership. This transformation molded it into a form and modus operandi, which, while by no means set in stone, nevertheless indicated the character and likely needs of the industry. And it was with this state of affairs that Roosevelt had to engage when he came into office. U.S. civil aviation was still an infant industry, but had already disclosed wayward behavior and its specific needs. There were strong political, defense, economic, and corporate forces at play with vested interests established and ambitions to pursue. The challenges of the industry, in other words, began to appear in clearer and complex form as 1933 approached.

The three key developments in this period were the introduction of government funding; improved infrastructure; and a raised profile among the general public and in government. In 1925 new airmail contracts provided increased funds; the following year the government-appointed Morrow Board recommended that the government should provide the necessary infrastructure for a national system of air lanes; and in 1927 Charles Lindberg made the first solo nonstop flight across the Atlantic. Other factors also lifted aviation's profile, notably the rise of Pan American World Airways to commercial dominance on America's overseas air lanes, but Lindbergh's feat more than anything else was an iconic moment that captured the imagination of the American people and helped to lay the foundations for a massive increase in popularity, interest, and investment. Such popularity and interest were most effectively exploited by Juan Terry Trippe, the head of Pan American, who expanded his airlines' operations across the Western Hemisphere and then most spectacularly all across the vast Pacific Ocean.

These were all key developments, but it was also vital to have facilitators for growth in both government and industry. Government help came primarily in the form of Herbert Hoover, secretary of commerce 1921–28 and president 1929–33. He provided government support that enabled the industry to exploit opportunities and develop policies that nurtured growth in civil aviation.[2] Hoover was convinced of the need for a national aviation policy and strove hard to create one. But, of course, all this would have been to no avail without the first generation of great pioneering entrepreneurs such as Trippe, and W. A. Harriman and C. M. Keys, who ran corporate predecessors of such celebrated airlines as American, Eastern, and Transcontinental, and Western, which later became Trans World Airlines (TWA) in 1950.[3] These entrepreneurs seized on the opportunities afforded by the system of airmail contracts to expand U.S. civil aviation.

THE IMPACT OF AIRMAIL CONTRACTS

Without government funding for aviation, not even the business acumen of Trippe could help the industry make headway. Eventually help arrived. Sponsored by Representative Clyde Kelly, chairman of the House Post Office Committee, HR 7064 was enacted into law on February 2 as the Air Mail (Kelly) Act of 1925. It authorized the postmaster general to award airmail contracts to private airlines and set the rates that were effectively levels of government financial support for the new industry. On June 3, 1926, the Kelly Act was amended and the rates were raised. Contractors were now to be paid $3 per pound weight of mail for the first 1,000 miles of carriage and 30 cents for each additional hundred miles thereafter. The rates were increased again the following year and aviation flourished. In 1928 Kelly introduced the Foreign Air Mail Act, many of the provisions of which had been influenced by Trippe and some of his business associates, who were, fortuitously, from Pittsburgh, Kelly's home town. The Foreign Air Mail Act extended the lucrative system of payments to overseas routes, and Pan American took full advantage.[4] It was the introduction of airmail contracts that provided the financial boost airlines needed to prosper, and would-be aviation tycoons such as Trippe grasped them eagerly.

Trippe was like a seventeenth-century buccaneer and a nineteenth-century commercial empire builder rolled into one. He was astute, ruthless, and well-connected. He came not from the richest of the lavishly rich, but was sufficiently well-heeled to move among the preeminent successes of the world of business and banking. As a student at Yale he linked with powerful bankers and commercial tycoons of the likes of the Mellons, Whitneys, Bruces, Vanderbilts, and Morgans. He married Betty Stettinius and into wealth in 1928: her father, among other things, had been a partner in the J. P. Morgan Bank and her brother, Edward, was chairman of U.S. Steel and later a senior official in the State Department during the war and for a brief period secretary of state. Trippe also had friends in Congress, most notably Owen Brewster, often referred to as the "senator from Pan Am." All these connections were important, but it was the way that Trippe exploited them, combined with his own drive and vision, that made him the dominant pioneer of U.S. international aviation and a figure to be reckoned with even by President Franklin D. Roosevelt.

Introduced to aviation as a navy pilot in World War I, Trippe returned to his studies at Yale when peace came. After graduation, he gained business experience working as a bond salesman for Lee, Higginson, and Company, but bored and yearning for the excitement that came with flying, he soon embarked upon what was initially an unsuccessful career in commercial aviation. However, Trippe crucially realized that the industry needed franchises and ideally exclusive ones and an injection of funds for it to thrive, and he immediately recognized the importance of the Kelly Act for the airlines.[5] Eventually, from the early contract awards, emerged United, American, TWA, and Eastern Airlines. They dominated the domestic market until the 1970s; in the international sphere Pan American did likewise.[6] The contracts were also symptomatic of what became commonplace, namely, close cooperation and mutual interpenetration of airlines and government, something that would become particularly distinctive of airlines that operated foreign routes. Of the five contracts initially awarded, the New York–Boston route went to Trippe and Colonial Airways. Ironically, he was soon ousted from the board for being too ambitious for fleet expansion. Undeterred and still determined to succeed, he managed to attract further financial backing for airline ventures, and most importantly of all, he bought out Pan American Airways in October 1927. Pan American had been created by senior members of the Army Air Service led by Henry "Hap" Arnold in order to try to ensure that the United States had a successful overseas operator that could preempt foreign airlines on strategically important routes.[7] By 1927 Trippe's focus had switched fully to the potential of foreign routes reaching into the Caribbean and Central and South America, and the acquisition of Pan American was crucial. It enabled him to acquire his first overseas airmail contract. Operating from Key West, Florida, to Havana, his airline was just in time for the extension of the Kelly airmail system into the international sphere. This was the beginning for Pan American, and other international airmail contracts soon followed.

Trippe learned much from these early days that abided throughout his career. In particular he sought to dominate any market he entered: monopoly of American presence was his objective. To achieve that often meant close cooperation or, at least, acquiescence of the U.S. government, which in turn meant astute politicking and diplomacy and at times serving the strategic interests of government in order to ensure favored treatment. When confronted with powerfully backed competitors such as Imperial Airways of Britain, it also often meant company-to-company collusion as well. At the same time Trippe felt he generally needed a degree of commercial freedom in order to deal effectively with other foreign competitors, and that was not always easy to reconcile with government policy. To his critics Trippe's policies seemed predatory and monopolistic and reliant upon unjustified government support, but Trippe had a different perspective. He had not only to provide services that could compete with foreign state-owned and subsidized airlines but also to create operational infrastructure, meteorological, and navigational aids for many of Pan American's routes. These were the kinds of things that the U.S. government provided as a matter of course after the Morrow Board in 1926 for U.S. domestic airlines, but the massive capital outlay for overseas routes came mainly from Pan American's own coffers. Those investments, so far as Trippe was concerned, needed to be protected, hence his obsession with monopolizing U.S. overseas air routes. It is the story of the rise of Pan American and Trippe's designs for guarding its de facto monopoly that sheds much light on the challenges that confronted Roosevelt and his ambition to give new direction to civil aviation. In one sense Pan American's story is atypical, because it specialized in developing foreign routes, but in other ways it epitomizes the regulatory, political, and strategic challenges that civil aviation in general posed for government.

Airmail contracts boosted the rate of expansion of U.S. airlines to a staggeringly high level, but serious constraints on the domestic system's efficient and profitable functioning remained. The key problem was the route configuration that had grown up haphazardly and was utterly Byzantine in its complexity.

> Theoretically, a passenger could travel from New York to El Paso by American Airways. But this involved, first a trip due north up the Hudson as far as Albany...; then along the Mohawk Valley to Cleveland (Colonial Western); on to Fort Worth (Universal); and finally to El Paso (Southern Air Transport). The Southern Pacific Railroad did the honors for the last part of the route into Los Angeles.[8]

When Herbert Hoover moved from Commerce to the White House in 1929, he and his postmaster general, Walter F. Brown, determined to reorganize both the route system and the airlines. President Hoover gave notice of changes to come in a press conference in October 1929 saying that the

Post Office was trying to devise "some form of rate structure for the air-mail service. Hitherto, as you know, the routes have been let by competitive bid, and a great many distortions have grown up as the art has made progress."[9] Brown's plan for ironing out those distortions was to encourage the emergence of a nationally integrated route system based on three or four major airlines that would be larger, more efficient, and more profitable. This opened up a huge can of worms that has never been fully resealed. Brown's aims of larger, more efficient, and more profitable airlines in the public and national interest compromised competition. His strategy was to manipulate the award of mail contracts through new legislative authority, which he received through the passage of the McNary-Watres Act of 1930, sponsored by Representative Laurence H. Watres of Pennsylvania.

> The Postmaster General is authorized to award contracts for the transportation of air mail by aircraft between such points as he may designate to the lowest responsible bidder at fixed rate per mile for definite weight space....
>
> The Postmaster General, when in his judgment the public interest will be promoted thereby, he may make any extensions or consolidations of rates which are now or may hereafter be established.[10]

This conferred huge discretionary powers upon the postmaster general, and he proceeded to exercise them vigorously in what later became known as the "spoils conference" to rationalize the industry by privileging existing airmail carriers and encouraging their growth. There soon emerged from this what later became the domestic megacarriers: Eastern, TWA, United, and American Airlines. Total airmail miles flown by the industry increased dramatically from 10,200, in 1929 to 35,900 in 1932–33. Airmail costs per mile to the government decreased from $1.26 to $0.26. And passenger numbers rose from 165,000 in 1929 to over 550,000 in 1933.[11] On foreign routes Pan American emerged as the industry leader and soon acquired its de facto monopoly by ruthless expansion and as a result of favored treatment from government, though, as we shall see, that did not involve taking part in the "spoils conference" system.

The result of all this was that the United States rapidly retrieved its world leadership in civil aviation lost to its European counterparts during the First World War and in the decade that followed. The phenomenal growth on both U.S. domestic and foreign routes in themselves would have posed challenges for Roosevelt, but there were aspects that emerged in the way the industry developed that raised questions that went beyond those that might arise for purely commercial enterprises. Many of these issues took on sharper focus in the deliberations and consequences of the Morrow Board.

THE MORROW BOARD, HOOVER, AND THE NEED FOR A
NATIONAL AVIATION POLICY

Before becoming president, Herbert Hoover served as secretary of commerce under the successive presidencies of Warren Harding and Calvin Coolidge, 1921–28. He worked hard to improve the department's performance and prioritized close cooperation between government and industry to encourage new enterprise and expand America's commercial reach abroad.[12] The U.S. civil aviation industry was embraced by this sense of priority, and from the outset he sought to develop a national policy, but success did not come readily. Early attempts to strengthen aviation failed, but Hoover was undeterred and continued to pour his considerable energy into the cause. He was a man of faith and believed in aviation's future and moreover that it was important for national defense. While Congress remained inactive, he followed his own convictions and tried to bring different parts of the industry together to consider safety and standards issues. He had some success, but in the end it was the Morrow Board that provided him with his most effective platform for reaching out and influencing not only Congress but also the general public. It really made things happen.[13]

The Morrow Board was spawned by a confluence of rather different but connected politically controversial developments all concerned with fears about the United States lagging behind other countries in aviation. Many attributed this to the federal government's failure "to provide machinery to encourage and regulate the use of aircraft in commerce."[14] In particular there was growing anxiety among and criticism from members of the Army Air Service. These criticisms were the most vituperative from Brigadier General William "Billy" Mitchell. A First World War hero and leader of the American expeditionary air force in France, he was a man fully committed to the importance of airpower. He admired the way that Great Britain had established an independent service with the Royal Air Force, but actually wanted to go farther in the United States and create a Department of the Air under his control that would take authority over both military and civilian aviation. This idea of military control inflamed opinion and resulted in strong opposition from members of Congress and the airlines and almost everyone else who wanted to see civil aviation flourish. The Morrow Board Report later damned the idea: "The union of civil and military air activities would breed distrust in every region to which our commercial aviation sought extension."[15] Mitchell was his own worst enemy with his volatile and intemperate personality and addiction to courting publicity. During the 1924 presidential election campaign and on into 1925 before congressional committees and from other public platforms, he continued to harangue the administration.

It had little impact on the electoral fortunes of Calvin Coolidge, the Republican candidate for the presidency: Coolidge won with an overwhelming majority, but Mitchell had certainly stirred things up. The Lassiter Board followed by the House of Representatives' Lampert Committee both criticized the government, and in December 1925 there were cries for the creation of an independent air force. That same year the great philanthropist Daniel Guggenheim donated $500,000 to New York University to speed up the development of aerial navigation. In the following year "Guggenheims," stipends given to aeronautical engineering departments to promote research, began, and during the 1930s some ten universities benefited. There was now more awareness and concern about aviation and America's poor performance. In the light of all this and at Hoover's urgings, Coolidge thought it prudent to appoint the Morrow Board in June 1925 as the best means of examining how to develop and apply aircraft in national defense, but it was also meant as a sop to critics such as Mitchell. However, Mitchell, cushioned by private wealth and unconcerned about consequences, continued his criticisms unabated. In the end an exasperated Coolidge authorized proceedings against him and he was duly court-martialed in 1926, but by then the Morrow Board had taken its course.

Dwight Morrow, future father-in-law of Charles Lindbergh, held extensive hearings and was presented with information and recommendations from a wide range of people and organizations, none more influential than Herbert Hoover in his testimony on behalf of the Commerce Department. Ironically, while the Morrow Board was convened specifically to address concerns about defense, it did far more for the future of the civilian sector. Hoover argued that the needs of the industry were comparable to those of waterborne commerce, and just as government had helped maritime commerce, so it ought to help air commerce. "The Department of Commerce has been confident these last two years that the development of the flying art has reached a point where it is near the possibility of self-supporting application to commercial transportation in the United States." He went on: "In this belief we have advocated the creation of a Bureau of Civil Aviation that the Government might undertake to give services to commercial aviation comparable with those which the Government has over a century given to commercial navigation."[16] The bureau would regulate technical and safety standards and license pilots. This was the first of three main demands that Hoover made. The second was that the system of mail contracts should be enlarged, and third, that the United States should develop a national system of airways, navigational infrastructure, and airports with funding for these developments provided by federal, state, and municipal government.

The fact was, and continued to be so, that civil aviation was just too important to be left to the vagaries of the marketplace. Bottom line after

1926 was always that American civil aviation had to flourish, and if that meant subsidies, then so be it. But rather characteristically of American general attitudes toward the marketplace, there was resistance to recognizing this reality. Hoover insisted that subsidies should only be a temporary measure, and the Morrow Board emphasized that the infrastructure developments proposed would involve indirect and not direct subsidies of the kind that many foreign airlines received and that were "un-American." "Un-American" direct subsidies may well have been, but, if they were, they were nevertheless going to be provided in America through airmail contracts. The whole issue of government financial support—direct or indirect—and regulation of pricing in the industry were later to become huge issues, and their handling has not always been accurately explained. Objective judgment would probably have to describe some of the resolutions eventually arrived at as "un-American."

Hoover's justification for subsidies and huge government expenditure on infrastructure was largely in terms of commercial payoffs from a well-established and thriving civil aviation industry. However, he had another line of argument, which connected strongly with defense—the original motor behind the creation of the Morrow Board.

> I need not emphasize the importance of commercial aviation as an arm of defense. While it is not possible that the actual commercial plane will be much use in actual battle, yet the building up of the manufacturing industry behind such aviation is of the most vital importance. And we must develop the airways across our own country...for purposes of defense.[17]

In 1939 if anyone had cared to comment on the now discredited Hoover, they might have noted his common-sense prescience, at least here. From the outset, civil aviation always involved defense and strategic as well as commercial considerations, and it still continues to do so. Research and development and manufacturing capacity are probably the two most important factors, but there are more specific ones as well such as the U.S. Civil Reserve Air Fleet, which provides uplift capacity from civilian airlines for transporting troops abroad in times of crisis. The interface between civil and military aviation was another huge issue that complicated the development of civil aviation.

The board recommended that a Bureau of Air Navigation under an additional assistant secretary of commerce should be established with broad regulatory authority and the wherewithal to develop infrastructure, that the system of airmail contracts should be expanded, and that encouragement should be provided to air manufacturers. Largely reflecting the convictions of Hoover, the board justified its demands in both commercial and defense terms.

> Progress in civil aviation is to be desired of and for itself. Moreover, aside from the direct benefits which such progress may be expected to bring us in our peace-time life, commercial aeronautic activity can be of real importance in its effect on national defense. It creates a reservoir of highly skilled pilots and ground personnel. Whatever is done to increase the use of aircraft, to expand familiarity with aircraft among people, and in general to develop "air mindedness" will make it easier rapidly to build up an expanded air power if an emergency arises.[18]

All this energized the Congress to pass the 1926 Air Commerce Act, and the Air Corps Act of July 2, 1926. The latter changed the nomenclature from Air Service to Air Corps and provided for its expansion over the following five years.

> Appropriations for aircraft began to rise, as did negotiated contracts authorizing experimental aircraft. These appropriations and the system of negotiated contracts allowed the aircraft industry to avoid many of the deleterious effects of the Great Depression that began in 1929.[19]

At the end of the five-year period, U.S. expenditure on military aviation had risen by 140 percent, albeit from a very low base, and the Air Corps' force level stood at 14,650 personnel and over 1,600 aircraft. Aviation defense issues, however, were only partially and rather ineffectually addressed by the changes wrought by the Morrow Board. Military aircraft and flying capability were soon left way behind by civilian aviation, and this was to be tragically exposed in 1934.

In accordance with the Air Commerce Act, the Commerce Department now became empowered to regulate and nurture civil aviation. William P. McCracken Jr. became the first federal aviation regulator as assistant secretary of commerce for aeronautics. This was a major institutional step forward, but its substantive impact was limited and regulation remained rudimentary for another decade. McCracken had powers to license pilots, grant airworthiness certificates for aircraft, and help provide infrastructure in terms of navigation and communication and the development of airways. The industry gained new shape and direction as a result of both federal and municipal government action and expenditure. Among other things, this helped to erode suspicions of a skeptical public that traveling by air was unviable and unsafe. Above all else, however, the main consequences of the Morrow Board and the Air Commerce Act and later amendments were not in governance but in increased funding through airmail contracts and direct investment in infrastructure. The 1929 air-expenditure estimate of the U.S. federal government was 125 percent above the 1925 level and stood at $145 million. In addition, there were also large expenditures by state and municipal governments. For example, the Commerce Department estimated that when the 890 projected airports were completed in the United States and their capital expenditure added to that already expended on the 726 existing airports, the total would be around $200 million. Most of this money came from local not federal sources.[20]

In the current age of widespread firsthand familiarity with mass air travel, it is not easy to grasp what it might have been like before all this came to pass: but it was very, very different. A feel for just how different and how dramatic these changes were comes from a flurry of court cases that arose in the United States as airports appeared like a rash across America and flying increased exponentially. The 1926 Air Commerce Act established the right of interstate travel through airspace above a minimum height prescribed by the Commerce Department, but this still left a number of uncertainties to plague the infant industry. It was not until the 1938 Civil Aeronautics Act, for example, that it was confirmed that the public right of freedom of transit extended to intrastate as well as interstate traffic. There were also plenty of people ready to challenge these rights. When Atlanta's first airport, Candler Field, was opened in 1927, Clovis Thrasher, who lived nearby, sued the city for nuisance and overflight trespass. During the case before the Georgia Supreme Court, Justice Bell slipped into philosophical musings: "What is the sky? Who can tell where it begins or define its meaning in the law? When can it be said that a plane is above the sky or below it?" In the end the court decided that so long as nothing had been built to impede things, aircraft could fly through available space. However, the Georgia legislature subsequently passed the Uniform State Law for Aeronautics, which stipulated that overflights below fifty feet were trespass and effectively overturned the decision in the Thrasher Case. Gradually it became accepted that flights were permissible provided that they were not too low and did not damage those who owned the land below.[21] But it was not until the case of *United States v. Causby* in 1946 that the threat of trespass was lifted on low flights.[22] The only recourse for those below flight paths now was to prove that they suffered some actual harm as a direct result. Among other things, this brief detour into rather arcane legal cases demonstrates just how novel flying was in the 1920s and 1930s and how important it was to raise its profile.

PROFILE

There were two important aspects to the profile of civil aviation in the United States in the 1920s and early 1930s: one was public and had obvious implications for developing the market; the second was to do with the way government in the United States perceived of the importance of civil aviation abroad and in particular its potential for affecting strategy and defense.

Between May 20 and 21, 1927, Charles Lindbergh made the first solo nonstop flight across the Atlantic in the *Spirit of St. Louis,* a single-engine Ryan monoplane. He flew from Long Island, New York, to Paris, covering 3,610 miles at an average speed of just over 107 miles an hour, and the journey took him thirty-three hours and thirty-nine minutes.[23] He became a national hero overnight and popularized what was still frequently referred to as "the art of flying." One scholar has gone so far as to claim that Lindbergh was one of the two men to usher the United States into the air era, the other one being Dwight Morrow.[24] It is difficult to assess the precise impact that Lindbergh had because other important developments such as the Kelly Air Mail Act and the consequences of the Morrow Board were all bringing important changes to the industry, but there is no doubt that the rise in civil aviation's profile received a massive boost as a result of his achievement. It may very well have influenced the choice of transport to the Democratic National Convention in Chicago by the party's nominee for President Franklin D. Roosevelt five years later. Well before that, though, the achievement of the solo flight across the Atlantic and Lindbergh himself were both used by Juan Trippe to boost the profile and hence the fortunes of Pan American. The progress of his airline rode in tandem with mounting concerns about the possible consequences for U.S. national strategic and defense interests and brought the company and government into a close if often troubled relationship.

Latin America was there for the exploiting by civil aviation, but in the decade after the First World War with the United States falling further and further behind the European airline industries and with Britain and France preoccupied with developing imperial routes, it was left largely to Germany to take advantage of the situation. By 1927, when U.S. airlines finally began to pick up, Germany was entrenched with Lloyd Aéreo Boliviano in Bolivia, Condor and Varig in Brazil, and Sociedad Colombo-Alemana de Transportes Aéreo (SCADTA) in Colombia. All prompted concern for the United States military, but particularly the focus was on SCADTA, which operated near the Panama Canal, which was the main security concern of the United States in the Western Hemisphere in the interwar period.[25]

The U.S. government was always wary about the vulnerability of the canal, so crucial to its ability to concentrate naval forces in either the Atlantic or the Pacific. When Captain Peter Paul von Bauer, the head of SCADTA, approached Washington in 1926 for landing rights in the United States to complete a route from Bogota via Barranquilla, "Hap" Arnold, the future commanding general of the Army Air Force 1941–44, and already a senior officer in the Army Air Corps, got wind of it and expressed his dismay in no uncertain terms to the U.S. postmaster general. He argued against granting anything to SCADTA and proposed instead that a U.S. airline should be formed to operate routes to South America. The airline he and other like-minded colleagues sponsored was Pan American. In the meantime his argument proved persuasive and von Bauer was denied landing rights.[26] With the situation in Europe unsettled, the decision to prioritize security over the Panama Canal looked prudent, but matters were also fluid as Pan American under Trippe's tutelage made rapid progress in Latin America.

Between 1927 and 1933 Pan American emerged as America's dominant overseas carrier and occasioned renewed attention to the state of the international aviation regime. Trippe had helped influence Clyde Kelly regarding the substance of the 1928 Foreign Air Mail Act, and after a faltering start, like his domestic counterparts, he rode to commercial success on the back of airmail income. He expanded his route system quickly by taking over local airlines, extending Pan American's reach across the subcontinent, and as it went, mail revenue brought huge profits. He made successful mail contract bids on routes to the Panama Canal Zone and to Mexico, and by 1929 Pan American's airmail revenue exceeded $2 million. The following year, while Pan American still only carried a modest number of passengers, less than 7,000, it had a guaranteed income of $4 million from mail carriage.[27]

Trippe's grand strategy was easy to discern: it had three important tactics. First, care was taken to nurture good relations with government. This was important for securing airmail contracts and also for help in handling foreign governments to obtain favorable operating rights. One of the main dilemmas facing private airlines was the diplomatic job of negotiating with foreign governments, and while Pan American had much success in doing so, most notably with Portugal in developing the southern transatlantic route, the backing and sometimes the diplomatic skills and political pressures that the State Department could wield were invaluable. Second, Trippe had the vision and the commercial courage to commission route surveys, to develop radio-assisted navigation, and to invest deeply in new design for technologically advanced airplanes.[28] In 1965, in what was to become his largest investment in technological development and his final bequest to the airline industry before his retirement, he negotiated the specifications with Boeing for what became the Boeing 747 jumbo jet. Third, Trippe set out to dominate and in the end monopolize U.S. international routes. In pursuit of that objective, he sought to expand Pan American's reach rapidly by buying over twenty airlines, mainly in South America, and entering into partnership with the W. R. Grace Shipping Lines to form Pan-American Grace Airways (Panagra). With this expansion and his well-connected political base in Washington, he was able to sweep the decks on foreign mail contracts. And this was far from being uncongenial to the U.S. government of the day. The government had become nervous about the development of foreign and usually heavily subsidized airlines in Latin America, particularly in proximity to the Panama Canal, and wanted U.S. airlines to be able to compete with them. This was the main motive for the passage of the 1928 Act. It was not a huge jump to move from those concerns to the idea of a "chosen instrument" status for Pan American. In short, for strategic and security reasons, Pan American would be built up with government support to become a strong U.S. carrier to counteract the spread of operations by airlines under foreign ownership. This security concern had been brewing for some time and was to catapult the importance of civil aviation onto center stage, and in doing so it strengthened the working relationship between government and Pan American. There were several aspects to this intermeshing. First of all there was the question of the structure within which airlines operated in the international sphere: whatever it might be it was always likely to bring the airlines and government into close relationships. In fact the Pan American Convention on Commercial Aviation that convened in Havana in 1928 was the first attempt to construct something in the Western Hemisphere. At the time, no international agreement applied, partly because the United States had never ratified the Paris 1919 Convention Relating to the Regulation of Air Navigation, which provided rudimentary governance over aviation for most of Europe. President Coolidge dignified the Havana proceedings by addressing its opening session on January 15. The outcome of the conference was the Havana Convention signed by twenty-one American countries and later ratified by eleven, including the United States. Havana followed the Paris Convention regarding the principle of air sovereignty: "The High Contracting Parties recognize that every Power has complete and exclusive control of the air space above its territory."[29] Otherwise, however, it fell somewhat short of the achievements of 1919.[30] Even so the Havana Convention placed further onus on the U.S. government to ensure that it had a viable policy to cope with the opportunities that beckoned.

Another aspect that has already been noted was the 1928 Foreign Air Mail Act, which extended the same generous subsidies to overseas carriers that had been available domestically since 1925. It helped Pan American compete and counter the threat from foreign airlines operating in areas deemed strategically sensitive by the U.S. military.

A third kind of intermeshing with government came with Trippe's penetration of the Latin American market. One way of helping him to accomplish this was to employ the celebrity status of Charles Lindbergh. Pan American hired Lindberg, and he and Trippe toured South America together in September 1929 negotiating landing and other rights. It was such negotiations and their outcome that meshed with U.S. government concerns. Trippe extracted, wherever he could, extremely favorable terms through what came to be known as Form B Contracts. These were drawn up by Pan American's lawyers and stipulated that Pan American should be granted twenty-five-year franchises and the right to establish its own terminals in foreign countries; that it should be accorded customs and clearance privileges for its passengers and baggage; that it should be awarded exclusive airmail carriage contracts; and that it should be granted immunity as far as possible from local taxation. An additional stipulation was that flying and ground equipment should be bought in the United States.[31] These contracts were negotiated by the company, not by the State Department, but they benefited U.S. official policy in several ways. They advanced Pan American and drove away competitors, which was good for American commerce and for American security. They bolstered U.S. manufacturing and they avoided the United States having to grant reciprocal rights to other countries to fly into the United States because the agreements were private and commercial, not intergovernmental. Mutual benefit for both Pan American and the United States was thus achieved.

Finally, the most important development in terms of entangling the fortunes of the airlines and government arose both out of Trippe's plans for welding his operations more closely together in Latin America and from the U.S. government's growing fears of foreign airline operations. This was a complex development, which eventually made Pan American's operations of central concern to Washington and led directly to the U.S. government treating Pan American as a de facto chosen instrument.

A serious obstacle for Trippe was the fact that Colombia stood in the way of linking up the two arms of his operations in Latin America: Panagra on the west coast and Pan American in Central America and the east coast. There now took place a pincer movement to deal with this problem. Attitudes in Washington began to change and shift in favor of an agreement with Colombia. Several officials, and in particular Assistant Secretary of State Francis White saw new opportunities for the United States to exploit now that they had an airline that could compete and compete particularly with SCADTA. White became a significant and important supporter of Pan American's interests. The U.S. military also now reversed themselves. Arnold had helped Pan American enter South America, and he confessed that he could see much benefit if a U.S. airline could be the main link between North and South America. Negotiations on a bilateral air service agreement with Colombia were revisited with White leading the U.S. delegation. Matters proceeded satisfactorily, and on February 23, 1929, they were consummated in the Kellogg-Olaya Pact granting reciprocal landing rights. This was the first bilateral air service agreement made by the United States. Two years later Trippe moved to deal with SCADTA more directly in the second part of the pincer movement. In a secret deal with its owner, Von Bauer, in the spring of 1931, Trippe bought 84 percent of SCADTA's shares and took control, but left Von Bauer nominally in charge. The deal was kept secret for years from the Colombian government and only senior members of the State Department were informed.[32]

In retrospect it is clear that 1929 was an important turning point in the way the State Department, and hence the U.S. government, dealt with U.S. overseas air carriers. Up until then, while the industry had little profile or importance, the State Department had always adopted a stance of benevolent impartiality, but it now began to provide direct diplomatic support to U.S. airlines in their pursuit of operating rights and commercial advantages on international routes. That change was pushed along by the Post Office. In July 1929, Francis White considered a Post Office request that active diplomatic support be given to U.S. airlines and their overseas operations. He came out in support, largely because a hands-off policy might result in several weak U.S. overseas operators competing against one another with the net effect that they would all be damaged and weakened and then fall prey to heavily subsidized foreign competition. This would not only damage American commercial interests, it would also threaten the United States' security. U.S. mail should be carried in U.S. planes, and foreign airlines should be kept away from the Panama Canal and, ideally, from the whole Caribbean area. In a proposal that uncannily anticipated the reasoning of Walter F. Brown and the rationalization of the domestic route system, White suggested that the United States should have a chosen instrument policy, that is, Pan American should be given preferential treatment and rendered support by government. White's views did not necessarily entail delivering a monopoly to Pan American because he also spoke of supporting other U.S. airlines in the overseas passenger market, but Pan American was to be singled out for particularly favorable treatment as the current U.S. market leader. Any criticisms about discrimination that might arise could always be deflected, he said, by arguing that the mail contracts had been put up for competitive bidding and that Pan American had proved to be the only capable airline to come forward. In Cabinet on July 12 President Hoover agreed to the Post Office's request, but he entered the caveat that this new policy should not prevent support being given to other companies as well as to Pan American.[33] However, any qualms about Pan American developing a monopoly on U.S. overseas routes seem to have been suppressed later when Postmaster General Brown fully approved of a Pan American takeover of its only viable rival "New York, Rio, Buenos Aires Airlines" in August 1930.[34] Within a year of Roosevelt entering the White House, Pan American flew 55 percent of the total air miles flown in Latin America.[35] By 1937, while "a few foreign lines to Canada and Mexico... [were] conducted by other companies," on overseas routes Pan American held an effective monopoly.[36]

DRAWING IT ALL TOGETHER

In the depths of the Great Depression, precipitated by the Wall Street Crash in 1929 and with which the hapless Hoover was ill-equipped to cope, there emerged a somewhat unlikely ray of hope in the form of Franklin Delano Roosevelt. Successively New York Democrat senator, assistant secretary of the Navy during the First World War, presidential running mate in 1920, and governor of the State of New York since 1929, Roosevelt had progressed well politically. Even so, he was widely seen as something of a maverick and not entirely trustworthy, but he fought an impressive campaign for his party's presidential nomination in1932 and on July 1 the Democratic Party Convention in Chicago chose him as their presidential candidate.

As Roosevelt now moved ineluctably closer to entering the White House, what awaited him in the field of civil aviation? For many it was already plain that civil aviation had acquired a surprisingly broad raft of problem issues for such an infant industry and, notwithstanding the reforms that had occurred in the aftermath of the Morrow Board, that the regulatory and governmental framework that oversaw the airlines was still very basic. The Aeronautics Branch of the Commerce Department under McCracken was seriously challenged by a maze of intractable problems. These included the role of subsidies, the scope of government regulation, and the appropriate level of commercial competition. There was also the close relationship that had developed between airline operators, members of Congress, and government officials and the question of how those relationships should be managed. There was a palpable tension between public service and national interest on the one hand and commercial autonomy and self-interest on the other. There was also a problem with the system of vertical holding companies whereby airplane manufacturers owned most of the airlines as subsidiaries and dictated the aircraft that they bought. Altogether these problems begged questions as to whether the existing domestic airline regime and its system of governance were sufficiently robust.

The international sphere posed even more daunting challenges. The airline system there had little structure and that which did exist was not uniform. There were different conventions governing Europe and the Americas, and tentative attempts to try to reconcile their differences eventually crumbled away under the force of U.S. Isolationism. At the very point at which airlines were about to bridge the Atlantic, there were no common rules for their meeting, apart from provisions for accident compensation set by the Warsaw Convention. For international aviation to flourish a way had to be found to build some kind of order out of this chaos. There were already deep worries in the United States about foreign airlines—often heavily subsidized and able to draw on cheaper labor—and their operations from both the perspective of competition with U.S. airlines and security. In the midst of all this there were self-seeking corporate leaders such as Trippe who were already significant forces in their own right, and whose power bourgeoned as the airlines continued to grow commercially and as their strategic importance was emphasized by the deteriorating world situation. Was a monopoly on foreign routes the best way to deal with foreign competition and strategic challenges? Should Pan American continue to be the chosen instrument? How should Trippe be dealt with? How competitive should airlines be allowed or encouraged to be in the international sphere? Should the airlines negotiate with other governments for their operating rights, or should the State Department do this? What shape should an international regime take and how could it be established?

These were the kinds of questions that were to arise to confront Roosevelt from the domestic and the international civil aviation regimes during his time as president, but in the meantime Roosevelt made his own mark on aviation history. After he had been nominated by the Democratic Party National Convention in Chicago, he did something no other candidate for presidency had done before: he flew to the convention.

As part of political ritual all previous nominees had waited some weeks before receiving notification of their nomination and delivering their acceptance speeches; none as candidate had flown in an aeroplane. As he had planned for weeks, Roosevelt early the next morning boarded a plane, although he did not relish flying, and flew to Chicago to address the waiting delegates. Since World War I Roosevelt had not trusted aeroplanes, and the flight against head winds was particularly slow and bumpy.

The flight was in fact several hours late. Buffeted by strong head winds and refueling first in Buffalo and then Cleveland the plane flew on through air turbulence strong enough to lay Roosevelt's son John low with travel sickness. The flimsy "Tin Goose" Ford Tri-motor was a well-seasoned workhorse, but conditions in the air were still primitive. There was a symbolism in what Roosevelt did. He was making several points about setting aside cumbersome traditions and conventions and also identifying himself with the future of transport, which lay in the air. When Roosevelt landed he rather inaptly remarked: "I was a good sailor," but at the time it was quite common to talk in maritime terms about commercial flying, so one should not read too much into Roosevelt's comment. Indeed, if one were to do so, it might conjure up an impression that he had little understanding of and feel for civil aviation, and these would be major errors.[37] It is difficult to think of a better entrance onto the highest political stage for someone who was soon to set about transforming civil aviation.

CHAPTER 3

AN UNEASY START: CIVIL AVIATION 1933–37

> The relationship between civil aeronautics and the Federal Government is so close...that a sound Federal policy is essential to success.[1]

ROOSEVELT WAS SWORN IN ON MARCH 4, 1933. The prospect he confronted was truly bleak. Agriculture was in free fall. Farmers were going bankrupt in their thousands and fleeing the land. During the 1920s, as prices collapsed, gross farm income dropped catastrophically from $17 billion to $5 billion by 1932. In 1933 those farmers that remained on the land were burning crops to ward off the winter cold. One in four American industrial workers was unemployed. The country was turning into an agricultural and industrial wasteland, and at the heart of the problem was the fount of capitalism itself: the banks. The day before Roosevelt's inauguration, banking reeled with more and more closures. The day after his inauguration, the great financial center of New York shut its doors and thereafter states whose banks were still open followed suit.[2] The country teetered on the brink of chaos.

What followed was "the 100 days," a period of concentrated, experimental reform in which the Congress passed an enormous raft of legislation to fight the Depression. In this first intense flurry of activity, Roosevelt's New Deal delivered an Emergency Banking Act to bring in new regulation. The Emergency Farm Mortgage Act, the Farm Credit Act, and the Agricultural Adjustment Act collectively brought relief to farmers. A civilian conservation corps employed hundreds of thousands. The Tennessee Valley Authority renewed a vast area of the South. Measures to provide direct grants to the states for unemployment relief and help for mortgage holders were enacted. Industrial relations were brought under government regulation through the National Industrial Recovery Act albeit temporarily. And so it went on, a helter-skelter of legislative action and a proliferation of government agencies.

However, Roosevelt was no great economic theorist. Some measures were mutually contradictory, and throughout the period leading up to the Second World War, he often changed tack or reversed direction. Mistakes were made, including in aviation. Nevertheless, his legislative program had two plain objectives: to ease the pain for ordinary folk and to reform the structure of capitalism. From now on, capitalism it would be regulated into responsibility. At the heart of the New Deal was a pragmatism that had faith in the free enterprise system, providing it operated responsibly. If it did not then it was government's job to make it do so. In the 1930s this is what Roosevelt brought to the domestic U.S. economy; in the Second World War he sought to apply the same principles internationally for when peace came.

Amid all this activity, policy developments touched upon the future of civil aviation with the president's aim to address the issue of a national transport system. If the economy were now to be treated on a national basis, rather than being left as the preserve of the states, then transport also beckoned for reform. Exactly how aviation should be treated within this broader transport strategy, however, remained elusive, and not just for Roosevelt, but for virtually everyone else. Aviation was a new and unique industry and no one had ready answers for the challenges it posed. For several years Roosevelt appears to have classed it as just another form of transport to be regulated along similar lines to the railways and the maritime industry. His first action to affect civil aviation was a proposal for more national transportation coordination. He asked for "emergency railroad legislation under which a coordinator of transportation would be authorized to promote or compel action by carriers to avoid duplication of service, prevent waste, and encourage financial reorganizations."[3] This was a principle Roosevelt wanted to apply throughout the sector. He wanted an integrated whole, and aviation should be subsumed under the broad heading of a national transport policy. Ultimately, he failed to realize this ambition and later changed his mind about how civil aviation should be handled; nevertheless, this early foray into rationalizing the transport system had an impact on developments.

In addition, New Deal initiatives highlighted the need for administrative reform and this also influenced civil aviation's development. One of the most significant cumulative effects of Roosevelt's New Deal was a massive expansion of government responsibilities that required a commensurate administrative structure. In the opinion of one of the leading scholars of the New Deal, "Roosevelt's most important formal contribution [to the development of the modern presidency] was his creation of the Executive Office of the President on September 8, 1939," which provided the means for more effective control over what was now a huge bureaucracy.[4] But that reform was a long time coming. It started in late 1936 when Roosevelt enlisted the help of experts led by Louis Brownlow to set up a Committee on Administrative Management and make proposals about reorganization. The aims were to increase efficiency and effectiveness and to solve some of the anomalies that had arisen with independent commissions, such as the Interstate Commerce Commission (ICC), that took executive actions but were independent of the president. After the publication of the Brownlow Report in 1937, Roosevelt commended it and measures to Congress, but in April 1938 the House of Representatives threw them out.[5] This was a staggering defeat for Roosevelt. Furthermore, this all connected with civil aviation reform as a particular instance of the need for Executive Branch reorganization. So, as Roosevelt consistently insisted that aviation should be dealt with according to principles recommended by Brownlow, many in Congress directed similar objections at aviation reform to the ones that they had leveled against the reorganization plan: they thought that the proposals gave too much power to the president. Civil aviation now became something of a government stalking horse for action in the broader area of government reorganization, which culminated in 1939 with the creation of the Executive Office of the President. Being a stalking horse further complicated the passage of what eventually became the Civil Aeronautics Act of 1938.[6]

Both the idea of an integrated transport system and administrative reform were significant for civil aviation and affected the medium-term development of policy, but before they gained traction another issue propelled civil aviation into the limelight. The administration created a furor with its airmail policy, which prompted heated debate, hasty action, and divisions within itself about how best to proceed.

CANCELLATION OF DOMESTIC AIRMAIL CONTRACTS AND THE 1934 AIR MAIL ACT

Roosevelt inherited a tripartite regulatory system established by the Air Commerce Act of 1926. The Commerce Department's Aeronautics Branch had authority over safety, the power to license aircraft and pilots, and the duty to develop airways and provide navigational aids and air traffic control. The Post Office controlled the award of airmail contracts and routes. And the ICC controlled mail and freight rates. Early in 1933, modest reform, driven by the need to economize, remodeled the Aeronautics Branch into what subsequently became the Bureau of Air Commerce. This was a rather cautious beginning by the administration for what came to be seen as a hugely important industry, but things soon changed and forced a major reassessment. The motor for this emerged out of concern with the "spoils conference" system of Walter F. Brown.

In September 1933 Senator Hugo Lafayette Black of Alabama chaired hearings before the Special Committee on Investigations of the Air Mail and Ocean Mail Contracts. They provided the catalyst for what proved to be a disastrous move by the administration: the cancellation of all domestic airmail contracts. Black was senator for Alabama from 1926 until 1937, when he joined the Supreme Court and eventually became one of its most distinguished judges. He was a gifted and tenacious man, and when fed information from Fulton Lewis Jr., a reporter with the Hearst Press, of extensive corruption in the award of airmail contracts under Brown, he pursued the matter relentlessly. In January 1934 Black reported that Brown had not awarded contracts on the basis of competitive bidding, that rates were often highly inflated, and that there were corrupt relationships running through the industry because of interlocking interests, including the vertical holding of subsidiaries by airplane manufacturing companies.[7] In the context of the failure of capitalism, which had inflicted so much pain on the country, and amidst the crusading reformism of many in Roosevelt's administration, these findings could spontaneously combust. Legal advice from Karl Crowley in the Post Office recommended cancellation of contracts. In preparation for that, Deputy Postmaster General Harllee Branch had sought and received assurances from General Benjamin Foulois that the Army Air Corps had the competence to take over airmail deliveries. Postmaster General and head of the Democratic National Committee Jim Farley was close to Roosevelt and influential, but on this occasion when he advised against cancellation his counsel did not prevail, the arguments of Black did. Evidence unearthed by Black seemed compelling. The existing arrangements were "collusive and contrary to law."[8] Brown was never convicted of any wrongdoing, but Roosevelt agreed that the contracts should be ended. At 4 p.m. on February 9, 1934, domestic airmail contracts were duly cancelled: tragedy ensued.

At the time, "Hap" Arnold, then a senior officer in the Army Air Corps, wrote to his wife explaining what happened and why it was a disaster.

> The Army Air Corps was asked to take over a system of air routes covering the entire U.S. We didn't have enough experienced pilots to carry on and had to use inexperienced flyers who lacked the mature judgment, who were afraid to turn back, who did not know when they were getting into trouble and who had too high an opinion of their own capabilities. Add to that the lack of intimate knowledge of the air routes, the lack of knowledge of details of weather changes which occur so rapidly in winter and the desire of the airlines to see us fail....[9]

The brutal reality was the Army Air Corps was not up to the job. In both training and equipment it lagged far behind its civil aviation counterparts. Fatalities occurred, and on March 10 Roosevelt ordered the Army Air Corps to stop. They resumed a modified service on March 19 and continued until June 1, but then temporary contracts were again issued to private airlines.[10] Soon after, the Baker Board was appointed under former secretary of war Newton D. Baker, to investigate what had gone wrong, and from its findings came important developments. One scholar believes that in retrospect "the Air Corps air-mail service [was]...a pivotal event for the development of American airpower." General Arnold's views, while not as sanguine, do not contradict the fact that things improved.[11] Certainly from 1936 onwards appropriations for the Army Air Corps increased incrementally. Something further that emerged from the Baker Board had more direct consequences for civil aviation. Edgar Gorrell, war veteran and aviation enthusiast, served on the Baker Board and his role was noticed. He was later recruited by airline tycoons Jack Frye of TWA, Eddie Rickenbacker of Eastern, William Patterson of United, and C. R. Smith of American to be the first president of the Air Transport Association of America. This represented the airline industry and provided it with a more powerful and more unified voice than had been expressed during the domestic airmail crisis. Gorrell was to play a significant role in developing civil aviation policy.

The 1934 airmail crisis provoked outrage among politicians and the general public at the decision to cancel, at the deaths, and at the lamentable state of the Army Air Corps. Roosevelt had not made a good start in civil aviation. Views poured into the White House from the public, politicians, and the industry, and they continued to do so throughout the 1930s. They give an interesting insight into the way the nation perceived of the industry and its shortcomings. There were strong views that it needed further rationalization and protection against the dangers of cutthroat competition, but at the same time the virtues of competition were also praised as indispensable to efficiency. There was a growing swell of opinion, and not simply from the armed services, that thought civil aviation should be strengthened for strategic and defense reasons and should not be allowed to fall behind foreign competitors. The parlous and inadequate state of the Army Air Corps exposed by the airmail contract cancellation crisis did much to fuel these concerns. And certainly in 1934 there was widespread belief that the government had damaged the industry by the cancellation of contracts and needed to do something positive to redeem the situation.[12]

The airline industry, though lacking any unified voice until the creation of the Air Transport Association, was nevertheless up in arms at the administration's actions and feared that if government backtracked and simply returned the contracts to private airlines, there would be "the greatest possible confusion" unless it were accompanied by a clear plan for the industry.[13] It is important to note that the industry itself wanted regulation. This was never a simple matter of government calling for regulation and industry professing the virtues of the free market. It was always a much more complex conundrum for government to deal with than that.

Roosevelt had blundered, but the patent shortcomings of the industry and the inadequacy of the regulatory framework had been revealed and doing nothing was never an option. Roosevelt had clearly not got the first move right, but the question abided: What to do? There was a spate of proposals introduced into the Congress including ideas from Democrat Senator Pat McCarran of Nevada. McCarran played an important role in civil aviation reform over the coming years, but his relationship with Roosevelt was never easy. He was later classed by Roosevelt as a member of "The Hater's Club," who opposed the president's policies in the second term.[14] He was always a force that had to be reckoned with and was soon at odds with Roosevelt over the issue of an independent regulatory body for civil aviation, but on this occasion in 1934 he lost the initiative to Senators Black and McKellar, who were prompted to and supported in action by the administration. The senators proposed what soon became the 1934 Air Mail Act.

In the midst of the crisis Roosevelt wrote to Senator Kenneth McKellar of Tennessee, chairman of the Senate Committee on Post Offices and Post Roads, to his counterpart in the House, Representative James M. Meade of New York, and to Senator Black. Roosevelt explained that his general goals were "to avoid the evils of the past" and to encourage through government regulation "the sound development of the aviation industry." This was all rather vague generality, but Roosevelt's objective was that aviation should function responsibly like other components of the economy. Exactly how that should be achieved he might still not have resolved, but he did set out in further broad brush strokes several guiding principles.[15] In a two-page letter to McKellar, Roosevelt used the word competitive or competition no less than six times. He wanted regulation, but not as in the past when it compromised competition and allowed "monopolistic control which...often influenced them [i.e., airlines] to buy planes and other equipment from associates and affiliates."[16] In the future, regulation would be directed at achieving beneficial competition. So, while anything that prevented free competitive bidding should be seen as grounds for canceling a contract, steps should be taken to ensure that bidding was really and truly competitive with specifications for appropriate equipment, speed, load factors, and safety all being taken into account in awards. Later Roosevelt came to believe that these ideas about beneficial competition were not sufficiently adequate for the complexity of the industry, and he moved to support the tighter regulation expressed in the 1938 Civil Aeronautics Act. On interlocking companies, however, he never changed his mind: they should be prohibited and manufacturing separated from airline operating. For a while, until competence could be clearly established, Roosevelt proposed that only short-term contracts be issued. Companies tainted by corruption under the Brown regime should be debarred from receiving contracts and the ICC should take charge of setting mail rates within guidelines prescribed by the new act. Finally, in a clause that has great resonance in the twenty-first century in the aftermath of the international banking crisis of 2008–9, Roosevelt called for the exorcism of the evils of excessive salaries, unearned bonuses, and illegitimate expense accounts that were detrimental "to the interests of legitimate stockholders and the public."[17] What goes round comes around: governments in 2009 were again engaged in trying to formulate appropriate and effective forms of regulation for swathes of economic activity without eliminating competition, just as Roosevelt and his advisers did in the 1930s during the last massive crisis of capitalism.

The Black-McKellar Air Mail Act 1934 was passed on June 12 and closely mirrored Roosevelt's guidelines.[18] Bidding for contracts became more competitive though the provision to exclude former contract holders had little effect. Postmaster General Farley had been worried about the changes from the outset, and a blind eye was turned when the companies simply rearranged their governing boards and changed their names: American Airways became American Airlines, Eastern Air Transport became Eastern Airlines, United Aircraft and Transport became United Airlines, and TWA simply added "incorporated" to its name.[19] Even so, there was a broader distribution of contracts, and the lower airmail rates encouraged more attention to attracting passengers.

Increased competition fostered by the act did not always have positive short-term effects, and there arose widespread fears of cutthroat competition and predatory behavior that demanded further reform. But that was some time coming, and in the meantime, the 1934 Air Mail Act disturbed the financial stability of the industry that had been fostered by Brown, and bankruptcies and serious difficulties were commonplace until the war. However, amid all this turmoil, the international airmail routes remained largely untouched even though Farley had written to Senator Black:

> It is clearly evident that the Pan American Airways has been shown favoritism by former officials of the Post Office Department. Probably their contracts were not obtained as a result of genuine, open competitive bidding. In every instance the time allowed for bidding was entirely too limited and prospective bidders were not given proper opportunity to survey the route, negotiate with the countries over which the route passes for the necessary concessions and agreements and make the proper financial arrangements.[20]

Foreign airmail contracts had not come under the cancellation order in February, partly because Trippe had kept Pan American away from the "spoils conference," but there was no doubt of Brown's preference for Pan American in the award of contracts. It appeared as something of an afterthought when on July 11 Roosevelt issued Executive Order 6792, directing the postmaster general to make an investigation of them. Eventually the enquiry found that cancellation would be contrary to the public interest as it would disrupt services to Latin America and might result in "great harm" to trade relations in the Western Hemisphere. Some minor changes were effected, and slight reductions in payments for airmail contracts were made, but essentially the de facto monopoly of Pan American remained intact.[21]

> The most significant "interlocking" of all airline boards in the 1930s was that of Pan American, whose very profitable overseas mail contracts had come through the air mail cancellation crisis unscathed.[22]

This was quite an extraordinary contrast with what had happened to the domestic industry and highlights the emerging complexity facing regulators: the domestic and foreign spheres of civil aviation operated under very different conditions. There was no illusion about what had been going on as far as the foreign airmail contracts and Pan American were concerned. During the Black investigation, when Postmaster General Brown was asked if Pan American had been accorded preferential treatment as standard policy, he replied: "Well, perhaps it was. I would not dignify it with the term 'policy' but, that is the practice we certainly followed."[23] In fact, it was indeed policy and *was actually* dignified as such after discussion between the Post Office and the State Department in 1929 led to Pan American being designated as the government's chosen instrument for overseas routes, though not necessarily its exclusive chosen instrument. Thus, in the foreign field, there were compelling reasons of foreign and strategic policy for favoring Pan American. There were also embarrassing episodes involving government collusion that could be revealed if regulatory reform adverse to Pan American's interests were to go too far. There were all kinds of strategic and defense complications that muddied the relationship between Pan American and the government, and they largely led Farley to his decision. The same entangling relationships and concerns would return to pose Roosevelt with serious challenges during the war when he sought to find a way to implement his principles of responsible capitalism, competition, and freedom in the sphere of international aviation.

The 1934 act was clearly rushed through to cope with crisis. It tried to address the main cause behind the reason for cancellation, namely, corruption and anticompetitive practices, but it was obvious to all that this was a temporary measure and left many issues to do with civil aviation unaddressed. So far as Roosevelt's own views were concerned, the dispersal of authority between the ICC, the Post Office, and the Commerce Department did not sit comfortably with his aim of creating central direction of a rationalized national transport policy. In fact, just where authority in civil aviation ought to reside was something that troubled Roosevelt over the next four years, and this was an aspect of aviation policy where he seemed to dither and then eventually change his mind. The broad question of how the aviation industry should be regulated and a mass of other specific issues that are subsumed by the issue of regulation were not satisfactorily answered by the 1934 act. In an important way though there was recognition of that by the act itself because it granted the president power to appoint a Federal Aviation Commission to examine the future of civil aviation and report back to him no later than February 1935.

THE FEDERAL AVIATION COMMISSION

The Federal Aviation Commission was chaired by Clark Howell, an eminent journalist and editor of the *Atlanta Constitution*. A Pulitzer Prize winner in 1931 for helping to expose corruption in Atlanta and a high-profile Democrat, he also had bipartisan credentials having served on commissions of investigation before for both Presidents Harding and Hoover. He was not chosen by Roosevelt as an expert, but as a chairman to arbitrate between conflicting views. Someone who was definitely an expert was Vice Chairman Edward P. Warner, a widely respected man in aviation circles who had taught at the Massachusetts Institute of Technology and edited the *Aviation Magazine* for a time. He had also been assistant secretary of the Navy for aeronautics 1926–29 and was well aware of the important connections between civil and military aviation. The other aeronautics expert on the commission was Jerome C. Hunsaker, an engineer and also an avid advocate of aviation. The rest of the commission was made up of Albert J. Berres, whose brief was clear as an official of the American Federation of Labor, and finally Franklin K. Lane Jr., whose father Roosevelt had known when he was undersecretary at the Navy and Lane Sr. secretary of the interior in President Woodrow Wilson's administration. The commission reported on January 22, 1935. Its recommendations were detailed and wide-ranging.

The commission proposed government action in both the domestic and overseas aviation markets on mail contracts, subsidies, and infrastructure and recommended specific help for the airlines in negotiating with foreign governments for overseas operations. More significantly in some ways, it recognized the unique nature of the industry and decided that intervention was necessary in the three key domains of free-market operations—route entry, capacity (determined by size of aircraft and frequency of service), and fares. The character of the airline industry, public service requirements, safety factors, and strategic and defense considerations were all evident drivers in producing the report. It was already very clear, to some at least, that civil aviation was no ordinary commercial enterprise. Following that acknowledgment it seemed appropriate, and the report duly proposed, that there should be an independent commission to regulate the industry.

The Federal Aviation Commission made recommendations intended to rationalize regulation of the industry. It proposed a nonpartisan aeronautics commission with authority over fares and finances and the power to audit what it intended to be a more transparent industry. The commission would have approval power for air service agreements with foreign countries and responsibility for safety and for overlooking those aspects of the industry covered by the National Industrial Recovery Act. The Commerce Department would be responsible for navigation and the general development of airways. It would take the lead in helping to nurture the overseas operations of U.S. airlines and encourage the market generally. One obvious reform to this end was to simplify immigration and customs procedures. The Post Office would award airmail contracts, and the ICC was charged with the power to set and revise mail rates as circumstances might require and was urged to attend to this as a matter of urgency. Although it was widely acknowledged that there was an important interdependence of military and civilian aviation, it was stipulated that there "should be no attempt to require the inclusion of military features in the design or equipment of transport planes."[24]

The policy principle that underpinned the report and became the consensus of wisdom throughout the ensuing debates about civil aviation policy during Roosevelt's entire time as president was that "a position of world leadership" should be maintained by the United States and that the government should "lend such aid" as was necessary to ensure that. This meant developing both the most modern equipment and methods of operation. Furthermore, this was not to be restricted to America's domestic market.

> The national policy of stimulating air transport should extend to the promotion of American-flag airlines connecting the United States with our territories overseas and serving our major trade routes to foreign countries. The time has now come when air transport can be regarded on a world-wide basis.[25]

The report said that government financial support for both the domestic and overseas operations of the airline industry should be provided according to whatever was deemed necessary to develop adequate transport services. The free market could not be left to its own devices in such a strategically important industry. On foreign services, the report specifically advised that "additional aid as may be necessary to build up and maintain proper service under the American flag outside the boundaries of the United States should be allocated...." [26] According to the report, responsibility for assessing how much was needed should be the job of the Secretary of Commerce, who should study ways and means "to foster American air lines to foreign countries." [27] This was to be no passive but a purposeful proactive policy. The airmail contracts were an important aspect of financial viability for the airlines, but they should be awarded on a commercial basis in line with the income received by the Post Office. The airlines were to be commercial enterprises as far as possible subject to market forces. Thus, the commission saw subsidies as a temporary expedient: they should always be geared to making the airlines financially independent and self-sustaining. The commission was trying to strike an appropriate balance between commercial viability and competition on the one hand and the need for government support and regulation on the other. The commission reiterated earlier findings that foreign airmail contracts should not be changed, but also recommended that until a new independent regulatory commission could be established for the industry the ICC should have the authority to raise or lower existing airmail rates as circumstances might warrant. [28]

As important as financial support was for the still-infant industry, equally important in the long-term were views that the commission expressed on the three vital aspects of free-market airline operations—route entry, capacity and fares, and on the way to develop U.S. airline operations to foreign destinations. On route entry the commission recommended that all airlines wishing to operate a route, irrespective of whether mail contracts were involved, should be issued with a "certificate of convenience and necessity," a Common Law term used for public transport franchises: competitive bidding was not deemed to be in the public interest. This was later to cause much difficulty in reaching agreement on new legislation. The government would control route access, though there was to be a presumptive right for airlines operating routes on December 1, 1934, to continue: their rights would be "grandfathered." Many saw this as beneficial to Pan American, but the commission made a further policy statement and one that would be important for the future if implemented.

> The status of American Air Transport, flying in foreign commerce, should in general, not be one of competition between American lines, but of carefully controlled regional monopoly. [29]

This was a policy that had great appeal to Roosevelt's pragmatism. There were persuasive arguments that airline competition should be regulated, but there was also a fear of monopoly. This proposal appeared to offer the best of all worlds for aviation. Pan American's monopoly could be broken in favor of several U.S. airlines operating abroad in their designated sectors with competition being provided by foreign carriers. Roosevelt promoted this with resolution and vigor over the coming years.

On capacity and pricing the commission recommended that

> provision should be made to specify a minimum quality of service and a minimum frequency on scheduled air lines. Rates of fare should be subject to government approval, and the financial structure of air lines should be supervised and their general conformity with the letter and spirit of the law watched over by appropriate government agencies.[30]

What was being envisaged here was a detailed and tight system of regulatory control. There were to be guidelines for pricing in relation to the quality and speed of service offered and overall control exercised by government. As we shall see, these arguments won the day in the domestic, but not for some considerable time in the foreign, domain. The reasoning behind these recommendations for economic controls and particularly certificates of necessity and convenience was laid out in the full report in a section on "Competitive Bidding."

> To attempt to allocate the right to run lines through a process of competitive bidding is to throw undue emphasis on economy at the expense of quality, and almost to assure on most routes that the winning bidders will be those who establish their operations on the most parsimonious footing. Competitive bidding is a demonstrably successful device for the finding of a contractor to carry on an undertaking for which complete plans and specifications can be furnished and which can be definitely finished and paid for within a reasonably short time. Air transport, as we see it, clearly violates both of those requirements. The air transport map cannot be redrawn every few years without utterly disastrous effect on the service. New lines ought to be created on a substantially permanent basis. An air line cannot be torn up and transplanted. The fixed investment, in land, buildings, and equipment, of major air lines ranges, according to the best information we can secure, from $200 to $500 per mile of route. While there are lines that have not a penny of such investment, and that depend entirely on rental of existing structures and services, they do not seem to us to offer an ideal example of the type of service that ought to be developed in the future.[31]

Such considerations laid bare the difficulties of airlines working within a normal free market, even before the introduction of the political and strategic imperatives that further justified government intervention. The questions to be resolved for both the domestic and international spheres of civil aviation were: How and through what institutional means should government intervene? What kinds of support should be provided? And what kind of regulation should be applied? The Federal Aviation Commission was clear about the answer to the first question. There should be a new independent regulatory aeronautics commission. But, on the other two issues, the proposals provided only general and at times contradictory, or at least difficult to reconcile, guidelines and principles. On the one hand, the report envisaged a tightly controlled commercial environment with regulation over route entry, capacity and fares, and, furthermore, an environment in which the U.S. airline industry could not be allowed to be anything less than a world leader. As a matter of course it would receive government financial and diplomatic support and if in difficulty whatever were necessary to make it flourish.[32] On the other hand, the merits and benefits of competition were not to be ignored.

> It should be the general policy to preserve competition in the interest of improved service and technological development, while avoiding uneconomical paralleling of routes or duplication of facilities.
> ...ownership of stock in airlines by corporations engaged in other activities, or the interlocking of diverse aeronautical interests, should be strictly controlled by the commission hereinafter proposed. Nothing should be permitted which would in any way reduce the effectiveness of any competition, the preservation of which could serve the public interest....[33]

There was a recognition that beneficial competition did not necessarily come naturally. It had to be carefully fostered given the nature of the beast, but exactly how this was to be accomplished was not easy to see.

In the international sphere the Federal Aviation Commission, while believing that the aviation industry should be treated as far as possible in the same way as the domestic industry, also recognized that there were differences that would require "modifications...necessitated by a fundamentally different political, legal, and operating status."[34] In particular, the foreign domain would pose problems for the scope of ICC regulation: the commission was interstate, not international. There were two major and distinctive problems with foreign airline operations. The first was posed by the sovereignty of foreign states and the need to negotiate rights of passage, stop, and commercial entry. The second problem was competing against foreign airlines that were often government owned, that were heavily subsidized, and that had access to relatively cheap labor. They posed a threat to U.S. private enterprise operations, and this was a real problem for Americans to tussle with. For the time being, the commission suggested that

> the policy of the United States should be to support and assist American air lines in their relations with foreign governments and with foreign competitors. It should be considered in the public interest to regulate and control

foreign air lines entering the United States with the purpose of securing for American air lines equality of opportunity in foreign countries.[35]

The report was rich in ideas and proposals, but to what extent was Roosevelt going to act on it? That question will be answered shortly, but first it is important to register the fact that the Federal Aviation Commission turned out to have been most perceptive in its analysis regarding several key issues: the need for a new commission in preference to using the ICC, which would have difficulties regulating widely different facets of industry such as civil flying and airport development, and especially in exercising jurisdiction over foreign operations; the need for a new organization free from presuppositions about what should be done for a unique and infant industry; and finally the need for certificates of convenience and necessity, effectively to regulate all commercial air routes. Eventually, the Federal Aviation Commission's recommendations on all these matters were implemented, but it took several years and much argument and backing from Roosevelt before they were.

ROOSEVELT'S REACTION TO THE FEDERAL AVIATION COMMISSION

There is no record of what the president explicitly thought of the Federal Aviation Commission Report, though the fact that it reflected many of the ideas he expressed when he set up the commission and that he commended the report to Congress suggests that he was generally happy with it. In addition, there is evidence of his more specific views both in the presidential message that accompanied the report when it was submitted to Congress on January 31, 1935, and from inferences that can be drawn from the longhand amendments that were made on the original draft of that message.

Roosevelt had four significant concerns. These were that any immediate arrangements could only be temporary and that more considered legislation was required for more permanent solutions. Second, he wanted a fully integrated transport policy.

> I earnestly suggest that the Congress consider these various reports [on transport] together in the light of the necessity for the development of interstate planning of our national transportation. At a later date I shall ask Congress for general legislation centralizing the supervision of air, water and highway transportation with adjustments of our present methods of organization in order to meet new and additional responsibilities.[36]

Third, he was concerned about airmail contracts and the proper relationships between government financial help, profits, and competition. Longhand alterations on the original draft highlight his concerns here and also show his determination to emphasize that the commission's proposal that the ICC should have powers to alter mail rates should only be temporary and

> ...subject to provisions against unreasonable profits by any private carrier. On account of the fact that an essential objective during this temporary period is to provide for the continuation of (the) efficiently operated companies and to safeguard against their destruction, (. It) it is only fair to suggest that during this period any profit at all by (these) such companies should be a secondary consideration. Government aid in this case is legitimate in order to save companies from disastrous loss but not in order to provide profits. [Underlined text indicates long-hand amendments; text in parentheses is deleted text from original draft.][37]

Roosevelt took a very pragmatic and practical line on government aid to industry. Civil aviation was too important to fail, but that did not mean inflating the profits of private companies at public expense. Ideally, a responsibly regulated industry would allow the dynamics of commercial competition to push the industry into a condition of efficient and commercial success. Finally, Roosevelt had concerns about administrative principles that should be observed in any new regulatory authority.

Roosevelt wanted a fully integrated transport system and as such he was against the idea of creating a new temporary regulator simply for aviation. But there was also another factor influencing him on this matter, namely, fear of independent commissions exercising executive authority beyond his control. Under the U.S. Constitution there are divisions of powers and duties. It is the president's responsibility to oversee the bureaucracy and the executive actions of government, but such responsibilities had become blurred in government organizations that also had judicial and legislative functions. Most worrying of all, executive functions were being exercised by some of these commissions, independently of presidential control. With the massive expansion of government responsibilities that came with the New Deal, it was important for Roosevelt to ensure the efficient and effective operation of government and that there were clear lines of authority, responsibility, and accountability.[38] With those needs in mind, but also above all the need to keep control over his own government, Roosevelt chose to disagree with the commission on one of its central proposals.

> The Commission further recommends the creation of a temporary Air Commerce Commission. In this recommendation I am unable to concur. I believe that we should avoid the multiplication of separate regulatory agencies in the field of transportation. Therefore in the interim before a permanent consolidated agency is created or designated over transportation as a whole,

a division of the Interstate Commerce Commission can well serve the needs of air transportation. In the granting of powers and duties by the Congress (ordinary) orderly government calls for the administration of executive functions by those administrative departments or agencies which have functioned satisfactorily in the past and (that), on the other hand calls for the vesting of judicial functions (should be vested) in agencies already accustomed to such powers. It is this principle that should be followed in all of the various aspects of transportation legislation. [Underlined text indicates long-hand amendments; text in parentheses is deleted text from original draft.][39]

Such principles were later to be reiterated in the Brownlow Report concerning general government reorganization.

It is clear from Roosevelt's response to the Federal Aviation Commission Report that he believed that much still remained to be done. The 1934 act was only the start. He was firmly of the opinion that air transport should be integrated with other forms of transport and be brought under a centralized form of government regulation. In this, as in so many other things, Roosevelt was ahead of his, or at least American, times: it was not until the 1960s and President Lyndon Johnson that the United States had a Department of Transportation that fulfilled the institutional setup envisaged by Roosevelt. Whether or not it fulfilled his policy objectives is another matter. There are a host of reasons why the integration and centralization Roosevelt envisaged in 1934 did not come to pass on his watch at the White House, including the vested interests of existing regulatory agencies, but the main factor was that Roosevelt came to recognize the distinctive and unique problems posed by aviation and that it needed its own regulatory authority. He became content with less radical and less far-reaching reform that was focused solely on aviation.

Roosevelt, in commending the report to Congress, concurred in the general tenor of its findings. He had already grasped the importance of civil aviation and that it had to flourish, not only for commercial reasons but also because of its contributions to national security. The report had spilt much ink going into the complexities of the industry and how free enterprise and competition needed to be nurtured: they provided essential dynamics and efficiencies for the industry. However, given the character of civil aviation, the market could not be relied upon to deliver benefits automatically. They would have to be nurtured through regulation that took heavy investment costs, safety factors, and imperatives driven by national security into account. This meant a tremendously difficult job of constructing a regulatory framework that would reconcile these different demands and practices. There had to be regulation. There was no question about that, but the problem was what form and content it should take. Where was the balance to be struck between the free market and government intervention and what was to be done in the international sphere? Roosevelt was sensitive to these issues and also aware, as his remarks about the temporary nature of existing provisions show, that the job had only just begun. There were still many questions to address and solve. Until 1938, much remained unregulated.

> No provision was made for the regulation of passenger and express rates. No economic regulation of non-mail carriers was provided. Air mail contracts were awarded not upon the basis of the need for the public for passenger and express service, but solely upon the requirement of the air mail service.[40]

Roosevelt expected that more detailed regulation would be quickly crafted, but there was hiatus between 1934 and 1938 as Congress and the various agencies and departments concerned with aviation fought and wrangled over how to develop policy and to decide which agency should oversee the industry. Part of the problem arose from misunderstanding of the president's message to Congress dealing with administrative principles. It appeared to some that Roosevelt, in opposing the Federal Aviation Commission's advocacy of a new commission, preferred regulation by the ICC. This was not in fact the case for the long term. As Edgar S. Gorrell, president of the Air Transport Association and a man with an astute understanding of the industry, observed after the enactment of reform:

> ...the President's message reveals the situation was not quite so simple. For even in 1935 the President was indicating a view that executive and judicial functions should be separated.[41]

Roosevelt thought that the ICC would be the best for the job in the short term, but for the long term he wanted an authority that would oversee all aspects of transportation and one that would conform to the constitutional division of powers. In short he wanted clear presidential control over the government administration of civil aviation. Roosevelt later changed his mind, as already noted, regarding the idea of a single regulatory authority for transportation partly because it seemed unachievable and partly because of the unique needs of aviation, but he held firm in his views about the need for a clear division of power and the establishment of his prerogatives over aviation.

After the initial rush of measures that were applied to civil aviation, there followed a lengthy and uneasy period of controversy in the Congress and between warring factions in the administration that lasted until September 1937. Difficulties were compounded by civil aviation regulatory reform becoming entangled in the broader issue of administrative reform in general and fears that Roosevelt was looking for autocratic power in his second term.

FAILURE TO GET LEGISLATION 1935-37

Edgar Gorrell claimed in 1940 that there had been virtual unanimity for five years "regarding the kind of regulation which should be provided for air transportation" and that the problem that stopped quicker progress was divining an institutional framework acceptable to the parties involved in aviation.[42] But this was only partially true. Where to locate authority for regulating the industry was a huge problem, but there were difficulties as well about substantive policy. These concerned presidential control over the award of foreign routes; pricing on foreign routes; "grandfathering"; monopoly and competition; private company agreements with foreign governments; transparency; and the general degree of regulation required. Also, departments had quite specific and differing objectives: airlines negotiating foreign air rights troubled the State Department, the Post Office became paranoid over losing any of its powers, Commerce was challenged by the details of reform and the legal requirement for competition, and the newly formed Maritime Commission wanted to break Pan American's monopoly and seize authority for itself over foreign routes. What emerged from all this between 1935 and late 1937 can only be described as a rather bewildering political and bureaucratic mess.

Two important political developments also muddied the waters for aviation reform at the outset of Roosevelt's second term. On February 5, 1937, Roosevelt dropped a constitutional bombshell when he proposed to Congress that Supreme Court justices over the age of seventy should be supplemented with younger justices. Much to his anguish, Roosevelt had suffered important setbacks during his first term when the Supreme Court struck down as unconstitutional major pieces of reform legislation intended to help recovery and ease the pain for working people. Roosevelt felt that the court was politically and conservatively motivated and that it was denying his popular mandate. The majority of the court felt that the president was overreaching himself and constitutional boundaries. The court argued that federal authority was attempting to encroach on the preserve of the states.[43] It was another replay of the battle between states' rights and federal power and it hurt Roosevelt. Opponents likened him to the autocratic authoritarians in power in Germany, Italy, and the Soviet Union. From now on fears about the bourgeoning power of the president became a recurring political feature regarding many of Roosevelt's legislative proposals.

It was in this context that the Brownlow Report was received. The president had set up the Committee on Administrative Management to look into the problem of reorganization in 1936, and it specifically addressed the problem of independent regulatory commissions. What troubled Roosevelt and others about such commissions was that they appeared to have grown up to become a fourth branch of government. In presenting the report to Congress on January 12, 1937, he commented:

> The Committee criticizes the use of boards and commissions in administration,...and points out that the practice of creating independent regulatory commissions, who perform administrative work in addition to judicial work, threatens to develop a "fourth branch" of Government for which there is no sanction in the Constitution.[44]

Roosevelt wanted, and the Brownlow Report recommended, that the executive functions of such commissions should be brought under direct Executive Branch supervision by nesting them in an appropriate department of the federal government. At the same time, any quasi-legislative or quasi-judicial functions exercised by such commissions could be hived off into an independent agency located for housekeeping purposes within an appropriate department, but independent of the president and in particular with him bereft of power to dismiss its members except on specified grounds. Not surprisingly, given the controversy over the Supreme Court, many now put the most paranoid of constructions on this. They condemned what they saw as further attempts by Roosevelt to expand presidential power. The Reorganization Bill was dubbed the "Dictator Bill" and roundly rejected by the Congress.[45] For civil aviation this was to have harmful impact, which was exacerbated by the fact that the main author of the Brownlow Report, Clinton M. Hester, assistant general counsel in the Treasury Department, also later had much input into the drafting of aviation reform legislation and spoke on this in hearings in Congress. For some there were just too many connections all running together in the direction of increased presidential powers.

While the executive offices of state wrangled over jurisdictional issues and aspects of policy, a series of proposals for reform were presented in Congress. In particular Representative Clarence Lea of California and Senator Pat McCarran of Nevada emerged as key figures in aviation reform and the latter tried to seize the initiative early on when he introduced a bill in 1934 to create an independent aviation authority as recommended by the Federal Aviation Commission. However, among other things, this threatened to diminish the powers of the Post Office, and Senator McKellar, chairman of the Post Office Committee, soon strode forth to organize opposition. When McCarran's bill moved nowhere, he tried again in 1935, but differences in the Congress and opposition from the Executive Branch made any progress slow and difficult. But ironically what emerged time and again was the need for extensive reform. A report in July 1935 from the Aviation Sub-Committee of the Committee on Interstate Commerce, chaired by Harry S. Truman, expressed the problems concisely.

In recent years there has been an extraordinary growth of transportation by air.

> ...competition has been carried to an extreme which tends to undermine the financial stability of the carriers and jeopardize the maintenance of transportation facilities and service appropriate to the needs of commerce and required in the public interest. The present chaotic transportation conditions are not satisfactory to investors, labor, shippers, or the carriers themselves. The competitive struggle is to a large extent unequal and unfair, inasmuch as the railroads and motor carriers are comprehensively regulated, the water carriers are regulated in lesser degree, and the air carriers are scarcely regulated at all.[46]

Notwithstanding the obvious need, the 1936 presidential election year was not a good one for legislation that required strong and united backing from the Executive Branch. Then, in early 1937, came the court crisis and the furor over Executive Branch reform. Out of all this it is important for an understanding of how policy on civil aviation began to take shape to focus on three important themes: the differing views of the key departments and agencies involved that led to a stalemate on legislation in the Congress in the autumn of 1937; the impact of lobbying by the airline industry and its representatives; and Roosevelt's developing views and actions, which, during this phase, also contributed to the difficulties that mired civil aviation reform in damaging disputes.

The four key government players during this stage were the ICC, the Post Office Department, the Maritime Commission, and the Department of Commerce. In the summer of 1937 views began to concentrate on HR 7273, the Lea-McCarran Bill, which, in accordance with wishes expressed by the president after the Federal Aviation Commission Report, placed the ICC at the center stage for the regulation of the industry. This provoked stiff opposition from the Post Office. Harllee Branch sent a memorandum on May 27, 1937, to Marvin McIntyre, presidential appointments secretary, in which he strongly opposed the Lea-McCarran Bill, arguing that the result would be that the Post Office Department would lose "a large measure of control over air routes."[47] Later in July he further explained:

> It would seem rather than abandon the present laws and regulations, which have been enacted and promulgated as the result of years of experience, and which provide many safeguards against the evils and abuses which previously existed, it would be better to perfect these existing laws by constructive amendments.[48]

Of course, constructive amendments meant further enhancing the Post Office bailiwick. The Maritime Commission's comments on HR 7873 sponsored by Mead and McKellar, respectively chairmen of the Senate and House Post Office committees, were: "This is the Post Office trying to outwit the I.C.C. in getting rigid control of foreign air trade."[49] This, the Maritime Commission was not keen on as it cut across its own ambitions. The position of the Post Office when closely scrutinized was clearly self-serving, but then so were the positions of the other players. The main problem, as Lea pointed out, with the Post Office proposals in their various guises was that they would leave everything apart from mail services unregulated. This was something that most, including the airlines, saw as unwise and intolerable.[50]

Interestingly, the Maritime Commission's views in some ways mirrored those of the Post Office in wanting only piecemeal reform, but they had other major obsessions as well, namely, visceral dislike of Trippe and Pan American's monopoly and a driving ambition to oversee the foreign operations of U.S. airlines. The Maritime Commission came into being in June 1936 with the passage of the Merchant Marine Act and replaced the U.S. Shipping Board. Its claim to authority in aviation was derived from the Maritime Act requirement that "the Commission...investigate application of aircraft to foreign trade and...make recommendations relative thereto" and the fact that seaplanes were still the main vehicle for transoceanic flight. The head of the commission 1936–38 was Joe Kennedy, already a powerful figure, father of the Kennedy political dynasty, a leading Democrat and major contributor to party coffers.[51] His senior adviser on aviation was Grover Loening. Previously a business associate of Trippe, Loening had now turned strongly against him. Kennedy also disliked Trippe, who would not succumb to his charms and insisted on plowing his own very independent furrow. Kennedy and Loening wanted domestic and foreign airline operations dealt with separately and the Maritime Commission granted authority in the foreign domain. In arguing their case to the White House, they brought to light the difficulties of coming to terms with two very different sectors of the airline industry, the domestic and the foreign. Moreover, Loening, in his vituperative attacks on Pan American's monopoly, provided much food for thought about the need for closer scrutiny of what was going on and for some action to counteract what he saw as Pan American's dangerous policies. The existence of a monopoly in itself was a problem, but also Pan American's private deals with foreign states and airlines were also cause for deep concern because Pan American generally sought "to acquire exclusive rights....This exclusiveness is largely directed specifically against other American companies...."[52] The foreign dimension now loomed ever larger in considerations about the industry's regulatory reform and had impact on Roosevelt's thinking. Crucially, for the future development of U.S. international aviation, the

1938 Civil Aeronautics Act granted the president control over the award of U.S. foreign routes.

The Commerce Department also had concerns about the Lea-McCarran Bill. Notwithstanding reassurances from Lea that many of the department's powers would remain intact, Assistant Secretary of Commerce Johnson still worried about the dangers of diminishing powers and overlapping and conflicting jurisdictions and was also troubled by Pan American's monopoly. In addition Commerce was piqued as it thought that it had not been closely enough involved in the development of legislative proposals fashioned by Lea. As for the ICC, as things stood, it looked as if it were all set to gain expanded powers and authority over the new industry in a manner similar to those it currently exercised over the railways.

This conflict and bickering within the administration was widely known and did not help matters. Roosevelt later explained in a press conference: "Of course you know that for the past two years every proposal that has been made on the Hill looking toward a permanent method of administering civil aeronautics has met opposition from one branch of Government or another."[53] This was further complicated by pressures from Pan American and Juan Trippe moving unceasingly behind the scenes and sometimes very publicly to promote his airline's interests. As a result several conflicting suggestions have been made about who authored the 1938 act; these include Clinton Hester, James Roosevelt, Edgar Gorrell, and Trippe's counsel Henry Friendly. It has also been claimed that Gorrell and Friendly were simply acting as the mouthpieces of Trippe. Friendly denied authorship of the act and it seems a rather overinflated claim for Gorrell as well, though he undoubtedly had substantial input.[54] Gorrell's position is rather difficult to read. He was clearly deeply motivated by a desire to see U.S. civil aviation thrive as a matter of national priority and was determined that government should provide an effective regulatory framework for safety controls and infrastructure. On economic controls he leaned to a conservatism that had much in common with Herbert Hoover's ideas on corporate capitalism. His default position was to oppose aggrandizement of the state, but he dubbed laments about the demise of laissez-faire as "empty nostalgia" and called for "relaxation of anti-trust laws and other legal restraints which will permit business to assume a greater degree of responsibility in the conduct of its affairs."[55] Much of this cast him in sympathy with Trippe's agenda, but to see him as the latter's puppet in feeding ideas into government officialdom is to exaggerate. His concerns spread wider than Pan American, and as we shall see, it was his plan for integrating the airlines into the war effort that introduced U.S. domestic carriers to foreign operations, much to Trippe's dismay, but directly in line with the wishes of Franklin Roosevelt.[56] For his part, Trippe's position was always dictated by a desire to expand Pan

American and safeguard its de facto monopoly, and he was clearly busy promoting Pan American's interests during the drafting of the Civil Aeronautics Act. One of the issues that caused him deep concern was the fact that the then current Lea-McCarran Bill did not cover overseas routes. This was a serious omission for Trippe because his mail contracts were due for renewal and he wanted regulations in place that would grandfather his routes and effectively guarantee the reawarding of the mail contracts.[57] One avenue of pressure that Trippe exerted to have foreign air routes covered by the bill was via Joseph B. Eastman, chairman of the ICC, to whom he wrote pleading his case on July 20, 1937.[58] The omission of overseas routes was amended later in the year, but even though Trippe had much influence, it was by no means entirely because of his lobbying. Furthermore, it is important to emphasize that his influence in the Roosevelt administration was far less potent than it was in the Congress, and even there it diminished over the years.

During 1936–37, Roosevelt's position on aviation reform is not easy to read. Roosevelt may have been in two minds about the passage of reform legislation on aviation in 1937 because of the broader issue of executive reorganization. If he were, then this could have been a contributory factor to the lack of progress. In July of that year Secretary of Commerce Roper wrote to him explaining that "at a Cabinet meeting some time ago you indicated that you desired to have action withheld on bills of this character [i.e., involving regulation by new executive powers] pending action of the Congress on your Reorganization Message." Roper presumed that the president did not want aviation legislation passed in the current session until the broader legislation on reorganizational reform had been safely passed.[59] This was contrary, for example, to what Congressman Lea believed Roosevelt wanted, but Roper may very well have been correct in his assumption. It was not uncommon for Roosevelt to leave different people with diametrically opposed views of what he intended.

There was also a widely held impression that Roosevelt wanted the ICC to play a major role in regulating the industry instead of a new independent authority. Many in Congress, including Lea and McCarran, and in the Executive Branch, held this perception of Roosevelt's position. It did not capture the full picture, as we shall see. Finally, out of all the cacophony of representations made to the White House, there gradually emerged a clearer pattern of the needs and challenges of the industry, and this altered Roosevelt's ideas about how it should be regulated. Roosevelt changed his mind between the views he expressed in his response to the Federal Aviation Commission Report in 1935 and the passage of the 1938 Civil Aeronautics Act. It is difficult to pin down the exact time of the change. It came over him gradually and began to tell in July 1937 and became clear in 1938, and it involved his decision to opt for a new independent aviation commission and a determination to develop policy for the international as well as the domestic sphere, which had been the main focus of the reformers up to the closing months of 1937.

Clearly, the problem of devising aviation regulatory reform was not solely to do with differences between departments and the pressures from Pan American, the Air Transport Association, and other mouthpieces of commerce and industry, Roosevelt himself was also part of the problem. The president had information at his fingertips if he needed it to give more robust direction to policy development. Clarence Lea sent him a detailed analysis of the differences between the Federal Aviation Commission Report, which Roosevelt had largely endorsed, and HR 7273, as it stood in July 1937.[60] Among other things, it noted differences on the regulatory authority and provisions for regulating international operations. Whether the president actually absorbed all this is unclear, but at this point he failed to take decisive action to cut through the difficulties and dispel uncertainties on how to resolve matters. For example, throughout all this, and as late as October 22, 1937, Roosevelt appeared to favor using the ICC in a major regulatory role. Secretary of Commerce Roper reported to Assistant Secretary Johnson, who was in charge of aviation, that at a Cabinet meeting that afternoon Roosevelt had called attention to the fact that the air bill, then being worked on to try to end the impasse that had developed over the summer, should have three objectives.

1. The Administration of all regulatory matters regarding pilots, beacons et cetera, should go to Commerce.
2. Matters touching transportation of mail to the Post Office.
3. Questions involving rates, etc., to the Interstate Commerce Commission.[61]

However, Roosevelt only ever intended a limited role for the ICC. His response to the Federal Aviation Commission Report had led many to believe that he favored the ICC over the creation of a new independent body to regulate the airline industry, and at the time that was probably true, certainly for the short term, but people were missing the main point, which was that no commission should independently wield executive powers. Those were the prerogative of the president. In May Roosevelt wrote to Marvin McIntyre that the "important thing is to prevent administrative duties being handed over to the Interstate Commerce Commission. I have no objection to giving them quasi-judicial or quasi-legislative duties."[62] Roosevelt was deeply unhappy with independent commissions exercising executive powers.[63] So far as he was concerned the ICC could never solve the problem posed by the airlines in its entirety, and by late 1937 there is some, albeit conflicting, evidence to suggest that he was turning against the idea that the ICC should have even a minor stake in aviation. On the one hand, in February and June 1937, Congressman Lea and Senator Truman, respectively, sent notes to Roosevelt indicating their understanding that they still thought that he wanted the ICC to play a significant role in aviation regulation.[64] And at the end of July, when Roosevelt began to think of establishing a new committee to try to end the impasse over legislation, he mentioned that the ICC should be represented. However, on the other hand, in the event, it was not represented, and in a semiofficial history of the genesis of the Civil Aeronautics Act, its author wrote: "Absence of any representative of the Interstate Commerce Commission was considered as showing that [it] 'was intended to have its feathers plucked,' and, of course, that is exactly what happened."[65] The fact is that Roosevelt was turning against the ICC as an aviation regulator, but that only became apparent in the autumn of 1937.

The demise of the Lea-McCarran Bill based on extensive powers for the ICC began to gather pace in June. An analysis by Lea of the differences between his bill and the Mead-McKellar Bill representing the Post Office was forwarded to the president in May by the Leader of the House Sam Rayburn. It indicated major conflicts abided between the two, symptomatic of the claims of rival government agencies.[66] On May 31 Roosevelt asked McIntyre to try to get Lea and Mead together to reconcile their bills, but differences continued to ferment, and a few days later, when Roosevelt was bombarded by complaints from the Maritime Commission and the Commerce Department, he wrote to Lea.

> I have had some very hurried protests from Assistant Secretary Johnson of the Commerce department and Mr. Joseph Kennedy of the Maritime Commission. Their objections are strong and vigorous, and before anything further is done in the matter, I think it would be wise to contact them and talk the matter over.
>   I also understand the Post Office is opposed to the bill....[67]

On July 30 Lea informed the president that he had consulted with the various interested parties, which he acknowledged he should have done before, and that as discussions progressed they realized that differences were "not nearly so great as had at first been suggested." However, the Post Office and Maritime Commission still clearly thought radical change was unnecessary, and in fact hopes for enacting HR 7273 without a major rethink was now highly unlikely.[68] Roosevelt was coming to appreciate the regulatory needs of the industry, and he was by no means persuaded that extant proposals for aviation were adequate. One clear example of that were the foreign operations of U.S. airlines. Concerns about them prompted him to make an important suggestion at a meeting with the Interdepartmental Committee on Civil International Aviation chaired by R. Walton Moore of the State Department:

> President said he might favor an entire new policy with reference to our foreign air services. There was some discussion of the advisability of appointment of a special committee to formulate policy.[69]

A few days later the president had made up his mind: there would be a new committee to sort things out, and it should incorporate overseas routes into its proposed regulatory framework. It has been suggested that this decision to expand the remit of reform to foreign air routes was directly because of lobbying by Trippe and Pan American, and as we noted earlier, this was an important matter for Trippe and linked with his ambition to secure his airmail contracts through a grandfathering of his existing route network. However, by the very nature of Trippe's devious maneuverings, it is difficult to ascribe relative, never mind absolute, responsibility for this change of policy direction. It seems something of an overstatement to claim that Trippe was the key factor. Certainly Roosevelt did not need to be told by Trippe directly or indirectly that overseas airline operations were gaining in strategic significance given developments particularly in Asia and Europe. Furthermore, as it eventually turned out, the expansion of regulation over foreign routes was to be vastly to the detriment of Trippe's ambitions for Pan American.

On July 31 Roosevelt wrote to Branch in the Post Office Department that he now thought that legislation was unlikely on civil aviation in that session of Congress. He was correct: the Lea-McCarran Bill was filibustered out in the Senate. Roosevelt suggested that the Interdepartmental Committee on Civil International Aviation should expand its remit.

> [It should] cover the whole aviation field, taking in the Interstate Commerce Commission if it is not already represented, and that this Committee charge itself with the preparation of a Bill for next session in January, covering the whole subject of aviation, including mail—both domestic and foreign. Such a Committee could well invite the Congressional Chairman to participate in their deliberations.
> What do you think of this for a course of action?[70]

Whatever Branch thought, this is what happened, except, as noted before, the ICC was not represented. The president authorized the formation of the committee in Cabinet on September 14, and it appeared later in the month as the Interdepartmental Committee on Civil Aviation Legislation with Assistant Secretary of Commerce Johnson as chair.[71] It was this committee, in close liaison with Representative Lea and with much input from Clinton Hester and White House personnel James Roosevelt and James R. Rowe, that was largely responsible for what became the 1938 Civil Aeronautics Act. But also important during its genesis between October 1937 and passage of the act in 1938 were further analyses that were fed into the White House about the needs of civil aviation from Pan American and representatives of airline interests and the changing mind of the president. Franklin Roosevelt had already begun to shift ground in the summer and early autumn of 1937, but there was more change to come before the Aeronautics Act took its final shape.

CHAPTER 4

THE PASSAGE OF THE 1938 CIVIL AERONAUTICS ACT

> There is practically no governmental regulation of American air lines.
>
> Business Advisory Council 1937

CIVIL AVIATION REFORM UP TO SEPTEMBER 1937 WAS A FIASCO, but things were then set to change. President Roosevelt gave aviation more attention and invested more resources in pushing it forward. The Interdepartmental Committee on Civil Aviation Legislation was his first move in those respects. It was a key player in developing the government's proposals, but many of its ideas were prompted and drawn together by the trio: Clinton Hester of the Treasury; James Rowe, administrative assistant to the president 1938–41; and James Roosevelt, the president's eldest son and secretary to the president 1937–38. James Roosevelt took up his post in the White House at the start of his father's second term: he resigned because of personal and health problems in November 1938.[1] But during that relatively short period, many gave him "the credit for getting departments together and sponsoring the framing of the legislation" that later became the basis of a revised bill introduced to the House by Clarence Lea, and passed as the 1938 Civil Aeronautics Act.[2]

Most of those revisions were drafted by Clinton Hester in consultation with Lea, with whom the administration liaised most closely in the Congress to advance legislation and who worked closely with Edgar Gorrell. The McCarran-Lea Act, as the 1938 Civil Aeronautics Act is often known, is somewhat of a misnomer. McCarran in fact opposed much of what Lea and the administration wanted, and it was Lea in the House, working closely with Hester and opponents of McCarran in the Senate, who secured the passage of the final act in a form that satisfied the White House. In terms of its actual content, it might better be named the Lea-Hester Act. James Roosevelt directed much of the overall political cajoling to propel things forward, and he had a good overall grasp of what was needed, but the technical expertise came from Clinton Hester and Gorrell, with Rowe acting as a general facilitator. Hester's expertise was desperately needed by the administration as aviation became entangled in the morass of issues and the political controversy that erupted around the government's plans for reorganization of the Executive Branch. Even without that, with six departments of government directly involved, with the ICC and the Maritime Commission still jockeying for position, with a variety of conflicting views held by influential members of Congress, the airlines, and representatives of the industry, and with clearer and more determined ideas only now coalescing in the Executive Branch, civil aviation regulatory reform was always going to be difficult to fashion.

Reasons for the eventual shape that the Civil Aeronautics Act took and its successful enactment in 1938 are not easy to marshal. Even setting aside or dealing only briefly with many of the technical issues and the bureaucratic turf wars that in the end had little bearing on the eventual shape of the regime, the nature and direction of developments are often difficult to grasp. It is a confusing story with changing positions and many comings and goings between the White House, Congress, executive agencies of government, and aviation interests, but on close examination four clusters of factors emerge that largely determined the course of events. The first is the coordinated teamwork that centered on James Roosevelt and the good relationship that was established with Clarence Lea. The second is the way that the foreign dimension of civil aviation began to loom ever larger as the international situation deteriorated. This not only provided more sense of urgency and focused minds on all aspects of aviation both civil and military, but it brought a better appreciation of civil aviation's regulatory needs. This worked as a catalyst for some of the ideas that fed into the 1938 act. The third is to do with President Roosevelt, who developed a clearer picture of what he wanted. He soon set aside any idea that he might have held that aviation reform should only come on the heels of Executive Branch reorganization and fell back on the idea of creating an independent commission for aviation, though for a time there was uncertainty about whether the ICC should be that independent commission or whether something entirely new should be created. These first three factors and how they interacted with views from the industry will unfold in more detail later in this chapter, but the fourth factor requires close examination now because it had broad impact and was an important component of the context within which much else happened: it is the assembly of ideas in the White House.

THE IMPACT OF IDEAS

Roosevelt was no great thinker, but he drew others who were to the White House and tapped into them for ideas and policies. One presidential adviser and speechwriter described Roosevelt as having a "fly-paper mind": ideas just stuck.[3] One idea often led to many, and this was particularly true in the presidential campaign of 1932. Casting around for informed ideas on important policy issues, Roosevelt, with the help of friend, speechwriter, and legal adviser Judge Samuel I. Rosenman, decided to establish a group of thinkers—ideas men, which was dubbed the "Brain Trust" by the press. Among the trustees were Rexford Tugwell, a leading agricultural economist, and Raymond Moley, also an economist and later an important speechwriter for the president, both from Columbia University, and Adolph A. Berle, a specialist on corporations and modern capitalism who became a key figure in international aviation policy as assistant secretary of state during the war.[4] The Brain Trust was symbolic of the readiness of Roosevelt to soak up new ideas and draw in advice from outside of normal government channels.

During the Depression and the war, the administration actively reached out to engage the help of organizations such as the Council on Foreign Relations, the Twentieth Century Fund, and the Business Advisory Council. There was a rich intermingling of membership between such organizations and government. For example, Berle, Francis Biddle, who served for a time as Roosevelt's attorney general, and John Winant, U.S. wartime ambassador to Britain, were all members of the Twentieth Century Fund established in 1919 by the Boston retailer Edward A. Filene to "promote the public welfare." The Twentieth Century Fund was a typical progressive organization committed to scientific improvement of the economy and society. The Business Advisory Council was set up to advise the Commerce Department in 1934 and again had a distinguished roll call of members including Edward Stettinius; Averell Harriman, industrialist and presidential envoy; Myron C. Taylor, who acted as a special ambassador for Roosevelt most notably to the Vatican; and Paul Hoffman of General Motors, who later became chief administrator of the postwar European Recovery Program better known as Marshall Aid. Hoffman was also a wartime member of the Twentieth Century Fund.[5]

While much of the advice and the recommendations that came from groups such as the Council on Foreign Relations and the Twentieth Century Fund were progressive, some even judged highly radical, Roosevelt was no revolutionary. He also consulted with the business community and bankers such as his long-standing friend Bernard Baruch, a "good Southern Democrat" and believer in balanced budgets and conservative fiscal policies. Baruch was no Keynesian and was often a critic of Roosevelt's policies, but he thought that the president was largely "a shrewd, practical and pragmatic politician."[6] He was correct. Part of that pragmatism was to defer when necessary to conservative Democrats such as his first vice president John Nance Garner and influential Texas senator Tom Connally.

Roosevelt came from the well-to-do and the well-heeled. The Roosevelt family home sat alongside that of the Vanderbilts' and the Morgenthaus' in leafy Hyde Park on the banks of the Hudson River in upstate New York. With the New Deal, some say that he betrayed his background and class; others that he saved them. The truth is more complex. He helped to change his class to make it more responsible and responsive to the needs of ordinary people and less corrupt. And he did this not by being an inveterate chameleon, but by abiding by strong underlying principles and pragmatically pushing along agendas where best he could in accordance with those principles. Kimball has quoted Roosevelt's own words to capture some of his elusiveness: "I am a juggler, and I never let my right hand know what my left hand does...."[7] But, needless to say, the juggler himself needs to know and Roosevelt did. Furthermore, as Kimball points out, Roosevelt acted in accordance with some deep-seated assumptions about the obligations and responsibilities of government and what folk should rightly expect of it. Of course, he was only human, and at times pique and prejudice would get the better of him, but generally he was a magnanimous man who could rise above such things. From the broad perspective, his actions and policies reveal a remarkable consistency. McGregor Burns in his classic study of Roosevelt put it thus:

> He had an order of priority which amounted to something of a political creed. He believed—most of the time—that government could be used as a means to human betterment. He preached the need to make government efficient and honest. He wanted to help the underdog, although not necessarily at the expense of the top dog. He believed that private, special interests must be subordinated to the general interest. He sought to conserve both the natural resources and the moral values of America.[8]

Some might read that and see Roosevelt as simply a rather conservative character reflecting the common decency of man; however, when one remembers the context of the Depression and the blight it inflicted on the mass of people, common decency can take on radical form. Within the lexicon of liberal capitalism with a social conscience, Roosevelt was a radical in his

time. In one of the first of his speeches to have national impact, he warned
the country of the dangers that threatened from concentrations of economic
power in the hands of the few. In such circumstances the "majority would
become serfs."[9] This was another idea like liberty that abided with Roosevelt
throughout his career, and notwithstanding the compromises he made for
the sake of war production during the Second World War, it led him on to
attack Pan American's monopoly of U.S. foreign air routes.

Assessing anyone's radicalism is all rather relative and often depends on
the social and economic challenges that are confronted. For Roosevelt those
challenges were huge and the stakes were high—the survival of a way of life,
and it was not just one for the rich and well-to-do, but also one that offered,
or should offer, improvement for ordinary folk. It was a way of life that had
to be changed while conserving continuity and the good and the positive.
For many he seemed to strike the right balance, but for those like Baruch,
what Roosevelt strove to do in the New Deal went too far in creating a
"nanny state" in which rugged individualism and self-help would atrophy.
Of Roosevelt's efforts Baruch commented:

> I was so often reminded of the story about two frogs who jumped into
> separate cans of milk, which were sealed and put on board a freight train.
> One frog called out, "Help! Help! Help!" The other cried, "Hustle! Hustle!
> Hustle!" When the cans were opened, the first frog was dead. But the second
> had hustled so hard that he had made a cake of butter on which he was sit-
> ting safely. Much of the New Deal, despite its good intentions, discouraged
> people from hustling for themselves.[10]

From Roosevelt's perspective the problems were that maybe frogs might not
know how to make butter cakes, maybe they might not have the strength
to make butter cakes, or maybe they might just jump into cans of vinegar.
Experience, time, and chance can be crueler than Baruch allowed. However,
even Baruch readily conceded that there had been damage wrought by unfair
competition and that business had failed "in joining with government in
making regulations which we know are quite necessary."[11] Many in the business community like Baruch recognized that capitalism needed to be more
responsible and required government help to that end through regulation.
Roosevelt was ready and willing to deliver regulation, though he rarely used
that word, and from late 1937 onwards he focused more closely on trying to
service civil aviation in that way. He called it cooperation between government and commerce.

Ideas counted in the Roosevelt administration, and ideas from many
quarters were incorporated into what became the 1938 Civil Aeronautics
Act. Representations were made directly from the industry by Edgar

Gorrell of the newly established Air Transport Association. Lea passed him a copy of the Civil Aeronautics Bill to make sure that it incorporated sufficient measures to ensure stability in the industry, and by mid-January 1938 Clinton Hester, in a note to James Roosevelt, observed that most of Gorrell's proposals had been incorporated into the bill drawn up by the Interdepartmental Committee on Civil Aviation Legislation.[12] Another important source of ideas and opinion was the Business Advisory Council. In November 1937 its Executive Committee approved a report on civil aviation regulatory reform, which caught the attention of James Roosevelt. He was so taken with it that he wrote: "Bring this to me when you bring me the air plan."[13] In several respects it reflected many of the views put forward by Gorrell and is suggestive of a consensus that was beginning to emerge among those not prejudiced by administrative vested interest or too politically at odds with Franklin Roosevelt. Significantly, Trippe was a member of the council, but the focus of the report, while encompassing foreign operations, was primarily on the domestic industry, and some of the recommendations were clearly at odds with Trippe's favored objectives. At the very least, the report gives a picture of what the Commerce Department and progressives in the business community were thinking, but maybe there is more. While it is not possible to connect the ideas in the report directly to President Roosevelt and the policies he subsequently approved, they are part of the context within which policy was formulated. That formulation process changed the provisions for civil aviation dramatically between September 1937 and January 1938 when an administration-sponsored bill emerged from the interdepartmental committee. And many of the proposals in the Business Advisory Council report were in fact incorporated in one form or another into that draft bill and from there into the 1938 Civil Aeronautics Act because they were either persuasive with senior figures in the administration or resonated with views that they already held, and this included Franklin Roosevelt.

The report pulled no punches and throughout there was a sense of urgency for action. The situation was lamentable. Apart from safety standards and the licensing of pilots and equipment,

> there is no government control over the number of American companies that may operate over a given route. In general, anyone can start an airline anywhere, provided its aircraft and airmen conform to the safety requirements of the Department of Commerce. A shoe-string company can be organized overnight to parallel another line, thus impairing public safety, jeopardizing the security of labor, and destroying invested capital.
>
> A strong airline is entirely free to put its competitors out of business by temporarily slashing passenger and express rates to uneconomic levels.

Conversely there is nothing to prevent an airline's oppressing the public by rates outrageously high.[14]

The result was that the "industry has reached the point where unbridled and unregulated competition is a public menace."[15] It was a public menace because it threatened the health and welfare of capital and labor and the safety of the traveling public.

> It is essential in the air transport industry that government shall provide proper control to discourage irresponsible competition and to encourage good management, sound capital investment and returns adequate to make generous provision for purchase and maintenance of the best and most modern equipment.[16]

Even more significantly it endangered two things, for which the airline industry was most valued: the economic welfare of the United States and its national defense. The diagnosis and general prescription were clear, but how were objectives to be cast into policy proposals and through what form of regulatory structure could they be implemented?

The report insisted that it would be unwise to await passage of the government's reorganization measures before acting on aviation regulatory reform. And there was no need because the Business Advisory Council's proposals conformed to the principles laid out by Brownlow. Steps should thus be quickly taken to establish a "unified system over the entire American transport industry by air—both the portion operating within the continental United States and that operating outside our borders...."[17] This was clear and uncompromising. International airline services might have been in their infancy, but from the outset of the thinking on reform it was strongly recommended that the domestic and foreign regimes should be as similar as possible and dealt with by one overarching system: this melding together of the domestic and the international spawned controversy and difficulties. To establish a unified system, the report advised that all administrative functions should be brought under the control of the Department of Commerce and all quasi-judicial and quasi-legislative functions under the ICC. Apart from squeezing the Post Office Department out of aviation matters, the allocation of powers to the ICC already pointed to some serious difficulties arising from the international sphere. If, as the report suggested, there were to be a unified regulatory system over both domestic and foreign civil aviation operations, it would be beyond the constitutional remit of the *Interstate* Commerce Commission to wield power over *international* operations. That problem was further compounded when it was appreciated just how much decisions about foreign operations of U.S. airlines would affect foreign policy. There was some ambiguity in the report about the possible role of the ICC, perhaps reflecting concern over these matters, and toward the end of the report it was simply stated that "regulation of the economic problems of the industry should be vested in a non-political, permanent agency of government.'[18] The ICC was not specifically named.

Economic problems of the industry were seen as threatening and severe, ranging from a complete absence of regulation over passenger and express rates to the "farce" of competitive bidding on mail contracts, and different practices in the domestic and foreign spheres. For example, domestic mail contracts had in effect become "perpetual franchises" but there was no provision of continuity of service for airlines operating abroad. The first reaction of the Business Advisory Council was to consider and then rule out as inappropriate government ownership for a new and dynamic industry and, as it was on the cusp of financial self-sustainability, even subsidies should only be temporary. The main remedy was conceived of in the form of government regulation by certificates of necessity and convenience, which would control route entry and be able to "outlaw piratical practices" while at the same time preserving healthy competition. In addition, rates for passengers and express services "both domestic and, to the extent possible, abroad, should be regulated in the public interest."[19] Cooperation between airlines should be allowed, particularly for interlining, under the watchful eye of the regulatory body.

Among other things, this was something of a power play by the Department of Commerce. If carried out to the letter the report's recommendations would have brought the whole regulation of the aviation industry under its framework, though not direct control. All administrative matters, safety, navigation, developing the airways, and foreign relations were to be bedded in the Commerce Department. As noted, the report was somewhat ambiguous about the location of economic regulation: at one point it mentioned the ICC, at others there was reference to a new independent commission, but in respect to the latter there was also the comment that if and when the reorganization plan goes forward then that commission would automatically be nested as an independent agency within Commerce. Perhaps the main point to be drawn out for future developments, however, is the insistence on following the principles derived from the Brownlow Report and the reorganization plan, namely, that all administrative and executive functions should be brought directly under Executive Branch and hence presidential control and that quasi-judicial and quasi-legislative functions should be separate. Sorting these issues out caused interminable debate and argument.

It began to become clear from these proposals just how intimately related the structure of regulation and the substantive regulatory system would be. If there were to be a comprehensive system embracing both domestic and foreign airline operations, it was difficult to see how the ICC could play the part that had been originally envisaged for it by the president and in the McCarran-Lea Bill that was filibustered out in 1937. Substance would affect the form of regulation. Fears, not just from outside, but also from within the airline industry itself, of unbridled competition led the authors of the report into recommending a comprehensive form of regulation for route entry in both the domestic and the foreign domain and also over pricing, though only if it were possible on foreign routes. Nationalization was ruled out, subsidies were frowned on and only tolerated as a temporary necessity, and competition was still envisaged as playing a major but tightly regulated and carefully nurtured role. The main worries were cutthroat competition, wasteful duplication, instability that frightened away investment and troubled labor, and a growing sense of the need that regulation of foreign operations had to go hand in glove with those for the domestic industry.

THE INTERDEPARTMENTAL COMMITTEE AND ITS DRAFT CIVIL AERONAUTICS BILL

In accordance with the president's express wishes, Secretary of Commerce Roper on September 15 set about establishing the Interdepartmental Committee on Civil Aviation Legislation: "I told them to go into a room and bring me a unanimous report ."[20] The committee came into being toward the end of the month with the specific task of formulating unanimous proposals from all the interested agencies of government on aviation regulatory reform and submitting them as a bill to the president.[21] Achieving widespread consensus on a bill was seen as imperative if legislation were to be successful and that imperative was to have an important consequence regarding whether or not price controls were to be imposed on foreign operations: something vehemently opposed by Trippe and Pan American.

Assistant Secretary of Commerce Colonel James Monroe Johnson chaired the committee made up of Second Assistant Postmaster General Harllee Branch, Assistant Secretary of War Colonel Louis Johnson, Assistant Secretary of State Judge Walton Moore, Assistant Secretary of the Navy Charles Edison, and Assistant Secretary of the Treasury Steve Gibbons. It heard evidence and considered views in hearings on eight separate days in October 1937 and studied the issues for a further two months before a draft was produced as a confidential print by the House Interstate Commerce Subcommittee of the Interstate and Foreign Commerce Committee. The draft embodied radical changes from the McCarran-Lea Bill of the previous summer.

As noted before, as late as October 22, 1937, Roosevelt still favored using the ICC in a major regulatory role, but just over three weeks later the interdepartmental committee had bypassed it in favor of creating a new regulatory body.[22] Hester reported to James Roosevelt on November 15 that the committee was heading toward the creation of a new body with authority over safety and economic regulation. This was further confirmed on November 26 when Monroe Johnson sent James Roosevelt a draft bill proposing a new three-man CAB having all powers over safety and economic regulation previously exercised by the Commerce Department and the ICC, but with the additional authority "to license operations abroad subject to Presidential approval."[23] He made the significant comment that "in general the Board will have authority to regulate completely the transportation of passengers and goods by air." Some matters would be subject to judicial review, but the rest would be under the direction of the president.[24]

James Roosevelt wanted a clearer picture of these developments and asked Hester to send him an analysis of the changes between the McCarran-Lea Bill HR 7273 and the draft produced by the committee. Hester obliged on December 30, 1937.[25] It was a model of analytical clarity that revealed significant developments.[26] The troubled story of finding or creating an appropriate administrative authority for civil aviation had taken what proved to be a decisive turn during the deliberations of the committee. Until the start of 1938 the ICC had held a central position; after the subcommittee print of the interdepartmental committee it did no longer. There were solid and substantive reasons for that, but there was also the fact that Roosevelt had become increasingly disillusioned with the ICC and its chairman, Joseph B. Eastman. The commission strongly opposed the January 1937 recommendations of the Brownlow Committee. It was pitted against the subsequent reorganization bill and became a significant factor in its failure in the Congress. The failure did not come about until April 8, but Roosevelt was aware of Eastman's position well before that. The political mood in Washington was dark with many moving against what they saw as attempts to seize unconstitutional powers and drive toward dictatorship, while the administration thought that the changes were needed for the sake of good and effective governance. James Roosevelt confronted these issues head-on in a speech in New York City Town Hall on January 20, 1938.

> Dictatorship comes, always, as a receiver in bankruptcy for parliamentary governments that have failed to govern.[27]

By February 1938 the press was commenting that the president's "special distaste for the lengths to which he thinks the Interstate Commerce Commission has insisted on asserting its independence also enters the maneuvers" to exclude the commission from a significant role in aviation. The article asserted that "the President opposed shifting aviation regulation to the Interstate Commerce Commission," and another publication also claimed that the president "is definitely opposed to the Commission."[28] In April, during a crisis in the railroad industry, the president told Congress that commissions such as the ICC in exercising executive functions were, in all probability, unconstitutional by effectively creating executive authority in a fourth branch of government. Assistant Secretary of State Berle noted in his diary shortly afterwards that "he [Roosevelt]...really wanted the railroads handed over to some administrator with instructions to see that they got entirely clear from the ICC...."[29] Reports that the president had turned against the commission were true, but he had not done so simply out of personal pique arising from its opposition to government reorganization. There were sound substantive reasons as well for the demise of the commission's ambitions for civil aviation and these also influenced the president in his thinking. Roosevelt had been consistent in harboring no objection from principle to quasi-legislative and quasi-judicial powers being exercised by the ICC; however, as the complexity of civil aviation became clearer it was apparent just how difficult it would be cleanly to separate judicial and legislative powers from executive powers in this sphere. The last thing Roosevelt wanted was for executive power to be wielded by such an independent body as the ICC, especially when they spilt over into foreign policy.

The interdepartmental committee wanted the role assigned to the ICC by HR 7273 to be taken by a new agency, eventually named the Civil Aeronautics Authority (CAA). The substantive reasons behind that change were that a CAA would centralize both economic regulation and all safety matters under its authority, whereas under HR 7273 safety matters would have been divided with private flying safety going to the Department of Commerce and airline safety to the ICC. "It is believed that this rapidly developing industry should be regulated by an agency vested with power to regulate all branches of aviation and which can devote its entire time to such regulation."[30] Such a view was bad news not just for the commission but also for the Post Office and the Commerce Department. The powers, held by the trio of agencies that had overseen aviation in the past, were to be stripped away and relocated in a new independent agency whose executive powers would be directly under the control of the president. This change was also deemed advisable because so much of the work envisaged by the new legislation would involve executive functions. One of the most crucial of these executive functions would pertain to spheres of particular and growing concern and those that were clearly in the domain of the presidential prerogative, international relations, and national defense. "Therefore, it was believed essential that these functions be exercised under the direction of the President rather than by an agency completely independent of the President as in the Interstate Commerce Commission."[31] In the areas of foreign relations and national defense, even quasi-judicial and quasi-legislative matters were firmly in the hands of the president and the CAA chairman who would be directly responsible to the president and removable at his will. All other quasi-judicial and quasi-legislative matters would be dealt with by other members of the CAA acting as an independent body.

On the substance of regulation, HR 7273 remained silent on a series of important issues that the interdepartmental committee felt needed robust action, while on others it sought to perpetuate the status quo, often to the benefit of Pan American. So, HR 7273 sought to grandfather existing operations, give preference to airlines operating foreign routes if they had previously negotiated foreign landing rights, to prohibit government from interfering with any obligations or privileges granted by a foreign country to a U.S. airline, and to restrict the secretary of state to powers of consultation only in the granting of overseas operating rights. It was widely suspected that many of these provisions were due to the direct intervention of Trippe. In marked contrast, the interdepartmental committee insisted on making grandfathering subject to the public interest and refused to give automatic preference to airlines that had previously negotiated landing rights with foreign governments. That would have been tantamount to privileging Pan American, which would have been "unwise," as it would have excluded "other American carriers" and prevented "the healthy development of such commerce."[32] Similarly it was deemed "unwise" to give a blanket exemption from government interference in privately negotiated agreements between airlines and foreign countries when such agreements might have a bearing on the foreign relations and the defense interests of the United States. Finally, the secretary of state was accorded negotiating powers, with the CAA authorized to grant overseas operating rights to U.S. carriers and rights to foreign carriers for entry into the United States, but all subject to presidential approval.

Both HR 7273 and the interdepartmental committee agreed on the need for certificates of convenience and necessity to regulate domestic airline operations, but beyond that there were significant differences. The committee wanted tighter domestic regulation and hence it required that the CAA would have to authorize any change or abandonment of operations. There was agreement on rate regulation in the domestic market, but HR 7273 was silent on foreign operations. This was a difficult issue, and the committee gave no clear-cut recommendation. Some on the committee wanted to leave matters alone as per HR 7273, but others wanted to extend rate regulation from the domestic to the international sphere of operations, and this eventually became the administration's and the committee's preferred position. On a raft of other minor policy and technical issues, the committee leant toward more regulation of mail schedules, mergers, and acquisitions, and disclosure of stock ownership. It proposed leapfrogging over the district courts for appeals and going directly to the Circuit Court of Appeals. On safety it was in two minds whether or not to reform wholesale the 1926 Air Commerce Act or to wait to see how things went within the CAA before addressing the possibility of safety reform. But all these were fairly minor matters. The key differences were on where to lodge authority over civil aviation, how to regulate overseas airline operations and specifically whether or not to control rates, and whether to run two parallel systems or seek a more comprehensive regime that would create a single harmonious whole embracing both domestic and foreign airline operations.

As the interdepartmental committee bill began to make the rounds, it became clear that the Maritime Commission was strongly opposed to its proposals, and there were fears that both Lea and McCarran would turn the bill aside as too radically different from their own agendas and then simply fall back on their own versions.[33] But there was support from elsewhere in the administration. The president's Committee on Administrative Management generally endorsed the bill, and the president himself was preparing to throw his full weight behind it. By mid-December 1937 he wanted to talk personally with McCarran and Lea to try to bring them on board.[34] The president "called Senator McCarran and Congressman Lea to the White House and informed them informally on 4 January [1938] that he now desired to adopt Senator McCarran's idea of a separate commission to regulate all phases of aeronautics."[35] This was pleasing to Lea and McCarran, but they were both concerned that members of Congress would object to the new commission being placed within the Commerce Department and many would still wish to use the ICC as the regulatory body.[36] These views about the danger of placing the new authority within the Commerce Department were to affect the way the aviation bill was redrafted. But that came later. The main point of the meeting at the White House was tactical to make a gesture to flatter both Lea and McCarran—the senator in particular. McCarran was later to make the point in Congressional hearings that "the substance of the conversation [with President Roosevelt] was that he had come to the conclusion that the first idea I had presented in 1934 was correct.'[37] However, it would take more than this massaging of his ego to appease the senator and resolve the general differences between him and the president. The main substance of those differences were to do with what McCarran saw as the bourgeoning powers of the president, which, among other places, he saw reflected in the aviation legislation. McCarran had a deep distaste for Roosevelt, fuelled by his suspicions that the president was constantly angling for more power. McCarran was a populist and with rhetorical ability to wax lyrical on his pet topic.

The innovations of executive power...indulged in by Jackson, promoted by Lincoln, expounded by Garfield, declared righteous by [Theodore] Roosevelt and philosophically promulgated by Wilson, appear to have been but fore-runners, rivulets, as it were, contributing to the flood that now sweeps on, submerging the utopian doctrines and theories of Jefferson and conferring unheard of and unfettered expansion to the executive.[38]

A man with views such as these was not going to be easy to handle, but for a while things went deceptively smoothly.

On January 7, 1938, Hester reported to James Roosevelt that he had met both McCarran and Lea in "very satisfactory conferences." Lea in particular was most cooperative and was very sympathetic and anxious to put legislation through that would reflect well on the administration. It was because of Lea's reaction and the fact that he was actively promoting the interdepartmental committee bill that Hester described the meeting as "one of the most satisfactory I have ever had with any member of either House of Congress." McCarran, on the other hand, did not like the bill and was continuing with his own efforts for a five-man board that would be independent of the president and executive departments. He wanted the new agency separated from the president and the Commerce Department to ensure its independence. Notwithstanding this difficulty, Hester was quite sanguine about the possibility of a compromise and that the president would achieve the kind of control over executive matters in civil aviation that he desired.[39] James Roosevelt forwarded this memorandum on to his father with the note that nothing further needed to be done at this time, and sure enough, on January 18, Hester reported to James Roosevelt: "We are getting along splendidly at the Capitol on the Civil Aviation legislation."[40] McCarran and Lea had accepted a whole raft of substantive regulatory changes to the version of the bill that they had sponsored in the summer of 1937. They had agreed to abandon "any idea of vesting in the Interstate Commerce Commission control over civil aviation" and now agreed that a CAA should exercise executive functions with a chairman designated by the president to act as executive officer, that its members should be removable at will by the president, and that matters affecting foreign affairs and national security would be subject to the direction of the president. There was some question as to whether it should be a three- or five-man authority, and they would not accept that the agency be housed in Commerce with the secretary having control over housekeeping matters, but Hester commented that the Committee on Reorganization were content with this as the arrangements still followed the principles of the Brownlow Report.[41] On locating the independent agency outside the Commerce Department, McCarran had got his way, but he had apparently conceded on much else.

On most significant issues that separated the committee's draft and the McCarran-Lea Bill, accommodation was reached in favor of the administration's position. The grandfather clause was made subject to the public interest, and automatic preference would not be given to airlines that had privately negotiated foreign-operating rights. The position of the committee was accepted on judicial appeals, consolidating all safety matters in the CAA and limiting the life of certificates of convenience and necessity if it were found to be in the public interest to do so, and there was some movement on modifying the position on existing private agreements between U.S. airlines and foreign countries. There was also acceptance of measures to prevent monopolies and collusion in domestic and foreign operations, but in the final act these prohibitions could be waived at the discretion of the CAA: airlines could be granted antitrust immunity. Accommodations were also reached in a number of other areas of less significance or of more technical nature, for example on interlocking directorates; however, some areas of disagreement remained.[42]

Redrafting of the Lea-McCarran Bill now had momentum, and Hester was optimistic that all could be resolved. Some of the differences between the administration and McCarran, however, were in the public domain and that further complicated matters. The main sticking points were whether or not the Post Office should fix airmail schedules, disclosure of stock ownership and private agreements between airlines and foreign governments, and the insistence by the administration on the requirement that the president approve the issuance of certificates to existing airlines authorizing them to operate in foreign air commerce.[43] There was also the question of controlling rates on foreign routes, and on this neither Lea nor McCarran was in favor. Their position was that the Senate and House Interstate Commerce Committees had both held hearings on the proposal to control rates on overseas routes, the Senate twice, and on all three occasions had rejected it.[44] However, in a long conference meeting with Clarence Lea and representatives of Senator McCarran on January 22, Clinton Hester managed to narrow down the differences between the administration's proposals and what McCarran was prepared to accept, almost to insignificance.

> They accepted without modification the two which deal with private agreements between our airlines and foreign countries and the disclosure of stock ownership, but desired a slight modification with respect to the other two.

In effect what the understanding on private agreements meant was that airlines could continue to fulfill obligations, but only so long as they did not unduly restrict the actions of the U.S. government. On the last two outstanding problems:

...gentlemen reluctantly agreed PO fix schedules, but subject to 30 days notice in which can appeal.

...gentlemen agreed to control rates on overseas routes but argue for a one year "pioneering stage" where would not be controlled.

...these are the two that are still contentious.[45]

Sadly the euphoria that these developments occasioned was short lived. On January 24 Hester informed James Roosevelt that McCarran had "reneged" on what his representatives had agreed and would not accept Post Office power over schedules and stops or regulation of overseas rates. However, McCarran's behavior was beginning to isolate him: Lea was prepared to accept what McCarran was not. McCarran wanted to leave things for a couple of weeks while he was away on a trip back home to Nevada, but Lea wanted to move on with the bill that James Roosevelt and the administration were promoting.[46] The committee made some accommodations in particular on overseas rates where it effectively agreed to McCarran's request for a year-long pause, but on Post Office control of airmail schedules it urged the president to uphold the Post Office's powers.[47] These conciliatory gestures were too little and too late for McCarran. He fired his advisers and turned to lawyers from the ICC for help. In the meantime he abandoned Washington for his home state Nevada and stayed there, not ten days as he had indicated he would to Hester, but for a month. While he was away there was a flurry of articles in the press that stirred matters up further and entangled the proposed aviation legislation more directly with the administration's broader proposals for government reorganization.[48]

In fact, while the substantive issues that bothered McCarran—namely, the Post Office's role in fixing airmail schedules, regulation of international rates, and presidential control over the allocation of overseas routes still seemed to some at least to be at issue—the main problem lay elsewhere.[49] What remained to trouble the passage of legislation were concerns over presidential power and hence the location and extent of his powers in civil aviation. The flurry of articles referred to above were all full of these issues, not the substantive ones that really counted for the future of aviation. As one industry publication put it:

It...appears that the aviation industry is placed more or less in the status of a guinea pig to find out how the Congress will go with the administration in its proposed plan of reorganization of Government agencies. In view of the growing opposition of Congress to the plan this promises to be a bitter fight in which much needed regulation of aviation may be submerged.[50]

Throughout February 1938 the administration worked to find a way forward. Hester frantically lobbied and cajoled members of Congress to try to sustain momentum on aviation legislation and to try to isolate McCarran. And he had some successes. In particular he targeted the Interstate Commerce Subcommittee on Aviation and most gratifyingly was able to report to James Rowe, James Roosevelt's assistant, that Representatives Bulwinkle and Crosser, who had previously strongly favored the ICC, were now prepared to support the administration's proposals.[51] These were hopeful signs, but on March 3 a new drama unfolded.

Back from Nevada, McCarran struck out alone. It was only now that the administration became aware that at the end of January McCarran had sacked his long-standing advisers on aviation and called in lawyers from the ICC. The result was made public on March 3. Without any premonition on the part of Hester or James Roosevelt, McCarran had introduced his own version of an aviation bill without consulting the industry, the interdepartmental committee, or any member of government and it "contains very few, if any, of the recommendations of the Administration."[52] What was equally annoying was that "Senator McCarran gave a release to the Press this afternoon in which he stated that his bill was based upon recommendations made to him by the President. Of course...this is not an accurate statement."[53] Simultaneously with the appearance of his bill, McCarran wrote to James Roosevelt and to Clarence Lea in a rather feeble attempt to justify his actions. The story for James Roosevelt was that it was all in keeping with the conversation that he had had with the president and with James Roosevelt on several occasions. For Lea, he explained: "It may not be necessary for me to state that this entire piece of legislation refers back to my earliest draft, when in 1934 I attempted to have Congress approve the regulation of aviation by an independent commission."[54] No one was taken in, and James Roosevelt, Rowe, and Hester moved to work with allies in the Congress, most notably Clarence Lea, but also Senators Barkley and Truman, to head off McCarran's bill and propel Lea's forward. Ironically, one of the concessions that McCarran had wrung out of the administration, namely, to move the CAA out of the Department of Commerce as a stand-alone independent commission, was now to prove troublesome in the Congress. And it was largely issues to do with executive power, where they should be located, and how they might be limited that proved to be the areas of controversy over the following three months, but there were also two other important issues that had to be resolved: a play for power by the Maritime Commission and the question of extending rate controls over foreign air routes.

The Maritime Commission's position had been weakened by the departure of Joe Kennedy to become U.S. ambassador to the Court of St. James in

London. Even so Loening worked with shipping interests such as American Export Lines, which wanted to enter the overseas airline business, to consummate amendments proposed in November 1937 to the Maritime Act. Those amendments would have grasped power over overseas routes for the commission. Loening's arguments in favor of the Maritime Commission, and in the course of which he had robustly and sometimes venomously attacked Pan American's monopoly, were not without influence. They helped publicize the nature and needs of U.S. overseas aviation routes; however, he was just not able to muster sufficient support for what on any objective reading would have been a most awkward division of power for the industry, especially when most parties were trying to rationalize and centralize its regulation. The outcome on regulation of overseas rates was much more ambiguous. McCarran had reneged on the concessions made in January, and there were thus serious political problems likely to arise in the Congress. Equally worrying and likely to inflame the matter of foreign rate controls was the fact that Trippe was bitterly opposed and the matter was still unsettled even though the interdepartmental committee had voted unanimously in favor of extending rate controls over foreign routes.[55] Rowe reported to James Roosevelt on March 3, however, that there appeared to be a shift in Trippe's position. After consultations between Trippe and his counsel on the one hand and Johnson and Hester on the other, Hester was convinced that a compromise that would allow the aeronautics bill to move forward without destructive controversy was now possible.[56] The compromise in its final form was a commitment to revisit the issue after the act had been in operation for a year combined with vague references to economic controls that did not specifically empower the government to extend rate controls over foreign routes. This was the clearest victory that Trippe achieved in the Civil Aeronautics Act, and it appears to be a price that the administration was prepared to pay to ensure smooth progress of the bill.

The day following McCarran's little surprise, Clarence Lea introduced HR 9738 proposing the substance of what had been agreed in January, embodying the vast majority of the administration's substantive regulatory preferences, but with a five- rather than a three-man authority and with the CAA standing outside the Department of Commerce, and with no powers whatsoever reserved to the Secretary of Commerce. Instead the CAA would be answerable to the courts and to the president: Section 801(a) stipulated that the "exercise and performance of the powers and duties of the Authority which are not subject to the review by courts of law shall be subject to the general direction of the President."[57] For those in the House ill-disposed to what they saw as the Executive's desire to expand its power, this was too vague and too dangerous. In hearings in the House that followed, Clinton Hester appeared as the first witness and was given a very rough ride. No clear line could be drawn prior to court decisions as to what fell within the scope of executive power and what fell outside, and Hester was obliged to admit as much. The bill now went through a further iteration and in its new form presented on April 20: Section 801(a) had been deleted and an administrator was introduced into the equation who would carry out executive and administrative functions. He was to be appointed and could be dismissed by the president at will in order to conserve executive prerogative over executive and administrative matters. In contrast, the members of the authority who would be in charge of all quasi-judicial and quasi-legislative functions could only be dismissed for good cause. Representative Bulwinkle took much of the credit for the idea of an administrator, but in fact this had been suggested back in December 1937 by Dr. Harris, director of research of the president's Committee on Administrative Management.[58] While the House Committee was willing to concede that executive functions had to be exercised efficiently, hence the administrator, it was also determined to limit such powers tightly. The "fear of Presidential control, expressed so outspokenly in Congress in connection with the Brownlow Plan for reorganization of independent regulatory agencies, led the House Committee to reserve to the authority full discretion over the work which it might delegate to the administrator."[59] There was to be no mission-creep. The bill passed in the House and that was almost the end of the matter, but not quite.

After introducing S. 3845 to the Senate on April 14, McCarran was now pushing this version of his bill along, and among other differences with the House bill sponsored by Lea was a matter of principle concerning the power of the president to dismiss those who wield executive and administrative powers. In McCarran's bill there was no mention of an administrator, instead all powers were to be wielded by the five-man authority. A clause in McCarran's bill provided that members of the authority could be dismissed by the president on the grounds of "inefficiency, neglect of duty, or malfeasance in office," and while this, at first glance, seemed to empower the president, it actually curtailed his power by restricting grounds of dismissal to those causes. In the Senate Harry Truman tabled an amendment from the floor, which sparked off a fiery debate between administration supporters and those, like McCarran. who feared an expansion of presidential power. In the end Truman and his supporters won by a vote of thirty-four to twenty-eight and the clause was removed. It was a victory of sorts and made a point. It also made Truman and McCarran bitter enemies for the rest of their political careers, but it was of no great effect on the legislation that was finally enacted into law.[60] In the House-Senate Conference Committee to iron out differences between the McCarran- and Lea-sponsored bills, the Senate provision was replaced by the House's proposal for an administrator. Other minor changes were effected, and McCarran had a further, albeit temporary, victory, in that an independent agency, the Air Safety Board, was set up within and to run alongside the CAA. Otherwise the Lea House version went through virtually unscathed. It may be known as the McCarran-Lea Bill, but McCarran's version underwent "radical" changes from the original he introduced, and in the end it was much more a Lea than a McCarran bill.[61] And that was how it all ended. The Civil Aeronautics Act was duly passed and entered into law on June 23, 1938.[62]

THE CIVIL AERONAUTICS ACT 1938

From being virtually unregulated except for matters pertaining to airmail, civil aviation in the United States was now set to become one of the most regulated of industries. The cries of the industry for regulation, the views of experts that the industry was unique in its regulatory needs, the president's conviction that it must play a vital part in the nation's transport system, and its rising importance for national defense and U.S. relations with other countries had all conspired together to deliver the 1938 Civil Aeronautics Act. Its declared policy was the "encouragement and development of an air-transport system properly adapted to the present and future needs of the foreign and domestic commerce of the United States, of the Postal Service, and of the national defense."[63] Tellingly, of the four objectives identified, two spoke to the foreign domain: foreign commerce and national defense.

The administrative setup embodied many of the painstaking compromises that had been struck over the months. A five-man CAA and an administrator were to be appointed by the president with the advice and consent of the Senate: the former could only be dismissed by the president for "inefficiency, neglect or malfeasance in office," whereas the latter could be at will. The administrator was to execute and administer under the direct authority of the president, and the members of the authority were to carry out the quasi-judicial and quasi-legislative duties of the CAA as a free-standing and independent body. Within the CAA, but also independent of it, was nested a three-man Air Safety Board that would continue operating under the safety provisions of the 1926 Air Commerce Act. Ironically, this administrative structure, which had been so difficult to construct, lived less than two years: the substance of regulation crafted lasted much longer.

The CAA effectively drew most powers unto itself for the regulation of aviation, but there were still some difficult areas of overlap, particularly with the Post Office and airmail carriage, and there were powers within powers as in the case of the Air Safety Board. However, the real meat of the act lay in the CAA's economic regulation of the industry. After the passage of the act, every route and every stop on a route for every airline had to be certificated by the CAA. No transfers of routes were allowed without permission. No abandonment of a route was allowed without permission. And no certificate could grant exclusive rights. Certificates for foreign operations were subject to presidential approval and the secretary of state was empowered to advise and consult on negotiations for foreign routes and rights, and all foreign airlines operating into the United States had to have permits. Nothing could move without the CAA's approval and in the international sphere without the president's as well. Deference was made to existing operations, and the default position was to grandfather such routes unless the service could be shown to be "inadequate and inefficient." These rules applied to U.S. international operations with only minor concessions. Designation of stops on international routes would be made only in so far as practical. The CAA would respect agreements made privately between U.S. airlines and foreign governments but only insofar as they did not clash with the public interest. And on regulation of fares, while the CAA was empowered to reject fares published by carriers in the domestic sphere, fares on international routes remained unregulated with simply a proviso that this matter be revisited after a year.

> The Authority is empowered and directed to investigate and report to the Congress within one year from the effective date of this section, to what extent, if any, the Federal Government should further regulate the rules, fares, and charges of air carriers engaged in foreign air transportation, and the classifications, rules, regulations and practices affecting such rates, fares, or charges.[64]

In other words, after a year, there could be further consideration of whether or not to legislate to empower the government to regulate international rates applied by U.S. carriers. This was the so-called compromise that had been struck to avoid further damaging controversy that might have prevented passage of the bill, but in effect it turned out to be a clear victory for Trippe: there was no government authority to regulate rates on international routes. However, later in the act, it was clear just how interventionist the CAA could be in domestic fares. If in the opinion of the CAA domestic rates were

> ... unjust or unreasonable, or unjustly discriminatory, or unduly preferential, or unduly prejudicial, the Authority shall determine and prescribe the lawful rate, fare, or charge....[65]

Abuses such as uncompetitive mergers, interlocking interests, any lack of transparency in stockholdings were all subject to regulation and oversight.

However, at the same time that monopolies and collusion were made subject to prohibition, there were explicit provisions to override such prohibitions. Sections 408, 409, and 412, dealing with the CAA's authority over pooling and fare-fixing, interlocking relationships, monopolies, and airlines owning other airlines or other parts of the civil aviation business, were all open for exemption from the antitrust laws.

> Any person affected by any order made under sections 408, 409 or 412 of this Act shall be, and is hereby relieved from the operations of the "antitrust laws," as designated in section 1 of the Act entitled "An Act to supplement existing laws against unlawful restraints and monopolies, and for other purposes," approved Oct. 15, 1914....[66]

Monopolies and industry fare-fixing were possible if condoned by the CAA. Monopolies were not ruled out for some considerable time, and thereafter there was a further period in which U.S. airlines were not in direct competition with each other. The Declaration of Policy in Title I of the act had made due obeisance to the god of competition, but it was a god now constrained by the needs of "regulation for safety and sound development."[67]

No one could any longer say: "There is practically no governmental regulation of American air lines."[68] The government had truly taken the industry in hand, and given the threat from destructive competition in the domestic market and the growing crisis internationally, most were agreed that this was appropriate. In an address to the National Aviation Forum in January 1939, the president made clear what his view on the priorities of aviation were and how they had been addressed in the 1938 Civil Aeronautics Act: he also indicated the reasons why the structure of regulation had taken the configuration that it had.

> Civil aviation is clearly recognized as the backlog of national defense in the Civil Aeronautics Act which set up the effective machinery for a comprehensive national policy with respect to the air.
>
> Underlying the statute is the principle that the country's welfare in time of peace and its safety in time of war rest upon the existence of a stabilized aircraft production, an economically and technically sound air transportation system both domestic and overseas—an adequate supply of well-trained civilian pilots and ground personnel.
>
> This new national policy set up by the Congress views American aviation as a special problem requiring special treatment. Aviation is the only form of transportation which operates in a medium which knows no frontiers but touches alike all countries on earth.
>
> One fact which stands out is that hardly another civil activity of our people bears such a direct and intimate relation to the national security as does

civil aviation. It supplies a reservoir of inestimable value to our military and naval forces in the form of men and machines, while at the same time it keeps industry so geared that it can be instantly diverted to the production of fighting planes in the event of a national emergency.[69]

The special problem requiring special treatment was largely the reason why Franklin Roosevelt had switched away from the ICC to a new independent agency. And much of the reason why aviation was special arose from considerations of national defense and the way overseas airline operations had impact and implications for foreign policy. Just how important these considerations were needs to be examined further because there were many developments in the actual and potential operation of U.S. airlines in the foreign sphere as the 1930s drew to a close. They would have to be taken into account as the administration began to pay more attention to an international civil aviation regime.

CHAPTER 5

THE CHALLENGES OF INTERNATIONAL AVIATION 1933–39

Aviation is the only form of transportation which operates in a medium which knows no frontiers but touches alike all countries on earth.

Franklin Roosevelt[1]

The bomber will always get through.

Stanley Baldwin[2]

TRIUMPHS IN THE AIR AND THE MORE PERMEABLE THEY MADE FRONTIERS brought a new poignancy to humanity's vulnerabilities as the tragedy of the 1930s unfolded and global war approached. The development of civil aviation in the United States took place within this context, and that meant more than ever that it could never be seen as just another commercial enterprise.

World affairs began to deteriorate dramatically in the 1930s. Events moved first in Asia, where Japan laid siege to Mukden in September 1931 and then later contrived to go to war with China. Hostilities began in earnest in 1937, and in October 1938, after the Rape of Nanking and running amok in much of China, Japan withdrew from the League of Nations in protest at being branded an aggressor, whilst simultaneously looking even further afield for military expansion. Actions were speaking louder than words. In Europe it was the same story. Benito Mussolini in Italy and Adolf Hitler in Germany came to power in 1922 and 1933, respectively, and both propagated forms of extreme nationalism and mongered after war. In Spain a similar nationalism fuelled the Civil War, which entered its final phase in 1938–39 and culminated in victory for General Francisco Franco. In 1938 Italy consolidated its military gains in Abyssinia as Mussolini pursued his ambition to recreate the Roman Empire. And in the same year Hitler moved inexorably onwards to smash the last vestiges of the Versailles Peace Treaty and the existing political configurations in central Europe. He sought the breakup of Czechoslovakia by pressurizing Prague to grant autonomy to the Sudetenland, and in September, betrayal at Munich left Czechoslovakia indefensible militarily and the Sudetenland absorbed into the Third Reich. Events in Asia and Europe were a collective harbinger of worse to come. The world was on the edge. The last fatal moves were about to be enacted that would pitch the whole world into war. Militarism in the form of Japanese warlords, Spanish Falangists, Italian Fascists, and German National Socialists had seized the initiative in world affairs.

Democracies and democracy were under threat. Plagued by self-doubt and buffeted by one international crisis after another, they fell into weak and often rudderless foreign policies. But this was not universally the case: there were some in both the United States and Britain who had little truck with self-doubt and who knew what needed to be done. Unfortunately, they lacked the power to do it. In the United States they formed around Franklin Roosevelt, but he was constrained by Isolationist public opinion and, apart from the Navy, the parlous state of the U.S. military establishment. In Britain they formed around Winston Churchill, but the appeasers held him isolated from power on the backbenches of the House of Commons. To many, it looked as if all that those who would oppose aggressive militarism had were words, and while Roosevelt famously said in his first inaugural speech that "the only thing we have to fear is fear itself," not succumbing was far easier said than done. And the great fear that infiltrated so many souls of the well-intentioned Isolationist and appeasement camps, respectively, in the United States and Britain and paralyzed them from robust action was the prospect of a devastating war that would overturn the world order and destroy civilization. A key component of that potential for devastation was aerial warfare.

Hugh Montague "Boom" Trenchard, commander of the British Royal Flying Corps in France during the First World War and father of the Royal Air Force (RAF), observed in 1916:

> Owing to the unlimited space in the Air, the difficulty one machine has in seeing another, the accident of wind and cloud, it is impossible for aeroplanes, however skilful and vigilant their pilots, however numerous their formations, to prevent hostile aircraft from crossing the line if they have the initiative and determination to do so.[3]

It was an insight that Stanley Baldwin paraphrased sixteen years later as "the bomber always gets through," and by then bombing capabilities had expanded enormously and also there had been considerably more thought invested in what airpower could do. Interestingly, it was the United States that established the first center for strategic thinking about airpower when in 1920 the Army Air Service founded its Tactical School. The Army Air Service also had a high-profile publicist in the shape of General Billy Mitchell, who incessantly called for more resources and an independent air arm. He took a holistic approach, recommending the development of a wide range of functions for airpower. Later, in 1946, General "Hap" Arnold, an old friend and admirer of Mitchell, argued in a similar vein, saying that airpower consisted of "a nation's ability to deliver cargo, people, destructive missiles, and war-making potential through the air to a desired destination and to accomplish a desired purpose."[4]

It is never easy to trace the origin and interaction of ideas that result in full-blown strategic doctrines, but there is little doubt that ideas from Trenchard and the Italian Giulio Douhet seeped through much of the strategic thinking in the interwar years. Douhet, who is generally recognized as the first major theorist of airpower, in his book in 1921, *The Command of the Air*, emphasized the importance of bombing and its ability to inflict terror on the enemy population and undermine its morale.[5] Such ideas were later developed by an air marshal of the RAF for much of the Second World War, Arthur Travers "Bomber" Harris, who in turn had influence on many others. Furthermore, the ability of the bomber to get through and to inflict terror was brought home vividly to the world in the Spanish Civil War. On April 26, 1937, the Luftwaffe Condor Legion and the Italian Fascist Aviazone Legionaria bombed the Basque town of Guernica to rubble. Local authorities reported over 1,500 casualties, a figure that has now been scaled back to 200–400, but too late to prevent the propagation of the imagery of terror captured in iconic form by Picasso's famous painting *Guernica*. The impact was huge and frightening.

In the 1930s it was this picture of the destructive might of heavy strategic bombing wreaking havoc on industry and infrastructure and terrorizing the civilian population that held sway in both the official and the public mind. Sir John Slessor, Harris's predecessor as air marshal of the RAF, was fearful in 1938 that the Luftwaffe had the capability to deliver a knockout blow through heavy strategic bombing against Britain and France.[6] In the summer of 1941 Chief of the U.S. Army Air Corps "Hap" Arnold envisaged the possibility of equally decisive results, though for a different target. In a paper for the U.S. secretary of war, he wrote that "the United States must build, as quickly as possible, an Air Force capable of waging a decisive air offensive against the Axis powers in Europe, and this Air Force must consist of Heavy Bombers."[7] By the late 1930s the fear of the bomber always getting through was hugely augmented by knowledge of its payload, which could

destroy whole towns and cities. It was only with the development of sophisticated radar and improved performance of fighter interceptors that any kind
of credible balance emerged between the bomber as an offensive weapon
and the fighter's defensive capability. In the 1930s, before that happened,
strategic thinking was obsessed with the capabilities of heavy bombing, and
this was very evident in the philosophy and teachings of the U.S. Air Corps
Tactical School.

> The possibility for the application of military force against the vital structure
> of a nation directly and immediately upon the outbreak of hostilities is the
> most important and far-reaching development of modern times.[8]

What, one might ask, has all this to do with the development of civil
aviation policy in the Roosevelt administrations of the 1930s? The answer is
simple: a great deal. British prime minister Ramsay MacDonald may have
been waxing a little whimsical when he told the Disarmament Conference
in Geneva that civil aviation "in the twinkling of an eye, on the receipt of
a telephone message, could be transformed into a fighting force"; however,
he captured a certain truth, a mood of the era and its fears.[9] Civil aviation
was inextricably connected with a nation's airpower capabilities in terms
of research and development, equipment, the building of domestic infrastructure that strengthens a nation's economy, the development of overseas
airways that can be used for strategic purposes, and pilot and technical
skills. These features of the way civilian connected with military aviation
influenced the way civil aviation's future was considered by Roosevelt and
his advisers. Of paramount importance was the need for a thriving civil aviation industry and that could not be left to the vagaries of the marketplace.
Aspects of national defense and the conduct of America's foreign relations
would play important roles in determining how civil aviation policy would
develop, and Roosevelt recognized this from the outset.

After the president presented the Federal Aviation Commission Report
to Congress in January 1935, there were further developments that affected
how U.S. overseas airline policies would mature. The Federal Aviation
Commission had taken national defense specifically into account when
drawing up the report, and the connection between civil and military aviation capabilities was widely acknowledged and valued accordingly. The
foreign policy implications remained less understood. In June Roosevelt
moved to address this failing. He ordered the creation of a committee to
give "constant effective consideration...to the development of American
air transport lines in foreign territories." It was tasked further and required
to make "observations and gather information pertaining to civil international aviation in all its phases and to submit such recommendations as may

seem called for."[10] The result was the Interdepartmental Committee on Civil International Aviation, chaired by R. Walton Moore, undersecretary of state, with Assistant Secretary of the Treasury Steve Gibbons, Second Assistant Postmaster General Harllee Branch, and Assistant Secretary of Commerce John Monroe Johnson as its members. Although the War and Navy Departments were not originally members of the committee, they were frequently and closely consulted.

The committee first met on July 15, 1935, and it was an important forum for the discussion of difficult and important matters bearing on civil aviation, including talks with the British in December 1935 for the establishment of a transatlantic air service. However, it was primarily a talking shop and an educational forum. After over eighteen months it had never complied with that part of its brief that called for it to make "recommendations" to the president.[11] Nevertheless, the committee proved to be a useful vehicle for discussions, discussions that were frequently informed by Trippe and that propelled officials of government along a steep learning curve. In particular, the committee addressed three very important issues.

The first two are closely interwoven. They dealt with a collection of national security concerns and Pan American's de facto monopoly on foreign routes. How civil airlines operating abroad might contribute to U.S. security was a huge issue, and in practice this referred to Pan American. Its success on U.S. foreign routes had been assisted by government subsidy and favored instrument treatment, largely because of a felt need to have a strong and able competitor to deal with foreign airlines. The principle of competition had already fallen foul of the needs of political priorities, but the relationship between Pan American and the government proved to be a difficult and uneasy one as time went by. The government was well aware of the help Pan American rendered American foreign and security policies, but there was a growing uneasiness with Trippe's vaunting ambition to secure an unassailable and privileged position for Pan American in part by excluding other American airlines from foreign skies, and it made him powerful enemies.

Entwined in all this was Pan American's de facto monopoly on U.S. foreign routes and questions as to whether such a monopoly was legal and desirable in principle and in practice. What the nature of the competitive environment should be had arisen at an early stage of the development of civil aviation in the domestic realm. There were concerns at the Brown "spoils conference" system that had been used to rationalize and consolidate domestic airlines effectively into four dominant carriers. That system had subsequently been disrupted in the early Roosevelt years, but with the 1938 Civil Aeronautics Act, it became possible for the regulator to control all aspects of the industry and hence determine how competitive it might be. There were always those who objected that this kind of regulation was "un-American" and contrary to the principles of the free market, but fear of cutthroat competition, safety concerns, the need to protect capital and encourage investment, and the goal of creating a comprehensive and efficient national transport system for both economic and national security reasons overrode such objections. And in some ways this was all very well in the domestic domain because the U.S. government could dictate the form of regulation and apply it in a uniform manner that would at least provide common rules for the airlines; this was not possible in the international realm. There, American operators were confronted most frequently by government-owned or at least heavily subsidized airlines. In this environment, competition would always be on an unequal playing field, and moreover, the scope of operations would also be determined by agreements struck one way or another with foreign airlines and the governments of their parent countries, which could lead to preferential treatment for some and discrimination for others. These issues presented further complications for devising policies for the operation of U.S. airlines on foreign routes.

Trippe, however, had a ready answer to all problems: quite simply—Pan American. From one perspective this was understandable. Trippe gambled with huge investments, particularly in the Pacific, and knew that potential profits would disappear if there were competition from other U.S. airlines, especially if it turned destructive and cutthroat. In that eventuality American foreign civil aviation in general would be the victim and foreign operators the beneficiaries. Trippe was always quick to use such patriotic arguments to get his way with officialdom. So for him it made eminent sense that Pan American should be the chosen instrument of the United States abroad and built up even further as a strong international operator, which could take on all foreign comers. Playing to the strength of America's lead in the production of long-range passenger planes, Pan American would come to dominate the world's airways. This would benefit the U.S. economy and enhance its national security. Furthermore, Trippe was more than ready to go further than this and directly assist the government in the development of strategically important routes to Europe, across the Pacific and later to Africa. However, as we shall see, particularly when it came to "de-lousing" SCADTA in 1940 of its German personnel, the commercial interests of Pan American and U.S. national security sometimes conflicted.[12] It was not just that Pan American had established a de facto monopoly on U.S. foreign routes and was commercially successful in the 1930s that posed problems for U.S. policy-makers, it was also the fact that they had to weigh in the balance that Pan American served U.S. defense and security needs (though not always), and at the time was the only airline positioned to do so.

Thirdly, and finally, there was the challenge of a transatlantic air service, which mainly meant coming to terms with the British, but there were wider ramifications to this than just reaching an agreement on a transatlantic route. Those ramifications ran to a very basic factor of international services and one about which the British would have a massive say. Unlike domestic air services, no country could play the international civil aviation game alone. There had to be agreement on landing, on refueling, on transit, and most important of all on entry into commercial carriage with other nations. Those needs placed Britain in a strong position. In the 1930s it controlled or had a major influence on access to over a third of the globe through its empire, commonwealth, and client states, and equally importantly it held strategic islands that were needed for transoceanic routes. Reaching accommodation with others for rights of entry could and often did affect the character of the commercial operation offered. The regime for U.S. airlines operating on foreign routes could not be solely dictated by American policy-makers. Discussions with the British in the 1930s revealed many of these realities.[13]

TRANSATLANTIC CROSSINGS

There were a number of false starts in the planning of transatlantic air services. At various times in the early 1930s, proposals and projects ranged from a joint Anglo-French-U.S. scheme to exclusive collusion between Pan American and Imperial Airways. The whole international system, if one could distinguish it as such, was confusing and complex, partly at least because Trippe and Britain's Imperial Airways under its chairman Sir Eric Geddes and general manager C. E. Woods Humphrey worked closely and often secretly together, at least in certain areas, developing policies and negotiating independently of their governments. Woods Humphrey, a difficult man with an autocratic and highly patriotic manner but also a strong sense of fair play, was the driving force for Imperial Airways. Between Trippe and Woods Humphrey there developed an understanding that together their two airlines should dominate the Atlantic on the basis of what they referred to as a "square deal," but these secret agreements did not always remain secret and came to be frowned on by governments, which eventually insisted on more say and involvement.

A key factor that drew the British government more directly into Imperial Airways' affairs was Trippe's attempt to negotiate independently with Newfoundland for landing rights for a transatlantic route. He kept in close touch with Imperial Airways, but even so this aroused concerns in Ottawa, where Canada was fearful of being excluded from what was expected to be a very lucrative transatlantic operation. Ottawa alerted London to its fears and the talks were brought to an end when Newfoundland fell into economic disarray and reverted from Dominion to British Crown Colony status in December 1933. Thereafter the British Government, in the form of Sir Francis Shelmerdine, the director general of Civil Aviation, and Sir Donald Banks, director-general of the Post Office, insisted on more direct government intervention and closer liaison with Woods Humphrey. This was unpalatable to Trippe because he thought that he could work more freely and to Pan American's advantage without governments being involved, and he knew that if the British government were involved then the U.S. government would not be far behind. Pan American and Imperial Airways continued to work together on the planning for a transatlantic route, but both sides were now aware that final agreement would likely be subject to government involvement and approval.[14]

As planning for transatlantic air routes developed, particularly from December 1935 onwards, when British officials arrived in Washington for discussions, it became evident that the interests and objectives of Pan American and the U.S. government were not in entire accord. Unlike the U.S. government, Pan American, Imperial Airways, and the British government wanted to exclude competition by restricting operations between Britain and the United States to Pan American and Imperial Airways, or a UK-Irish-Canadian airline under Imperial's control. The British would also exclude airlines of other European countries from servicing the Atlantic by denying them landing rights on both the northern and southern routes in Newfoundland and Bermuda, respectively. Not only was this generally anti-competitive, but it was also exclusive of any other U.S. airline, something that troubled some officials in Washington, especially in the Post Office, which was required by law to have competitive bidding for the award of airmail contracts. Imperial Airways and Pan American also wanted to operate on the basis of their square deal, involving commercial collusion that ensured, among other things, that Imperial Airways would receive an adequate share of transatlantic airmail revenue. Without some kind of pooling or quota arrangement, Imperial Airways would only harvest a fraction of the revenue taken by Pan American because of the larger proportion of mail originating in the United States.[15] Understandably this was not palatable to most Americans.

The Interdepartmental Committee on Civil International Aviation at its outset in July 1935 was pretty much in the dark as to what was going on and was unsure of what was likely to transpire.[16] Over the following five months, Trippe, who attended most of the committee's meetings, provided enlightenment, but it was always colored by the needs and objectives of Pan American. Problems likely to arise on the proposed transatlantic route were discussed at a meeting of the committee on December 2, with Trippe present. This was a couple of days before the arrival of the British delegation, and as it later transpired, Harllee Branch rightly predicted that the British would ask for an exclusive arrangement and a fifty-fifty division of airmail carriage: the former demand would be difficult to meet and the latter impossible without an act of Congress. Apart from this it seemed that the committee was still unsure of what to expect. They were aware that Pan American and Imperial Airways had been engaged in talks on and off for several years, but the members of the committee were clearly not privy to the details of those talks. They now in effect turned to Trippe for information, but before doing so, sensitive to the fact that Pan American was the only airline represented at the meeting, they were prompt to indicate that they had not changed in their willingness "to hear the views of all interested American transport companies."[17] Given the circumstances at the time, this was a rather empty gesture.

Trippe held forth about the history of planning that had gone on between Pan American and Imperial Airways for a transatlantic route. He did not mention that Pan American wanted to divide the market with Imperial Airways on the basis of an exclusive "square deal," but he did make it clear that he thought major concessions would have to be made if an American airline were to launch a service. Without access to British airbases on both the southern and northern transatlantic routes, airplanes would not have the range to operate. The British, he said, held the key, namely, refuelling stops: "Without access to these positions it would be impractical for anyone to operate in the North Atlantic for at least some years."[18] The British, however, could in the meantime mount a transatlantic service to Bermuda and Canada with feeder services to the United States. Trippe knew that the British wanted to take the transatlantic route to New York via Montreal because that could link directly with a British round-the-world service that would eventually cross the Pacific to Australia. And for their part the Canadians had ambitions to make Montreal the main receiving and distribution station in North America for transatlantic traffic. Completion of Imperial's round-the-world route would, among other things, pose a competitive challenge to Pan American's Pacific ambitions. Meanwhile, in the Atlantic, there was the danger that the British could sew up the market and the United States would simply be left with feeder services: as Trippe pointedly told the committee, the "United States should have a larger share in a transatlantic service than a mere shuttle to Montreal."[19] What he did not say was that to forestall anything like that, he was prepared to go along with the idea of a square deal and that he was also prepared to try to sidestep his own government and deal directly with the British if he felt that he had to.

Branch noted that there were only three things that they could trade on with the British: landing rights, the amount of business that the United

States might offer, and moral obligations owed by Imperial to Pan American. At this point the discussion of the transatlantic route drew to a close, but Branch went on to suggest close government and airline cooperation in developing overseas routes. This was some indication of just how much the administration now appreciated the need for cooperation with Trippe: it also reflected Branch's conviction that the government needed to keep a close eye on Pan American.

> Mr. Branch asked the Committee to consider the possibility of putting the Government in a closer relationship with any major air transport company operating extensively in the international field. He pointed out that the foreign air mail service tended toward monopoly at the present time and that for this reason it might be convenient for both the company and the Government if there were a representative of the Government such as an official observer, without vote, on the Board of Directors, who might keep track of developments in the company.[20]

Needless to say, given Trippe's views, this never came to pass with Pan American.

Most of the issues surrounding the launch of a transatlantic route began to emerge in discussions between members of Moore's Committee and the British delegation led by Sir Donald Banks, which arrived in Washington on December 4, 1935. Banks's team included Shelmerdine, Woods Humphrey, and representatives of Canada and Ireland. The British had held preparatory discussions with the Irish and Canadians and representatives from Newfoundland in Ottawa to establish a common understanding before coming on to Washington. And Woods Humphrey and Trippe had conducted detailed talks in New York, out of which, largely at Trippe's insistence, they had agreed to downplay the idea of a joint operating company on the British side in favor of continuing with Imperial Airways and its favored relationship with Pan American. The Irish and the Canadians were not well pleased with this, but the cooperative atmosphere of Ottawa soon reasserted itself.[21] The outcomes of the meeting between Trippe and Woods Humphrey will be revisited in more detail shortly.

At the first meeting in Washington, it did not take long for Banks to reveal what they ideally wanted.

> ...we feel that this cannot be a matter that can be left to any, shall we say, chance company that comes along.
> ...we must insure that we get the best possible operating instruments, that will give us both [i.e., the United States and Britain] efficiency, economy and safety.[22]

The "non-chance" companies were, of course, Imperial Airways and Pan American. Harllee Branch simply responded by saying that a clear picture was needed of the rights Pan American had requested and what the British would ask of the United States in return. It was quite clear that American officialdom still did not have much idea about what was actually going on.[23] Trippe explained that Pan American sought rights for a twice-weekly local service to Bermuda and landing rights there as well as in Canada, Newfoundland, and Ireland for a twice-weekly service to the UK. Assistant Secretary of Commerce Johnson followed up on Branch's point and suggested that Imperial Airways and Pan American should spell out the array of rights to be reciprocally exchanged so that the conference could then work on them as a basic agenda. Over the following week, meeting in smaller groups, largely dominated by Imperial Airways and Pan American officials, this was in fact what was done, and by December 12, 1935, a basic understanding had been reached.

The understanding looked to provide a fifteen-year permit to Imperial Airways and Pan American for each to operate twice-weekly transatlantic services running from the United States to the UK via Canada, Newfoundland, and Ireland on a northern route and/or from the United States via Bermuda and other country stops to the UK on a southern route. The other stops essentially meant refueling in the Azores and going on to landfall somewhere in southern Europe, but neither Pan American nor Imperial Airways held such rights in 1935. The understanding also envisaged a local route from the United States to Bermuda, Puerto Rico, and stops beyond. In principle there was supposedly no exclusivity, and also the understandings were based "upon the principle of full reciprocity between the countries interested. They do not operate to exclude similar arrangements between the United States and other countries."[24] It was hoped that experimental flights could take place in 1936 with the full service being inaugurated in 1937. This timetable turned out to be unduly optimistic.

Part of the problem for the U.S. government arose from Britain's strong position. A few months after the December talks, Moore confided fears to a colleague that mirrored those of Trippe and that had led him to the idea of accommodating the British at almost any cost.

> Personally, I have always had in mind the fact that the British have the whip hand, inasmuch as they are able to conduct a trans-Atlantic service without obtaining any landing rights in this country, the other European Governments being in a different situation.[25]

In fact, the British position was more constrained than Moore, and possibly Trippe, realized. The British were fearful of superior American equipment and Pan American commercial aggression, particularly evident in the Pacific, and already in 1935 there were wider political considerations in play that made the British wary of offending the United States by opening a transatlantic route whilst denying rights that would enable the United States to do the same. Given that Moore was not sufficiently sensitized to such considerations, one might say that the Americans did rather well in Washington—at least prima facie. They insisted on and achieved a commitment to reciprocity and had seemingly overcome the desire for exclusive rights for Pan American and Imperial Airways.

It turned out, however, that the understandings reached in Washington had not resolved everything and that in some areas that seemed resolved there was in fact more to come. One issue that had been left for later consideration on the insistence of the U.S. government was the award of airmail contracts. As things stood the U.S. Post Office did not have the legal right to award contracts because operating permits had not yet been issued, in effect services did not exist and there could not be competitive bidding. Also underlying all this was a refusal by Branch to meet British demands. This was to be one of the issues that returned to trouble developments. Other problems arose because of Trippe and the British government.

Unknown to the U.S. authorities, Trippe had already reached an understanding with Woods Humphrey before the outcome of the Washington talks. They met in New York the week before the talks in Washington, and Trippe identified the difficulties that the U.S. government would likely cause for their existing plans mutually to dominate the transatlantic routes.

> In the first place, political considerations (particularly the importance of the large Italian and German votes of the forthcoming Presidential election) would make it quite impossible for the Government of the United States of America to contemplate the conclusion of a formal agreement with any foreign Government on an exclusive basis. Moreover it seemed certain that the United States Postal authorities...would be debarred legally from entering into any agreement with regard to the mutual exchange of air mails in advance of the establishment of a service....In these circumstances, Mr. Trippe and...[Woods Humphrey] were agreed that the best...approach would be to continue negotiations between the two Companies with a view to producing a basis of common agreement.[26]

A month later, on January 25, 1936, Woods Humphrey in London and Trippe in New York signed, on a company-to-company basis, an agreement for each to fly two round-trips a week on the northern route via Newfoundland. They were to enjoy exclusive rights, neither could start till the other did, and everything was to be on the basis of a square deal that would, among other things, take care of Britain's disadvantage concerning revenue from airmail carriage.[27] U.S. commitments to nonexclusivity seemed to have been negated.

The U.S. government was unwilling to authorize exclusive agreements for Pan American on Atlantic routes and certainly did not want to be publicly associated with such a policy for fear of the criticisms it was likely to draw. However, there was continuing anxiety arising from what most in Washington perceived as Britain's "whip hand," which led on to a willingness to try to accommodate British demands. On January 22, 1936, Banks wrote to Moore making the case once again for Anglo-American exclusive dominance of transatlantic services. It was no coincidence that at the time a French delegation was about to descend on Washington to discuss the possibilities for transatlantic services.

> If I may express my personal view, in confidence, to you it is that the development of Transatlantic flying will require careful control of the initial stages if undue competition and chaotic conditions are to be avoided, and that their control, whilst not designed to exclude the operation of other interests mainly concerned, should be exercised primarily by our two countries, and principally in the direction of avoiding an undue multiplication of flights across the Atlantic before the traffic has developed sufficiently to warrant them.[28]

On February 19, 1936, the interdepartmental committee decided that it "would go no further with the French than it had done with the Germans," which was not very far at all. This might seem like supine cowardice on the part of Moore and his fellow committee members, but the harsh truth was that the British government could determine unilaterally at that time who and who would not fly the Atlantic. Later in the year this became very apparent when the British undersecretary of state for Air, Philip Sassoon, explained in the House of Commons on July 30 how Britain, Ireland, Newfoundland, and Canada had undertaken

> ... to grant the necessary landing and transit rights within its own territory to the joint company [i.e., British-Irish-Canadian airline controlled by Imperial Airways] and to Pan American Airways. It is contemplated that unless otherwise determined by the consent of the four Governments such rights will be exclusive in respect of transatlantic air services for a period of 15 years....[29]

The U.S. government could grant commercial air rights to as many countries as it liked, but if those countries could not gain access to the refueling stops controlled by Britain, then they would be unable to fly.

It was not just the continuing attempts to make the transatlantic route exclusive to Imperial Airways and Pan American that frustrated developments. Three other matters arose to complicate and delay things throughout

1936 and into 1937. These were mail contracts and the related matter of issuing permits for fifteen years that the British and Pan American wanted to be irrevocable, British and Canadian insistence on routing flights across the Atlantic via Montreal to the United States, and matters concerning a route between the United States and Bermuda, which the Americans feared might be used by the British as a feeder service, which would allow them unilaterally to expand their transatlantic services. All illuminated the difficulties of international operations.

The issue of airmail contracts had been so contentious that there was no hope of agreement in the December talks. Initially it was a legal question as to whether the Commerce Department could issue irrevocable permits for fifteen years to Pan American and Imperial Airways that impeded progress. In December 1935 the department thought it could issue such permits, but by April 1936 there were significant doubts. Branch felt that he could not go along with issuing the permits as they stood because "these permits and the carrying out of arrangements between the two companies, will, in all likelihood, make it impossible for any American company other than the Pan American Airways to bid for a trans-Atlantic mail contract when one is advertised."[30] Notwithstanding Branch's strong sentiments, there were moves to accommodate the British in June and July, largely because of fears that the British might go it alone. In principle it was agreed that there could be revocation, but in practice the conditions and the costs were such that it was unlikely ever to happen. Revocation could take place only for "the highest reasons of public policy," and if enacted would lead to the suspension of all transatlantic services.[31] Branch's concerns and the concerns of the president and others in the administration about Pan American's de facto monopoly and its extension over the transatlantic routes would have to be dealt with by a different method, and when the final permits were issued in May 1939, they were.

While the saga about irrevocability was progressing, Branch was also engaged directly in the matter of airmail contracts. The British, Branch recorded, had been "insistent upon inclusion in the flying permits of an arrangement for carrying mails under which we estimated that the American company during the tenure of the permits would perform $3,000,000 worth of free service for the British."[32] This issue rumbled on for some time, but in September 1936 Branch wrote to Assistant Secretary Johnson in the Commerce Department protesting at any arrangement that might benefit Imperial Airways in this way and he was successful: "Commerce refused to issue permits with such a provision."[33] For the time being this issue receded into the background and became centered on the private company agreement between Imperial Airways and Pan American for a square deal, but there were two other matters that grew to greater prominence, caused delays, and had to be resolved.

Both issues highlighted what was to become a long-standing problem for U.S. international civil aviation. They had the best equipment in the world for international operations, but if they could not get access to bases and markets there was little use to which they could be put. Once these issues were fully appreciated, they helped to persuade President Roosevelt, and even those in the administration who were less internationalist minded than him, to seek multilateral worldwide agreement on rights of innocent passage or overflight and a right to technical stop for refueling and repairs. The problems about to be brought into focus did not solely involve these matters, but they loomed large within them. What troubled the Americans was the status of the route from the United States to Bermuda and British and Canadian insistence on routing incoming flights into the United States via Montreal rather than taking a more direct route from Newfoundland. The Americans were vulnerable on both issues because they needed refueling bases in British and Canadian territory; so, fearful of endangering their aviation interests, they trod carefully.

Bermuda was the eastern jumping off point for services on the southern route to Europe. This was an attractive route, because, unlike the northern, it would not be closed down for lengthy periods each year by harsh winter weather, and it was a destination in its own right and an intermediate stop to places such as Puerto Rico and onwards. It was not close enough to Europe for a nonstop hop with equipment then available, but Trippe was fully aware of that problem and had ambitions regarding the Portuguese and landing rights in the Azores, which would solve it.

The meeting in Washington in December 1935 was by no means the first time the possibility of a United States–Bermuda route had been visited, but now it looked as if it would actually come to pass. However, as the Americans considered this further, they began to fear that the British might use the United States–Bermuda route as a feeder service for additional transatlantic services over and above the agreement to allow two round-trips a week each for Imperial Airways and Pan American originating in the United States or Britain and running between these two countries. It thus became important for the Americans to get a commitment from Britain that the United States–Bermuda route would only service local traffic. Again this brought to light an issue that was to have progeny. Eight years later at Chicago, Britain and the United States failed to reach agreement on commercial aviation rights because of British fears that the Americans would use its capacity for picking up what they, the British, considered to be local traffic in London for onward carriage into Europe and thus service customers that they felt should rightly be catered for by British airlines. Again there was something to learn here: in an international marketplace, there is no such thing as a local market. In the Bermuda case it was the Americans who insisted that there should be. The problem for the British was that if they adhered to the letter of what the Americans were demanding, it would be an infringement on their sovereign rights in Bermuda. There was in fact nothing in law or in their formal understanding with the Americans to prevent the British from mounting as many flights as they wanted between Bermuda and Britain, and if they wanted to feed into that service American passengers from the New York-Bermuda route, then so be it.

Between April and the end of June 1936 there was a flurry of telegrams between Washington and the British Foreign Office, which, among other things, exchanged views several times about the status of the United States–Bermuda route. In the end the Americans had to be content with the following.

> ...His Majesty's Government, while they naturally cannot agree to restrict themselves in their own use of territories under the sovereignty of the British Crown, desire nevertheless to assure the United States Government that they have never intended, nor do they intend, to use the local service between Bermuda and New York as a means of creating a separate Trans-Atlantic service additional to that provided for in the draft permits now under consideration.[34]

On June 18, 1937, Pan American and Imperial Airways began regular services. With the Bermuda problem resolved as best it could be, the routing via Montreal remained as the last high-profile problem preventing the exchange of permits. As Trippe had pointed out to the interdepartmental committee on December 2, 1935, the routing being insisted on by the British could mean that they effectively ran the transatlantic route with the United States operating little more than a glorified shuttle service to Montreal. At best it would be a lengthy and inconvenient detour for incoming U.S. planes. This proved to be an intractable problem for some months. In February 1937 Moore reported to Secretary of State Cordell Hull.

> The Department of Commerce has not thus far been able to obtain the assurances it desires from Canada that the American Company will be permitted to fly the most direct route across Canada and not be obliged to fly the longer route via Montreal.[35]

Lurking behind the inconvenience and commercial disadvantage of being routed via Montreal was also the knowledge that such routing of transatlantic flights would dovetail with British plans for completing a round-the-world "all red line" empire route. Imperial Airways began a regular airmail service to Australia in December 1934, and the ambition was to cross the Pacific and link first with Canada and then with a transatlantic service.

Importantly, to do that it would have to acquire landing rights in Hawaii in order to cross the Pacific, which it did not receive until after the Second World War. Even so, at the time, there was potential danger here for Pan American. Imperial Airways could pose competitive problems for its well-advanced operations in the Pacific: these will be explored shortly. Moore thought that either the negotiations might stumble on this routing issue and then the British would go ahead with the transatlantic route without the United States, or Montreal would have to be accepted, which would lay up problems for the future.[36] In fact, Moore was unaware that Trippe and his vice president, John Cooper, had made arrangements with Shelmerdine in London in November 1936 to resolve the problem, at least to Trippe's satisfaction. Trippe suggested that Canada issue permits to Pan American for routes to Montreal and Shediac. "The American government could not dictate where his airline flew, he argued, and once permits were exchanged, Pan Am would gradually shift its service on to the Montreal route. This way everyone would be satisfied."[37] The final comment was ingenuous to say the least, but the United States government eventually agreed to what it believed to be a compromise by which Imperial Airways would fly from Newfoundland to Montreal and then on to New York, and Pan American would fly from Newfoundland on the more direct route via Shediac, New Brunswick, into New York.[38]

On February 22, 1937, the British Air Ministry issued Pan American with a permit to fly in and out of the UK, Newfoundland, and Bermuda. On March 5 a similar permit was issued to Pan American by the Canadian authorities, and on April 13, Ireland followed suit. The permits were handed to Trippe on April 20 in the Commerce Department in Washington, DC. Simultaneously Trippe had been negotiating with the Portuguese Government on a company-to-government basis and had managed to extract from it permits to use the Azores for twenty-five years with a clause excluding any other American airline for fifteen years. The British negotiated similar rights, but Pan American clearly looked triumphant with the way now open on the northern and southern transatlantic routes.

The months that followed witnessed great activity including a series of conferences twice in Ireland and once in Canada, which addressed safety standards and meteorological and communication issues. Things were moving forward, but then political controversy in the United States, aircraft losses, and delays in the delivery of new equipment for both Pan American and Imperial Airways conspired to cause more impediments. Furthermore, these developments were now taking place as the profile of aviation was lifted by the moves in Congress and the administration to reform the regulation of the industry and at the point in time that opposition to Pan American began to gather force. One of its most virulent critics, as already noted, was the newly established Maritime Commission headed by Joe Kennedy, with his aviation adviser, Grover Loening. In July 1937 Loening was quick to pounce on the exclusive agreement that Trippe had negotiated with the Portuguese and point out the dangers in no uncertain terms to his boss, Kennedy. He later sent similar arguments to James Roosevelt, who passed them on to his father, the president. According to Loening, the danger was not just that of monopoly, it was the way Pan American operated that monopoly. He felt that Pan American was endangering U.S. interests with its collusion with Imperial Airways, most notably by agreeing to hold back services until Imperial Airways was ready and by offering Imperial help to get entry into U.S. landing grounds in Hawaii and possibly Panama as part of its deal to acquire entry rights into New Zealand. He also thought that Pan American had not shown much vision in its preparations for the Atlantic route. He alleged that not only had it ordered insufficient and inadequate equipment, but it had not supported U.S. aircraft manufacturing. The latest U.S. aircraft were now in fact going abroad to foreign airlines and not to Pan American.[39] There was always a personal animus when Loening wrote about Pan American, but there was also much truth in what he said as well, and this seeped into the public domain and began to add momentum to the criticisms leveled at Trippe and Pan American. There was growing uneasiness not just among some members of Government but also in the Congress, the industry itself, and the wider public. Responding to these concerns in an attempt to create new potential for overseas aviation operations, the government now encouraged American Export Lines, a shipping company, to forge ahead with plans for developing Amex, an airline that could also operate on the Atlantic. This was shortly to have important consequences. Trippe tried to buy out Amex, but the deal was prohibited by the CAA, and it therefore continued to menace Pan American's monopoly. At the very least it became the means by which the administration could try to dilute Pan American's dominance on routes across the Atlantic.[40] But all this was some way off in 1937.

Criticisms were mounting and the moves on what became the 1938 Civil Aeronautics Act provided a dangerous platform for them. Trippe now decided that he would have to take some countermeasures. In March 1938 he explained to Woods Humphrey that the square deal that looked to pooling airmail revenue and that stipulated that neither side would start the transatlantic service until the other was ready was compromising him politically in Washington. There was now also the added complication that Amex was entering the scene. The result was that Woods Humphrey agreed to amend their agreement and delete both the pooling arrangements and the simultaneous start.[41] This did not mean, however, that one side could necessarily start without the other. With the passage of the Civil Aeronautics Act in June 1938, Imperial Airways would have to be approved by this new regulator and the president before operations could begin. And for their part the British, with their control over Bermuda and Newfoundland, would always have the last say on whether airlines flew the Atlantic or not. At least that was the case until early 1939.

In early 1939, after protracted talks with the French, the United States took the first step to outmaneuver the British in their control of Atlantic routes. They announced that France had been awarded landing rights in the United States for a six-month period, and the draft agreements were exchanged in March.[42] That in itself was not sufficient to undermine the British position, but combined with the range of the new Boeing 314, it was. The Boeing 314 had a range of 3,500 miles, which was enough to allow it to bypass Bermuda and land at the Azores in one hop, refuel, and fly on to Marseilles. In March 1939, after problems and delays, Boeing finally started deliveries to Pan American. This not only meant that Britain was outmaneuvered, it also cast into gloom the picture of British equipment. The British had managed to fly the first transatlantic commercial flight to Canada when the Short-Mayo composite carried a small package of mail from Foynes to Montreal July 21–22, 1938. This was a rather strange pick-a-back plane: a large flying boat carried a smaller one aloft, which then took off in flight, but it had only tiny cargo capacity. Britain's other available planes the Empire Flying Boats could only traverse the Atlantic with in-flight refueling, and the De Havilland land plane that was supposed to be an alternative, rather appropriately named Albatross, sadly broke up on landing in an early test flight.[43] The British could not compete effectively, but they knew when they had been outmaneuvered, and with war now imminent, they were not willing to antagonize the United States by delaying Pan American's transatlantic operations any further. They announced this in the House of Commons on February 1, 1939.[44] Just over a week later, Trippe, realizing that the transatlantic route was almost within his grasp, took one further step to appease his critics. Whether this step was directly prompted by Moore is unclear from the record, but an undated draft note for him to send to Pan American strongly suggests that it was. The note pointed out that the CAA was directed by the 1938 Civil Aeronautics Act to consider competition to be in the public interest to the extent necessary to assure the industry's sound development. "In view of the provision cited, the Authority's attention is called to the extensive character of the contract between your company and the Government of Portugal...," and Trippe was invited to offer a statement.[45] In early February 1939, he did.

If the Civil Aeronautics Authority will confirm our understanding that it is now of the opinion that it would be in the interest of American aviation that Clause 3 [i.e., the fifteen-year exclusivity clause] of the agreement of this Company with the Portuguese Government be waived, our company will advise the Government promptly that it waives such Clause 3 in its entirety.[46]

The letter was given considerable publicity, and Trippe's fortunes seemed to be improving. But there was still to be a slight twist in the tail.

On May 18, 1939, Chairman Hinckley of the CAA, who had a healthy dislike of Pan American's monopoly, wrote to President Roosevelt sending him certificates for Pan American to operate on both the southern and northern transatlantic routes. They provided for two round-trip flights per week, and they could be apportioned to the northern or southern route as Pan American saw fit. However, this did not permit Pan American to fill the capacity available, because the United States had been granted two round-trips a week by Great Britain and four by France. In short the CAA had left the door open for a further American airline to operate on the Atlantic, knowing that Amex was in the process of applying for a certificate to do just that. That same month Amex applied to the CAA pointing out that the collusion between Pan American and Imperial Airways might be contrary to the Sherman antitrust laws and raising a question mark over Pan American's exclusive deal with Portugal regarding landing rights in the Azores.[47] Both the CAA and President Roosevelt wanted Pan American's dominance to be diluted. As Hinckley succinctly put it the letter of presentation of Pan American's certificate:

> ... the Authority has deemed it in the public interest, in order to preserve the possibility of competition and to prevent a single air carrier from monopolizing all existing landing rights, to limit for the time being the number of such landing rights which the holder of the certificate will be entitled to use in rendering service authorized.[48]

Later that evening, President Roosevelt signed off on the certificate. On May 20 and June 24, respectively, Pan American inaugurated regular mail and passenger services on the southern and northern routes. All that Imperial Airways could manage was eight mail flights by in-flight refueled Empire Flying Boats in August and September, after which operations were suspended because of the outbreak of war.[49]

In the spring of 1937, things had looked very good for Pan American, but over the following two years difficulties delayed the launch of transatlantic services and undermined the exclusivity that Trippe had so wanted. The reasons for such developments arose in a much wider context than the transatlantic route and had much to do with an upwelling of criticism of Trippe and Pan American and dislike of the idea that the United States should be so reliant on one overseas operator. At the same time one should not over-state Pan American's problems because its power and influence continued to rise as it performed national security tasks for the U.S. government. The problem was more to do with the rise to prominence of other airline forces in the United States and the clash of policy priorities that developed between Trippe, on the one hand, and powerful forces in the U.S. government, on the other, that in the end, though the end was a long way off in 1939, were to prove the more powerful. It is to these issues that the focus must now turn to see how they developed between 1937 and 1939, how they explain the rising difficulties that Pan American had to contend with, and what they tell us about the policies that the administration crafted.

PAN AMERICAN: ITS CREDITS AND DEBITS FOR GOVERNMENT

Pan American was quite a phenomenon and could not help but be a central component of any policy covering U.S. international airline operations. Whatever way one looked at it, the airline had racked up a whole series of amazing achievements. Even Grover Loening, Pan American's most bitter critic, had to concede that its networks in the Western Hemisphere and in the Pacific should be left intact: they were just too important to American commerce and security to unpick.[50] Even so, by late 1939, Trippe and his company had angered and alienated many important people in the Roosevelt administration by their maneuverings, by their blatant pursuit of maintaining Pan American's monopoly, and by the slow reluctance with which they removed German personnel from SCADTA. And, notwithstanding Pan American's contributions to U.S. defense capabilities, Trippe's enemies were now to be found even in the Navy and the Army. So far as relations went between President Roosevelt and Trippe, they were best characterized as having "bitter personal feelings" by 1940, but at the same time Pan American was the only existing U.S. overseas operator and thus the sole instrument available to the U.S. government for achieving certain national security objectives that could only be pursued by employing a civilian airline.[51]

It is important to gauge just how important Pan American was in its three spheres of operation, the Americas, the Pacific, and the Atlantic, and there are always two perspectives in play: its commercial success and the national defense dimension. It is also important to emphasize that commercial aviation and defense matters were so closely related in the minds of the U.S. military that it is difficult to disentangle them. In the mid-1930s the U.S. military was possibly more concerned about the United States losing its dominance of civil aviation in the Pacific than it was about foreign commercial airliners posing a more direct security threat by operating into Hawaii, where the U.S. Pacific Fleet was based. The interdepartmental committee, in conference with the Navy and War Departments in July 1935, was advised that they had "no objection... to foreign owned commercial airlines entering the lagoon in the vicinity of the Army fortifications in Honolulu," providing reciprocal rights were granted in return.[52] However, the attitude of the Navy and War Departments was not very consistent. That same month they opposed granting rights to the Dutch for entry into the Philippines not so much because of objections to the Dutch but because of fear that such action might oblige them to open up the Philippines to all comers and most significantly the Japanese. The State Department objected to this, arguing that granting rights of entry to the Dutch would not oblige them to grant similar rights to any others, a position that was not entirely in harmony with the State Department's, and in particular Hull's, bête noire—discrimination.[53] A year later the War Department lifted its objections and declared that it was not opposed to granting entry rights to the Philippines for the Dutch airline KLM, providing Pan American was given reciprocal rights into the Dutch East Indies; however, it now also emphasized that this should not be taken as a precedent and that the War Department would wish to be consulted and would consider any other case on its merits.[54] In fact KLM was not granted entry rights, and there was, of course, general concerns about foreign entry into U.S. Pacific possessions and that concern grew as the world situation deteriorated. By 1938, Chief of Naval Operations Admiral William D. Leahy thought that it was more important to keep foreign airlines, and that included Britain's Imperial Airways, out of Hawaii than to trade entry there for landing rights elsewhere in the Pacific. Interestingly, in the same discussions, the president still gave emphasis to commercial matters: he "did not want to consider letting the British into Hawaii which would give them a round-the-world service unless they would reciprocate by giving us rights to a round-the-world service of our own."[55] However, Roosevelt was also well aware of the more direct defense needs of the United States in the Pacific and had been robust throughout the 1930s in dealings with the British over disputed sovereignty rights concerning strategically important islands. Those dealings with the British were part of the government's wider strategy of developing air routes throughout the Pacific through the expansion of Pan American. This prospered American commerce, and it also provided routes and bases that could be employed by the military if the need arose.

Pan American's progress in the Pacific was spectacular and a great public relations victory for Trippe, which did much to strengthen his hand with the Roosevelt administration and Congress. With the president's hearty approval, Trippe began to plan for a transpacific route in 1933.[56] This involved landing rights at John Rodgers Field, later Honolulu Airport in Hawaii; Midway Island; Wake Island; Guam; and Manila in the Philippines.

The development of this route to the isolated U.S. outpost in the Philippines was strategically of the utmost importance. When Pan American started a regular mail service on November 22, 1935, it was accompanied with great public fanfare. Postmaster General Farley attended and read a letter from the president stating in part: "Even at this distance I thrill to the wonder of it all."[57] Passenger services followed a year later and were inaugurated on October 21, 1936. Both the United States and the Philippines printed special commemorative stamps in celebration. Further public recognition came in August 1937 when President Roosevelt awarded Trippe the Collier Trophy for Pan American's establishment of the transpacific route.

From Manila, Trippe sought to enter the British colony of Hong Kong and then fly on into China by connecting with his subsidiary China National Airways Corporation, in which he had bought a half share in 1933.[58] However, at first the British refused unless the United States would reciprocate by granting them entry into Hawaii to provide a staging post for their own attempts to bridge the Pacific from Australia to Canada. Washington baulked at this on the pretext that they could not grant Britain such a right and refuse it to others, most notably the Japanese.[59] What they really objected to was the possibility of losing their dominant position in civil aviation in the Pacific and Britain developing its round-the-world route. For a time, Trippe was thus unable to make headway, but he soon developed a strategy that persuaded Britain to open Hong Kong unilaterally. He might work amicably with the British in the Atlantic, where they seemed to hold all the cards, but this was hardly the case in the Pacific, where Trippe's ambition was to exclude all comers. In 1937 Trippe negotiated landing rights in Macau with the Portuguese and then raised the specter of outmaneuvering the British in Hong Kong by developing Macau as a great civil aviation commercial centre and jumping off point for entry into China. "As a result," Trippe later explained, "we were invited to Hong Kong.... From that day we stayed there."[60]

Trippe was equally energetic in the south Pacific, negotiating landing rights in New Zealand in 1935. The plans for the route sparked off a long-running dispute with the British about sovereignty over islands that would be important for refueling and for strategic reasons. The most celebrated controversy was over Canton Island, for which Pan American received landing rights in 1938. Roosevelt took a detailed interest in all this, and the United States formally annexed the disputed islands of Howland, Baker, and Jarvis in May 1936. The president also instructed Joe Kennedy as he left to take up his post at the U.S. Embassy in London to speak to Prime Minister Chamberlain about the Pacific islands in contention.[61] After both sides had acted robustly to assert their claims, in the end, with war now rapidly approaching, an agreement was struck for joint Anglo-American control over some of the most keenly disputed islands.[62] Meanwhile, Trippe had been busy with his eyes on the route to New Zealand, but he needed a refueling station. He first tried to gain access to the British Island of Fiji, but when the British would only countenance that in a trade for landing rights in Hawaii, he turned to the American Samoan Islands and developed a base at Pago Pago. In 1938 Pan American launched an experimental mail service to New Zealand with their chief pilot Edwin "Meticulous" Musick pioneering the route. Sadly, on the opening flight, the Sikorsky S-42 Seaplane developed an oil leak after leaving Pago Pago. Musick took a fateful decision to turn back, but as he began to dump fuel, it ignited, and the aircraft disintegrated in a terrifying explosion that killed all on board. A regular service was now delayed until 1940, but when it did start, it was the route for airmail not just to the United States but also on to Britain. Notwithstanding that eventual success, more immediate consequences were growing public criticisms of Pan American. On January 13, 1938, the same day that Musik crashed, Grover Loening, rather predictably, fired off a telegram to the press:

> This accident brings into focus the monopolistic aims of this one company in a tragic blunder of over-expansion, under-preparation and overworking of its personnel and of its old equipment. I have been almost alone in insisting for years that the worst thing for our aviation industry and for our advancement in foreign air trade is to allow this company to grow any larger.[63]

The loss of the Hawaii Clipper six months later between Guam and Manila made matters even more difficult.

Notwithstanding the tragedies and the adverse criticisms that they fueled, which contributed to Trippe's decision to make concessions in order to progress in the Atlantic, Pan American had triumphed in the Pacific. It had developed a network of routes that traversed the Pacific and made commercial sense, even though they still had to show a profit that would eventually come from airmail and later passenger carriage. It had developed routes and landing grounds that would be indispensable for the Navy and the Army Air Corps in an emergency. It had created a direct link with the Philippines that was politically important. And throughout, Trippe had masterminded a wonderful public relations exercise that made his company hugely popular and also held in awe by many, including some in Congress.

Pan American's story in the Atlantic was, as we have seen, rather different. Trippe's maneuverings and his deals with Imperial Airways and the Portuguese government led to considerable controversy and adverse publicity for the company. Well before those problems developed, however, the Navy took a major interest in the possibility of transatlantic routes, and interestingly, once again as in the Pacific, it consisted of concerns that closely interwove civil and military air operations.

Early in March 1936 Captain W. D. Puleston, director of Naval Intelligence, suggested that the War and Navy Departments should have representation on the interdepartmental committee in the light of the fact that he had been told that within two years there would be aircraft that could fly nonstop from Europe to the United States: "When this development arrives it will profoundly affect all military and naval measures of this country."[64] Just over a week later, the interdepartmental committee met with Puleston to hear the Navy's views on transatlantic air services. Puleston told the committee that the Navy was "vitally interested in any agreement" because of the possibility of converting civilian aircraft to military use and because of the prospect of bases being developed close to U.S. shores, such as the one projected for Bermuda. He noted that the British had protested when the United States had planned to build airbases near the Canadian border and he thought that the United States should take a similar line regarding the expansion of the airfield in Bermuda to ensure that it was developed solely for civilian purposes. Ideally the base there "should be under our observation and preferably under our control."[65] This probably smacked of naivety to the more politically savvy of those present, but it was little different to the interventionist plans that were developed in Washington to deal with Latin America. The only difference lay in the fact that Britain was still a great power: none in Latin America were.

Puleston developed arguments that he professed should not be taken to suggest that he was in any way "obstructionist to civil aviation," but they clearly demonstrated the inextricable way that civil and military aviation entwined and that military considerations should constrain policies that might be imprudent and prompted simply by the prospect of immediate commercial gain. The thrust of what he had to say was that the United States must maintain its dominance in civil aviation: "This country's position in aviation was so strong that we should trade privileges warily in order to preserve our present advantages. This was borne out by the fact that the British had come to Washington in December 1935 on their own suggestion." He went on: "It is quite possible that within a few years there will be American equipment capable of operating non-stop service across the Atlantic. In such a case the landing places offered by Great Britain will be unnecessary and consequently we should not now accept them if we have to make too many concessions."[66]

This was a pretty hard line and perhaps harder than some of his superiors seemed to favor at this time, but it was widely held, and the fears that prompted it grew in force as the international situation deteriorated. This line of thinking had two significant consequences for civil aviation, one immediate, the other more medium-term. The first was that the priorities of the War and Navy Departments were clearly not always identical with the policies that were determined by commercial considerations for Pan American. This clash never became pronounced in the Atlantic, but the story in the Western Hemisphere was different. The second was more complex. Understandably, with chronic international instability, the U.S. service departments were very focused on anything that might challenge the nation's security, and one such factor was the operation of civil aviation, hence their determination to sustain and expand U.S. supremacy wherever possible. This was also an ambition nurtured by many nonmilitary officials as well. But aviation was also a commercial enterprise and one in the international realm that was by its very nature dependent upon the cooperation of others. During the war, as Roosevelt and his administration turned to postwar planning for international aviation, the perception that the United States would continue to dominate civil aviation became common abroad and began to pose an obstacle to realizing the kind of international aviation regime that Roosevelt wanted. The very success of U.S. civil aviation and suggestions that it should be maintained and expanded threatened its potential to flourish abroad. Other countries would simply refuse to treat, stand on their sovereign air rights, and refuse transit, stop, and commercial rights. President Roosevelt was sensitive to this and determined that the fears of other nations in this respect had to be assuaged. That assuaging was not easy, but the main problem by 1943–44 was no longer the position of the armed services but rather that of civilian advisers and officials who wanted to promote U.S. aviation in a more nationalistic and unilateralist manner than Roosevelt.

In the Western Hemisphere the story was different from that in the Atlantic and similar and in some ways even more spectacularly successful than the story in the Pacific. But also, it was in this sphere that Pan American and national defense priorities clashed more sharply than anywhere else. Much of the story of Pan American's rise to dominance in Latin and Central America has already been touched on and does not require repeating here, but there were important developments at the end of the 1930s. They encapsulated the dilemma for the U.S. government: it needed Pan American, but at the same time it grew uncomfortably uneasy both with some of the policies of the company and with the idea of reliance on one operator for U.S. overseas operations.

Growing fears about German- and Italian-run airlines in Latin America were widespread in Washington and dominated the attention of G. Grant Mason, chair of the Special Interdepartmental Committee on the Development of Aviation in the Western Hemisphere. In the autumn of 1938 Mason signed off on a review of German and Italian aeronautical exports to Latin America, which was passed by the chairman of the CAA, Edward J. Noble, to the president in October. It made four recommendations. Two advocated strengthening research and development and promoting U.S. exports, the other two related directly to U.S. international airlines, i.e., Pan American. They recommended "close liaison and cooperation between heads of United States military and civilian aviation" and the provision of "further support for United States international airlines."[67]

It was in this atmosphere that verged on paranoia regarding likely threats from Latin America that Mason's committee produced a much more comprehensive report in the summer of 1939 entitled "Plan for the Aeronautical Development in the Western Hemisphere." It was approved by the State, Navy, and War Departments and by the CAA, and a memorandum by James Rowe summarizing its findings was passed to the president on August 4. The report followed the same convention followed in the report on German and Italian aeronautical exports by referring repeatedly to "American airlines" in the Western Hemisphere, but this was fiction. There was only one American airline operating there and that was Pan American. So, if throughout one were to substitute Pan American for "American airlines," one would form a pretty accurate picture of just how important the company was to U.S. official policy.

The objective, given that this was about civil aviation, was predictable enough, "to promote sound aeronautical development": the justification, for the sake of "national and hemisphere defense" was less so.[68] At this point in time the most important characteristic of civil aviation in the Western Hemisphere for the U.S. government was its bearing on U.S. national defense. The report revealed the ambition of the United States to dominate the entire regional airline network. It was envisaged that U.S. airlines would operate international routes with the American republics servicing them with domestic feeder lines. Aviation would be in the hands of "citizens or legal entities" of the American republics. Routes and operations would be partly financed by the U.S. Export-Import Bank. Pilots would be U.S. trained and the export of American equipment would be encouraged. And this was only the first of two plans.

> The second is to be developed after further study. Plan No. 2 will provide for development of a much more extensive program appropriate only in emergencies. In the case of war, aviation contracts held by European controlled airlines might be cancelled or abandoned. In such cases the opportunity should be seized, under the procedure of Plan No. 2, for transfer of those rights to United States companies or, if that should be impracticable, to established national companies in the American Republics.[69]

President Roosevelt approved the plan on August 7, 1939. Its success clearly depended upon "U.S. airlines", that is, Pan American, but serious problems with Trippe were about to come to a head. Their full magnitude can only be appreciated once placed in the context of these plans for the Western Hemisphere that were developed by the military and civilian departments in the administration.

The central security concern of the United States in the Western Hemisphere was the Panama Canal, and so the operations of SCADTA in Colombia, an airline dominated by German personnel, had been of long-standing concern. Furthermore, as early as 1934, Lufthansa had operated a mail service across the South Atlantic and that was cause for serious concern, especially when seen in conjunction with the German and Italian presence in numerous South American airlines.[70] In March 1939 Naval Intelligence reported that SCADTA pilots were in fact Luftwaffe reserve pilots.[71] Such concerns deepened as the international situation deteriorated and tensions cracked into war in Europe. The U.S. government, largely through the good offices of U.S. Ambassador to Colombia Spruille Braden, but also with help from General "Hap" Arnold and General George Marshall, had been urging Trippe to de-louse SCADTA of its German personnel for months, but without success. Trippe argued that he could not afford to fire the German pilots without financial help from government. In the meantime he ducked and weaved away from dismissing his German staff. Here was a conflict between the commercial interests of Pan American and U.S. national interest as defined in Washington and articulated in the plans drawn up for aviation in the Western Hemisphere. Braden soon became exasperated by Trippe's procrastinations, but eventually three developments forced his compliance with official demands.

The day after war erupted in Europe, a now totally exasperated Braden exposed the secret deal to the Colombian Government by which Pan Am had gained 84 percent ownership of SCADTA in 1931. With clear and public responsibility for SCADTA, Pan American's hand was now more difficult to play. It became even more difficult not to take action against German personnel when the Export-Import Bank delivered a loan to help Pan American buy equipment for Avianca, which Pan American jointly owned with the Columbian Government, and which was scheduled to take over SCADTA's routes. Even now Pan American still procrastinated, and so, finally, Braden issued an ultimatum in February 1940. Unless Pan American shed its German employees, he would "cable the [State] Department that I could no longer accept responsibility in connection with the Panama Canal. Moreover, I would denounce Pan Am to the President, to Congress, and to the American people."[72] Now Trippe acted and the de-lousing began, but this was very late in the day and his behavior had turned influential people against him. Assistant Secretary of State Adolf Berle, who played a key role in developing postwar plans for international civil aviation, confided to his diary: "I am beginning to think that the president of that company, Juan Trippe, ought to be thoroughly investigated."[73] Trippe was no longer the "blue-eyed boy" that he had been with the Navy and War Departments or indeed with the State Department: but he was still an essential instrument for the government and its preparations in case war came to America.

While Trippe's fashioning of empire continued, his inveterate critic Grover Loening railed at Pan American and its practices. Loening's most comprehensive damning of the company was a paper he prepared for Kennedy in 1937 entitled "The Pan American Foreign Air Monopoly." It is unclear whether President Roosevelt had sight of this or not, but much of the argument permeated out into general debate and policy discussions that surrounded the crafting of the 1938 Civil Aeronautics Act. Tellingly, after a devastating if somewhat intemperate attack on Pan American, Loening concluded:

> The only possible justifiable reason for our having a monopoly is to pre-vent rate wars and destructive competition amongst ourselves. Competition already exists with foreign companies. So rate wars may be looked for there or conferences arranged as in shipping to control them and they can equally well control rates between our companies. Healthy competition can be kept from being destructive amongst ourselves by the controls already in hand, such as granting of permits for foreign operations and particularly granting of subsidies and air mail contracts. The legislation on all this needs some clarifi-cation but because it does, is no reason for allowing a monopoly in a new and virgin field like this before it even has a chance to start.[74]

Shortly after this, Trippe was summoned to Joe Kennedy's family seat at Hyannis Port for a weekend stay and discussions. However, when Kennedy asked Trippe to testify before Congress that authority over international aviation should be allocated to the Maritime Commission and Trippe refused, the meeting was abruptly curtailed. Trippe was making powerful enemies.[75]

A few months later Loening had occasion to rehearse his arguments once again in protest at the award of the airmail contract to Pan American for the route to Bermuda. This time we know that his protests were forwarded to the president. As we have seen, Loening had all kinds of objections to Pan American: its success was due as much to Navy trained pilots and American manufacturing as to anything else, but now U.S. manufacturers were suffering because Pan Am had not ordered the most up-to-date equipment. Trippe used his political and public promotional skills to great advantage to buttress his fortunes, but all the while he was careful to exclude other American airlines from overseas operations and made agreements with foreign governments to that end, and at least with Portugal and New Zealand, contrary to U.S. national interests. And so the catalogue of sins of omission and commission went on, and they percolated through the Washington establishment and into the ears of Franklin Roosevelt. But in the memorandum that was forwarded to the president, Loening had produced a stroke of genius that could not but resonate with the president. What had prompted Loening's latest outburst against Pan American was the fact that the bidding for the airmail contract to Bermuda was a sham: no other U.S. airline had the rights to operate to Bermuda, the British would not grant any airline such rights, and even if they had, the time allowed for the bids was insufficient for another airline to comply with the requirements for the service. With mischievously cruel irony Loening wrote:

> It is clearly evident that the Pan American Airways has been shown favoritism by former officials of the Post Office department. Probably their contracts were not obtained as a result of genuine, open competitive bidding. In every instance the time allowed for bidding was entirely too limited and prospective bidders were not given proper opportunity to survey the route, negotiate with the countries over which the route passes for the necessary concessions and agreements and make proper financial arrangements.[76]

This indeed seemed to capture what had happened with the Bermuda airmail contract, but then Loening delivered his coup de grace. He revealed that this was actually a "quotation from the 1933 letter of Postmaster General Farley to Senator Black at the time of the air mail cancellations."[77] In other words this was a stark and barbed way of reminding the president that in 1933 he had felt that the system was so corrupt, working contrary to commercial good practice and in violation of the laws of the United States, that he should dramatically cancel all domestic airmail contracts. The clear inference was that if the situation then demanded and received such dramatic action, why was something similar not done to deal with Pan American now. In his report for Kennedy on Pan American's monopoly the previous July, Loening had been even more explicit in raising the possibility of dangers for the administration.

> A succeeding administration to this one, or even any powerful opposition, could find in the continued favoritism and help to Pan American by the various Departments, no matter how justified now, almost as much a source of scandal as the disclosures of rank favoritism by Postmaster General Brown in the Hoover Administration. And the pleasant and thrilling trip [on Pan American's new route] to Bermuda of officials, and of Senator MacAdoo and

Judge Moore could readily be twisted into a different meaning if a serious attack on Pan America's dominating position were to be launched.[78]

There were good reasons why President Roosevelt would not take Pan American head on at this time: the critical world situation and Pan American's de facto position in international aviation prohibited that. However, the position that Pan American held and that Loening so feared was actually beginning to change, sometimes still to Pan American's advantage, but in many cases to its long-term detriment.

Some publicity cards were beginning to stack up against the company. Criticisms about safety going back to the Senate Copeland Committee Report in June 1936, prompted by the TWA crash in May 1935 that, among other things, killed the famous football coach Rock Knute, resonated on throughout the 1930s. Fatal crashes involving Pan American aircraft such as the one off Pago Pago and of a Martin Clipper between Manila and Guam in July 1938 perpetuated safety concerns and began to put a little tarnish on Pan American's record. The tarnish crept further with the criticisms of Pan American's exclusive deals with Portugal and Imperial Airways and with the publicly expressed criticisms about Pan American's monopoly. Hearings held in the Congress by the House Committee on Merchant Marine and Fisheries gave further profile to these issues. It was clear that the company was now coming under some threat, and Trippe responded by abandoning the offending articles of his deal with Imperial Airways and offering to waive his exclusive rights in the Azores. Those actions helped mitigate the threat, but more effective still was deterioration in the world situation, because the more it deteriorated, the more the U.S. Government needed an immediate champion of overseas civil aviation, and Pan American was the only contender available.

Further bolstering of Pan American's position came with the Civil Aeronautics Act effectively grandfathering Pan American's routes. In addition the act failed to provide for control of rates on overseas routes. Both these outcomes favored two of Trippe's main priorities: safeguarding his monopoly and his mail contracts and leaving him with pricing freedom. However, the Aeronautics Act counterbalanced these provisions by conferring ultimate authority over overseas route awards on the president. This was crucial in determining the future development of American overseas civil aviation, and a telling episode that signaled just how important soon developed. In May 1939 Amex applied to the CAA for a certificate to operate on the Atlantic. As we have seen, the CAA, in granting a certificate to Pan American, had arranged things so that there was capacity for other airlines to enter that market, and now here was Amex. Most significantly Amex was strongly and persistently supported by Franklin Delano Roosevelt, and because of the 1938 act, he had the power to help. Already one feature of Roosevelt's priorities for U.S. international airline services was clear. He did not intend for the United States to be solely reliant on one operator, no matter how successful and how currently dependent it might be on Pan American for helping to buttress American airpower. There would be no monopoly. Between 1939 and United States' entry into the war in December 1941, this became very clear.

CHAPTER 6

THE COMING OF WAR: POLICIES, PREPARATIONS, AND MORE REORGANIZATION 1939–41

"*Quid desiderat pacem, praeparet bellum.*"

"Let him who desires peace prepare for war."

Vegetius, fourth century AD

"We must be the great arsenal of democracy."

FDR, "Fireside Chat" broadcast, December 30, 1940

ON SEPTEMBER 1, 1939, the armed might of the Wehrmacht swept into Poland. On September 3 Britain issued an ultimatum demanding that Germany withdraw, and when it was ignored, a state of war was duly declared. France followed suit several hours later, and the devastation and horror that were the Second World War had begun. That same evening Roosevelt somberly addressed the nation. America would remain neutral, though not necessarily in thought. "Even a neutral has a right to take account of the facts. Even a neutral cannot be asked to close his mind or his conscience."[1] Neutral in theory America remained, but it was clear where Roosevelt's sympathies lay and from where he saw future threats to the United States. Two months later America's neutrality legislation was amended allowing foreign purchase of American arms and equipment on a cash-and-carry basis. While the law was applied uniformly, its effects were not uniform. As Britannia still had pretensions to "ruling the waves," this clearly favored Britain with its capacity to pay for and uplift supplies. This was an important first step for the United States along the road to becoming the great arsenal of democracy and for preparing for the possibility of war. For the time being, though, this was as far as Roosevelt felt able to go, and in fact he did not have the wherewithal to do much else in 1939.

It is true that the U.S. Navy was a force to be reckoned with by any power with its fifteen battle ships, five aircraft carriers, and nearly forty cruisers, but on land and in the air the story was very different. Germany pitched 1.5 million into combat in the invasion of Poland and 2.5 million for the invasion of France and the Lowlands in 1940. The U.S. Army, excluding the Air Corps, stood at 161,000 and 240,000, respectively, in 1939 and 1940. But it is airpower that we are most concerned with, and here the story was of comic opera proportions. In 1939 the Army Air Corps manpower strength stood at approximately 21,000 compared with the RAF's strength of 175,000 and the Luftwaffe's 300,000. Furthermore, the RAF and the Luftwaffe had modern high-performance aircraft: the United States did not with the exception of a few modern heavy bombers. The rest of the fleet was more or less obsolete. There was a very obvious and dire problem here: What to do?

The response to that question was robust, if not successful on all fronts, with an expansion of defense expenditure and very significant contributions from the civil aviation sector. Airpower has three very basic requirements: pilots, equipment, and logistics. Civil aviation was able to contribute to all three. First, the CAA undertook responsibility to help train a vastly expanded pool of pilots. Second, the manufacturing capacity nurtured by America's successful civil aviation and automobile industries could now be turned to military production and that was soon fostered, not only by U.S. government orders, but more significantly by orders largely from France and later in 1940 by massive orders from both France and Britain.[2] In July 1940, after Lord Beaverbrook, British minister for aircraft rroduction, announced that Britain would buy 72,000 planes from the United States at a delivery rate that was projected to rise to 3,000 a month in 1941–42, U.S. treasury secretary Henry Morgenthau declared: "From the standpoint of our own industry and defense, this is the most important thing that has happened this year."[3] British and French orders did not simply take equipment produced by existing capacity; they financed new factories. On the back of such orders and the expanded manufacturing capacity that it nurtured, Roosevelt was able to announce an annual target of 50,000 aircraft a year in May 1940 and rapidly to keep revising the figure upward thereafter. Eventually the United States produced equipment of both quantity and, after substantial difficulties, quality required for effective combat in modern air warfare. And third, a major contribution to solving logistical problems of delivery and supply to potential war theatres was provided by Pan American as it developed air bases and routes through Latin America and across to Europe and Africa and across the Pacific.

At the same time as all this gained momentum and further emphasized the importance of civil aviation, it transpired that the framework within which the industry operated again needed adjustment, and in 1940 President Roosevelt responded with further reorganization. Not entirely unrelated to that, and certainly connected with the logistical concerns about airpower, Roosevelt also came to the conclusion that Pan American should not be the sole instrument of U.S. international operations. Amex was sponsored by the administration as part of a multiairline policy for U.S. international civil aviation. This policy was staunchly advocated by Franklin Roosevelt.

MORE REORGANIZATION

The Civil Aeronautics Act had experienced lengthy and at times traumatic birth pains, and there was widespread expectation that it would usher in a period of institutional and regulatory stability that would allow aviation to flourish. When the Interstate and Foreign Commerce Committee reported out the Civil Aeronautics Bill, it had expressed the hope that if it worked successfully it could be taken as a model for creating, on a larger scale, a department of transportation in which all existing powers from other agencies connected with transportation would be centralized.[4] If this had come about, it would have been the president's ideal dream come true. In fact it was not to be in his lifetime or indeed for a long time after, but in the meantime the president held high hopes for the CAA and what it might accomplish. He wanted it to be the center of aviation developments in both the domestic and international spheres, supplemented by his own inputs in the international sphere as and when required. As James Rowe explained in August 1940, under Section 801 of the Civil Aeronautics Act, the president must approve or disapprove of any CAB decision relating to carriers in foreign commerce.

> This is a rather unusual provision, because in effect it gives the President a veto power (and no more) over the Board's decisions.
> In practice, the President's approval has not been routine. I have been handling the cases and have made it a practice of checking carefully with the State, War and Navy Departments.[5]

The president clearly had an eye on the broader implications of developments in the international sphere, and this did not go down well with Pan American, which soon challenged the power he wielded over foreign routes. This will be considered shortly, but a more immediate matter was how the new authority would relate to the old structure embodied in the interdepart-mental committee. Within weeks of the CAA coming into being, Assistant Secretary of Commerce Johnson suggested to his boss, Secretary Roper, that it ought to have representation on the interdepartmental committee in order to receive the benefits of its expertise. Roper passed those concerns on to Walton Moore, who in turn raised them with the president. But Roosevelt thought it "unnecessary to make any change for the moment in the set-up of the Interdepartmental Aviation Committee."[6] In fact, within two months, the committee was dissolved as neither Roosevelt nor Moore thought that it was necessary after the creation of the CAA.[7] They may have been a little premature and oversanguine about the effectiveness of the CAA, because the hope for a period of stability and steady development after its creation was not realized, and international civil aviation policy planning suffered as a consequence.

Much of the substantive regulatory reform of the CAA did prove resilient and long lived, though, even here, certain matters needed further clarifica-tion by executive determination and judicial findings, but the institutional structure continued to occasion serious problems. This was partly to do with the structures themselves and partly to do with personality clashes. While these bureaucratic matters can become tedious if dwelt on at too great a length, it is important to prolong our visit with them for a little while in order to register yet again how military and civil aviation matters were conceived of as being so vitally interdependent. It was this sense of interdependence that helped to push the need for further organizational reform to ensure that civil aviation was developed effectively, not just for commercial reasons, as important as they were, but also because of military considerations.

Edward J. Noble was appointed as the chairman of the CAA with Harllee Branch vice chairman and Clinton Hester as the administrator. Problems immediately arose between Noble and Hester. As early as September 1938 James Rowe warned the president that trouble was brewing, and while the initial difficulties were temporarily patched over, muted discord rumbled on. By March 1939 Rowe was becoming more fearful of damaging reper-cussions issuing from difficulties within the CAA. He thought that there were two problems with the act, one concerning jurisdiction and the other the need for cooperation. Unfortunately Noble and Hester disliked each other so much they just could not cooperate, which was damaging because the structure of the CAA required smooth relationships between its compo-nent parts for things to work. Furthermore, Noble was not only exploiting jurisdictional grey areas to expand his bailiwick, something that might have been tolerable, he was carrying this to the extent of claiming authority in areas beyond the grey areas that were clearly not within his allocated juris-diction.[8] His behavior angered Hester and alienated the other four members of the authority. The resulting tensions seeped out into the public domain. In the Senate, Senator Byrnes was involved in what Rowe described as a "terrific row" about the CAA during a debate on the Reorganization Bill, which Byrnes was then steering through the Senate as a Roosevelt loyalist and chairman of the Select Committee on Government Organization. This was a much-watered-down version of the bill that had gone down to catastrophic defeat in the House in April 1938. This time round, in 1939, it would succeed but not before experiencing the terrific row about the CAA on March 22. During the course of that debate, Byrnes bluntly declared: "The fact is that the Authority is a house divided against itself."[9] Biblical wisdom tells us that such houses cannot stand, and this is precisely the lesson Rowe drew from these developments. He was fearful of the impact on Congress if it became fully aware of the splits in the CAA. "If this dissension goes to the Congress, it will open up the entire Act and may end in undoing all the good work the Administration has accomplished in getting the industry stabilized."[10]

Byrnes and Rowe knew that it would not be easy to tamper with the Civil Aeronautics Act, but both were convinced that the president would have to do something. Matters were helped the following month when Noble resigned and was succeeded on April 17, 1939, by Robert H. Hinckley, but difficulties continued to arise, this time between the Air Safety Board and the CAA. Characteristically Roosevelt continued to procrastinate, though to be fair there were other rather dramatic developments taking place on the world stage that demanded his attention. In the end it may very well have been those developments that forced his hand. In August 1939 M. A. Harlan, worried by the Air Safety Board problem, wrote to Edward "Pa" Watson, secretary to the president, urging that "drastic action" was now necessary.

> In view of the European situation and the fact that there should be, insofar as is possible, complete harmony in all Federal agencies, particularly those so closely associated with the problem of national defense, and the further fact that the President has evidenced deep personal interest in the Civil Aeronautics Authority and has given so much time and effort to it, I believe that the seriousness of the situation should be called to his attention immediately.[11]

It is unclear whether the president actually read this, but there is little doubt that he was aware the authority was experiencing serious difficulties given that Rowe had fired off several warning shots within the White House. From April 1939 the president had the wherewithal to act because the Congress had finally passed a much-modified version of the Reorganization

Bill, but even so it was not until after considerably more delay that the president requested the Bureau of the Budget's Division of Administrative Management to undertake a study of what was going wrong in the CAA. Work began on December 4 and a report was issued the following spring. The Civil Aeronautics Study made three recommendations and offered a significant and telling observation.

The report claimed that it was "essential" in order to carry out "the original intent of Congress" regarding the proper constitutional division of powers to transfer to the administrator a whole series of executive responsibilities, for example the implementation of the 1939 Civilian Pilot Training Act.[12] The pilot training scheme had been one of those areas that Noble had overambitiously tried to seize, much to Hester's annoyance. Whether such changes actually reflected the original intent of Congress is a moot point. Edgar Gorrell certainly doubted that they did, but Roosevelt was convinced that whatever the case these changes were needed if the authority were to function effectively.[13] The report also recommended that the Safety Board should be abolished and its duties transferred to the CAA, which should then be renamed the CAB and have the power not only of investigating accidents but also, unlike the old Safety Board, the power to take remedial action. Finally, the CAB should be incorporated into the Department of Commerce for housekeeping purposes while remaining fully independent operationally. One advantage of this would be that the CAB would then have the voice of the secretary of commerce to speak on its behalf in the Cabinet and the Congress.[14] The report concluded:

> Finally, the existing international situation makes it of all the more moment that everything be done to facilitate Presidential leadership in the administrative aspects of the civil aviation program. To regard civil aviation as something entirely apart from the aviation facilities of the Army and Navy would completely overlook the realities of the situation.[15]

In a press release on April 30, Roosevelt announced the implementation of the report's recommendations. He then turned caustically on the administration's critics, scorning those who profess themselves always to be in favor of reorganization for efficiency and then, "in selfish protection of their own special interests we always find particular groups who hitherto favored reorganization arising in protest."[16] Once again the fallout of criticisms from the administration's efforts at reorganization had impacted on civil aviation, and Roosevelt felt obliged to try to deflect them. He emphasized that after five months of investigation, it "became obvious that a change was imperative if we were to continue to move forward in civil aviation."[17] Days later, on May 4, the Civil Aeronautics Study was released and appeared in the

New York Times. It helped to drive home the administration's case with the public and Congress. Roosevelt could not have left the CAA where it was, and he was determined once the reorganization was announced that it should be robustly implemented.

> In view of the important defense implications of civil aviation and the technical nature of the reorganization provisions affecting the Civil Aeronautics Authority, I am particularly anxious that the Bureau of the Budget follow through in detail on the effectuation of the Civil Aeronautics Authority reorganization.[18]

Civil aviation was of great importance in its own right, but in 1940 it was also recognized as being so important for national defense as well, and it was largely a result of the sense of urgency derived from those considerations that the reform of the CAA was successfully consummated under the general provisions of the Reorganization Act.[19] Ironically, the reform compromised the president's much-argued principle of separation of executive, judicial, and legislative powers that he had deployed so robustly in the struggle for the 1938 Civil Aeronautics and the Reorganization Act. Instead the pragmatist Roosevelt had opted for a practical division of functions, even though they overlapped. As Gorrell observed about the administrator and the CAB, "Administrative functions are conferred upon both. Rule-making and adjudicative functions are conferred upon both."[20] Even so, it worked. Equally importantly for Roosevelt, it gave the Executive more power over this strategically important industry. The new institutional setup remained in place throughout and beyond Roosevelt's time in office. There was no more major reorganization for civil aviation on his watch, but there was further clarification of the presidential prerogative relating to decisions about foreign operations, and this will be considered shortly when the fortunes of Amex and Roosevelt's ideas about general policy for overseas air routes are examined.

PREPARATIONS

The Munich sellout of Czechoslovakia in September 1938 that would eventually deliver the whole of that unfortunate country into Nazi hands was a turning point in more ways than one. On September 28, a couple of days before the pact at Munich was signed, Roosevelt called senior military personnel and the secretaries of Treasury, War, and Navy to a conference at the White House. Also present was the president's closest confidant, friend, adviser, and personal envoy Harry Hopkins. Fear of the power of the Luftwaffe was an important and well-known component of the Munich crisis, but even so Chief of the Army Air Corps "Hap" Arnold was surprised at the vigor with which the president now advocated expanding U.S. military aircraft production.

> To the surprise, I think, of practically everyone in the room except Harry [Hopkins] and myself, and to my own delight, the President came straight out for air power. Airplanes—now—and lots of them![21]

He spoke of an actual production target of 10,000 planes a year and an overall capacity to produce 20,000. At the time U.S. production was still under 2,000 a year so this was a shockingly ambitious target. Arnold knew just how badly new planes were needed, not just in numbers but in quality. A few months previously he had suffered the ignominy of having to "detour round damp clouds" in the plane allocated by the Air Corps for use by the secretary of War: it was so obsolete, it was simply unsafe to do otherwise.[22] This meeting was symbolic and a start. Arnold left feeling that the Air Corps had "arrived," but others in the military and many civilians in government criticized Roosevelt's demand for a massive expansion of airpower. Some were just skeptics, others wanted more emphasis on ground and naval forces. At another meeting, on November 14, there was a further and more formal review of policy. Roosevelt argued:

> When I write to foreign countries I must have something to back up my words. Had we had this summer 5000 planes and the capacity to produce 10,000 per year, even though I might have had to ask Congress for authority to sell or lend them to the countries in Europe, Hitler would not have dared to take the stand he did.[23]

The force of the president's arguments and feelings may have been overstated for effect, as he later modified his plans, but his long-term ambition was clear, namely, to increase aircraft production and make aircraft available to the democracies.[24] On neither count were his military chiefs in full accord.[25] The War Department was difficult, to say the least, when on December 21, 1938, the President authorized the French to inspect and purchase the most up-to-date American war planes.[26] Public difficulties followed in January 1939 when a Douglas A-20 bomber crashed in California with a French purchasing agent on board. Roosevelt weathered the adverse publicity and Treasury Secretary Morgenthau, whom the president had personally put in charge, continued to facilitate the sale of arms to France and Britain. The military chiefs were fearful that such sales would deplete resources that they wanted for American forces. In fact, from now on, although competing claims for resources persisted, increased appropriations and orders from France and Britain rapidly expanded America's capacity to manufacture warplanes of ever-increasing technological sophistication and performance. Roosevelt, with strong support from Morgenthau and General Arnold, had set something momentous in motion. The target capacity of 20,000 planes a year that Roosevelt set on September 28, 1938, was raised to 50,000 for actual production in May 1940, an even more shocking figure, but in fact U.S. aircraft production peaked in 1944 at around 100,000 planes a year.

Planes were one of the three necessary components of airpower: the second was pilots. The 1938 Civil Aeronautics Act provided the means for funding the training of pilots, and soon momentum gathered for action. A CAA paper cautioned:

> Recent developments in Europe have made it clearly apparent that the United States must take immediate steps to strengthen its aviation resources unless it is to invite the ignominy and attendant grave national risk of becoming a second-rate power.[27]

By December 1938 it was clear that the CAA had risen to the challenge and was promoting civil flying, and the press wanted to know what implications this might have for America's defense potential. All this was still very sensitive. Isolationism and Isolationists were still a potent force and in Roosevelt's mind powerful restraints on what he felt able to do. He had to be careful not to provide fuel for their fiery criticisms.[28] In response to questions from the press, he explained:

> Of course the training of reserve pilots is all part of any program for an increase in the number of planes that the Government has available to go in the air.
>   … of course you train pilots in the same kind of plane for civil aviation as you do for military aviation when you teach them to fly.[29]

Edward Noble was keen to push for civilian pilot training, and he wrote to the president on December 19 proposing that six training schools should be opened at universities at a cost of $100,000 as a first step in a program envisaging a total cost of nearly $10 million. Roosevelt checked further with Noble and also with Daniel Bell, acting director of the Budget, before announcing in a press conference on December 27 a civilian pilot training program costing $9.8 million with a target of training 20,000 pilots a year. This was implemented in June 1939 with the passage through Congress of the Civilian Pilot Training Scheme. There were still some who doubted its worth even among the military, but with the onset of war in September 1939, it soon became universally accepted that the civilian training scheme was an invaluable feeder of pilots for the expansion of the Army Air Corps.

After American entry into the war, it became the War Training Service, and by 1944 over 400,000 pilots had been helped in their training under its auspices.[30] Civil aviation made substantial contributions to the war effort. In dedicating the North Beach Airport in New York City on October 15, 1939, Postmaster General James Farley spoke the sentiments of many when he praised the contributions made by civil aviation generally to the nation's defense.

> ...the very existence of these airlines with their excellent equipment and personnel, is a strong guarantee of the nation's peace and safety. One of the lessons to be learned from recent events abroad is the fact that a nation strong in air power is well fortified to prevent aggression from any source.[31]

In 1940, 3,800 landing fields were improved or created by state and municipal funding of over $500 million, and the expenditure on civilian pilot training rose from $4 million to $37 million. There were over 35,000 miles of federal airways, and building airports for defense was the biggest item of expenditure in the CAB's budget in 1941.[32] Perhaps, most remarkably of all, as war approached closer and closer, administration spokespeople justified this expenditure not only in terms of strengthening the defense of America but also in terms of advantage for the long-term commercial interests of civil aviation.

> These [airports] will form the rim of our air defense fields around the nation and are designed to aid American aviation long after the emergency has passed.[33]

In fact President Roosevelt and his military advisers were already thinking of how to push that rim further and further out both to exclude the possibility of direct aerial assault on the United States and to develop the logistical capability of taking firepower, bomb power, equipment, and supplies into the war zone across the Atlantic and, in case war were to come with Japan, out into the Pacific. For all this, they needed Pan American, which complicated an already complex and fraught relationship.

Pan American and Trippe ran into troubled friction with the Roosevelt administration and particularly with the State and War Departments during 1939–40 over the tardiness with which SCADTA was eventually deloused of its German personnel, but well before that there were serious tensions, and Pan American, as vital as it was rapidly becoming for U.S. defense preparations, did not always get its own way. In particular, and important for long-term policy developments, the president and his advisers stood firm over important provisions of the 1938 Civil Aeronautics Act.

Trippe had wanted private agreements between U.S. airlines and foreign countries to be fully respected; he wanted existing routes grandfathered, his monopoly consolidated, and preferential treatment for airlines in the award of new route certificates in countries where they already had landing rights. On all these important issues he either failed or only acquired in modified form what he wanted. Private agreements would not be respected if they adversely affected U.S. national interests; the default position was to grandfather existing routes to retain the principle that those persons who have assisted in the establishment of the U.S. air transport system should receive preferential treatment, but if there were evidence of inadequacy of service or inefficiency, the route could be assigned to a new operator in line with Roosevelt's insistence on a multiairline policy. Preferential treatment in the award of new routes was not allowed, and the president had ultimate authority over granting permits to whatever American airline he wished on foreign routes. It is testimony to the clarity with which administration officials and Roosevelt had grasped the essentials of aviation policy that they were able to counter Trippe's arguments as effectively as they did. At the same time as noting this, however, it is also important to realize just how vital was the role Pan American played in U.S. defense preparations.

Pan American could do things that the U.S. government officially could not. The U.S. government could not intervene directly in Colombia to expel German personnel from SCADTA; it could not develop strategic routes to Europe; and it could not develop landing grounds and bases in foreign countries that were necessary for operating long-distance routes of strategic importance. Even when the government built or acquired bases for long-range operations, as in the Pacific, it turned to the expertise and equipment of Pan American to develop the landing grounds and routes albeit with help from government funding and the U.S. Navy. Of course, much of this was secret and sensitive work while America remained neutral, at peace and politically limited by Isolationist political forces as to what the government could openly and publicly do. This gave Pan American extra leverage.

The surrender of France in June 1940 propelled Pan American to the forefront of American defense strategy. Interestingly, eight days before Marshal Pétain signed the armistice with Nazi Germany, Juan Trippe met with Roosevelt in the White House. What was said is not on record, but over the following two months, there were rapid developments involving Pan American acting as a shadow agent of the U.S. government.[34] The submission of France had raised a number of specters not the least worrying of which was the danger of Germany seizing the French fleet. If that eventuality happened, then, with its increased naval strength, it could use Dakar on the African bulge into the South Atlantic to launch attacks on Natal in eastern Brazil 1,900 miles away and on the Panama Canal. The British put paid to any threat from the French fleet on July 3, 1940, with an attack on its naval base at Oran, and in fact Germany never seriously considered a transatlantic attack, but fears of such possibilities were very real in Washington in July 1940, and it would have been folly for Roosevelt not to take preemptive and cautionary action.

In late June and early July, plans emerged for the development of strategic air bases running from Canada and the United States through the Caribbean and down into Latin America.

> The War Department proposes to have facilities of Pan American Airways and its affiliated companies in Mexico and Central and South America expanded for the use of the United States in the national defense.[35]

The plan was for Pan American to establish a subsidiary called Pan American Airports Corporation to which money would be funneled through circuitous routes from the monies provided by Congress "for emergencies affecting the national security," Public Laws 588, 611, and 703 of 1940. The money would be handled by the War Department and the Federal Loan Agency before going into Pan American's coffers.

> This massive air base plan had a built-in obstacle: officially the United States had no right to build bases in neutral nations anxious to stay out of any global conflict. But a privately owned airline could, and thus entered Pan Am, so solidly entrenched in many of these critical areas.... [36]

Not surprisingly, a confidential memorandum for James Forrestal, first undersecretary of the Navy, declared the content of the plan "political dynamite."[37] The contract with Pan American was signed secretly in November, and over the next four years involved construction or improvement of over fifty air bases. It was not the government's specific intent, but, nevertheless, Trippe was able to expand and consolidate further his hold on American foreign air routes. He developed both facilities at the government's expense and overseas routes almost at will. Whenever awkward questions were raised by the CAB, the Post Office, or the State Department, national interest and the president overrode them in favor of Pan American. In July the Post Office refused to pay Pan American for mail carried from Bermuda as it had no right to do so under "existing regulations." Trippe confidentially explained to Harllee Branch at the Post Office and Robert Hinckley in Commerce the reasons for Pan American's operations into and out of Bermuda. The record does not disclose the justification, but when Sumner Welles raised the issue with Roosevelt, it was clearly reason enough for him to approve. The president annotated in long hand: "SW, OK, FDR."[38] At the end of the month

Trippe also put the CAB in its place when he informed it that "as a matter of high policy," the administration wants Pan American to open a route from New York via Puerto Rico to Dakar. James Rowe raised the matter with the president.

> State knows nothing about it, and on first blush is not too enthusiastic. War and Navy are not very interested, except to say any airline flying anywhere aids national defense.
> The Board believes you may have discussed this with Trippe.[39]

Roosevelt responded: "Tell them OK, FDR." While the service departments might not have evinced much sense of urgency or need regarding the route to Dakar, a year later their attitudes were much different. Pan American continued to spread its wings. It sought authorization for Pan American Airways Africa Ltd. to develop routes that would soon be of much importance to Britain and began to develop a major capability for cargo, supplies, and manpower carriage with Pan American Air Ferries Inc. On September 2, Harllee Branch, now chairman of the CAB, reported to Roosevelt that prompt approval had been given to both, commenting that they amounted to "early inauguration of . . . services the defense agencies felt to be of greatest importance."[40] Needless to say, Roosevelt approved. The route in question in Africa was the Takoradi, which had been pioneered by the RAF. It was now modernized and developed by Pan American in order to improve the supply to British forces fighting the Italians and the Germans in the Western Desert. It ran from Takoradi, a port in the Gold Coast on the eastern side of Africa, via Nigeria and Chad to Khartoum and then on to Cairo in Egypt. There would later be extensions onwards to India and China. This was a major development for Pan American giving it access to Africa, the Middle East, and later India, all of which had previously been the preserve of Imperial Airways. Much was to follow from this as anxiety rose in London about Pan American's likely postwar civilian operations, and in fact its development of civilian carriage prior to U.S. entry into the war in December 1941.[41] Such fears contributed much to the context of Anglo-American negotiations for postwar international civil aviation.

The war in Europe emphasized America's need for strong airlines and that competition would have to be restrained if it threatened to be damaging, costly, or wasteful. A paper on aviation policy in the Western Hemisphere that emerged from the CAB in December 1940 made this very clear, and intended or not, a beneficiary of the policy had to be Pan American.

> In the present state of world affairs it is important for the United States to strengthen its lines of communication in Latin America, to eliminate strife

between U.S. controlled airlines and, where possible, to uproot activities of its potential enemies.

a) No U.S. airlines will be given a certificate of public convenience and necessity to provide service already being adequately rendered by another U.S. carrier.

b) No U.S. line will be given support (either financial or diplomatic) in establishing air transportation service in a Latin American country in which another U.S. carrier is already operating unless it can be shown that the new service will be supplementary to, or at least non-competitive with existing U.S. services.[42]

In short, government must be very circumspect in terms of allowing anything to disrupt the existing system, which for all intents and purposes amounted to the monopoly on Latin American routes held by Pan American. A review of developments abroad clearly showed that it had been "national policy to have foreign air transport operations conducted through a monopoly."

> When the Pan American System was built up, the various contracts were advertised for competitive bidding in technical compliance with the law. However, in actual practice, matters were handled in such a manner that no company but Pan American ever had a real opportunity to obtain a contract.[43]

At least that was the case until July 1940, when there was a change of policy with the administration backing Amex to compete with Pan American on the Atlantic routes, but even here the idea was that each airline would service specific regions, rather than compete head-to-head. The general idea was that competition would come from other nations' airlines, while the United States, for its part, would develop a multiairline regime, as time and circumstances allowed, with different U.S. airlines assigned to different market segments. This proved to be an attractive idea. It was not the first time that it had been raised by any means, and it was something Roosevelt strongly promoted, on this occasion by championing Amex against Pan American, even though, as we have clearly seen, his government and the country were so dependent on Pan American not just for America's overseas commercial airline operations but also for the development of a logistical infrastructure that the military services so desperately needed. How the tussle between Pan American and Amex played out illuminates the development of Roosevelt's early thinking about international civil aviation and the difficulties he would face in trying to break Pan American's monopoly.

PAN AMERICAN AND AMEX

The Amex saga is important. From the outset there were those in the Roosevelt administration and not just Loening who frowned on Pan

American's exclusive and dominant position, so it marks not so much a change of policy as the first concerted effort effectively to challenge the de facto monopoly of Pan American. It brought forth important statements from President Roosevelt indicative of the way his thinking was developing about the future of American international aviation, forced the courts to further clarify presidential powers over the foreign operations of U.S. airlines, and demonstrated just how difficult it was becoming to deal with Pan American.

Amex was established in early 1937 by the shipping company American Export Lines and was looked on with favor and encouraged by the government and especially by the Maritime Commission. It carried out transatlantic surveys and invested heavily in equipment and resources. After due preparation during 1939, it applied for certificates of convenience and necessity to operate several routes across the Atlantic. In their application to the CAB Amex's lawyers stirred things up by suggesting that the pooling arrangements between Pan American and Imperial were contrary to the antitrust laws (even though the 1938 Civil Aeronautics Act provided exemption from antitrust actions) and that Trippe's agreement with Portugal for rights in the Azores was exclusionary: no other U.S. airline could be granted rights for fifteen years.[44] In response Trippe mobilized the full lobbying power of Pan American (as well as taking conciliatory moves noted in Chapter 5), but by the summer of 1940 the CAB and all interested departments and agencies agreed that Amex should be awarded the route from New York to Lisbon. The president gave his approval on July 15 and urged Congress to appropriate funds for the Post Office so that it could provide Amex with the necessary subsidy to operate the route. This is when the real trouble began. Trippe's ability to influence Congress was greater than his ability to sway the administration.

By September the House had refused to appropriate for the Amex subsidy, persuaded by the argument that it would be a waste of public funds to provide subsidy for an additional service to that already provided by Pan American when there would be no additional airmail revenue. Amex was furious and "threatened to 'blow the lid off' Pan American relations with government if Trippe gets his way with this."[45] That could have been politically awkward, but members of the administration did not need this kind of blackmail to pitch them against Trippe and Pan American. Rowe explained to the president: "Harllee Branch and the State Department have both told me that they consider this an outrage and that Trippe is doing it. As a matter of fact, Trippe is in very bad odor with every government department he deal[s] with, particularly State, the CAB, and the Budget."[46] Trying to get Congressional approval of the necessary subsidy for Amex was troubled and complex. At one point when matters had moved to the Senate where

Senator Byrnes, an administration loyalist was managing things for the White House, Roosevelt instructed Rowe to tell him:

> I am all for the appropriation of funds to the Post Office for the American Export subsidy. Tell him that eventually, in my judgment, we will have five or six separate airlines—one for North Europe—one for the Mediterranean— one for South America—one for the Far East and one for Australia and New Zealand. When that time comes, the Government will own half of each company and be represented on the Board. The last part of this can wait, of course, but it is important to keep the American Export Airlines in business.[47]

Roosevelt might not have thought through the implications of all of this fully, particularly part-government ownership, but he had already become consistent in his view that Pan American should not be the only U.S. operator on foreign routes. There should be no grand monopoly for Trippe. However, Byrnes failed to get the subsidy through the Senate, and for the time being the monopoly was safe, and then to rub salt into the wound, Pan American challenged the actual route award to Amex in the courts.

It seemed that Pan American was deliberately set on blotting its copybook with government: it might have felt that it could afford to because of all the work it was doing for the War and Navy Departments, but it was laying up trouble for the future. Amex decided to retaliate by taking the fight to Pan American. It would challenge it in its own heartland. Amex applied for a route to Mexico and bought into a local airline Air Transport of Central America (TACA) run by a cavalier New Zealander, Lowell Yerex, as the beginnings of a strategy to develop a network throughout Latin America. Trippe's response was brutal. Working with another local airline, whose owners were close to the Guatemalan dictator Jorge Ubico, Trippe managed to get some of TACA's franchises revoked, and there were even more "unsavory incidents" with follow-up attacks on TACA, including what a CAB strategy paper referred to as "the 'hijacking' of its freight."[48] An official of the Commerce Department later put it more diplomatically for public consumption:

> The competitive struggle between Pan American and TACA was marked by several unsavory incidents which did not raise the prestige of the United States in Central America.[49]

Meanwhile, the administration was urging Congress again to consider the subsidy for Amex. On January 17 Hull expressed the State Department's support to Roosevelt for the Amex route to Lisbon.[50] At the end of the month, while the matter was before the House Appropriations Subcommittee, Rowe again wrote to the president repeating the allegations from CAB Chairman

Branch, Postmaster General Frank Walker, and the State Department that "Trippe is blocking this" and that he was now "persona non grata" with every executive agency, "but still seems to get his way."[51] Rowe went on to add that Pan American was fighting in the courts "tooth and nail" to try to challenge the president's authority over the award of certificates of necessity and convenience on foreign routes. These matters were close to the president's heart, and he was intimately involved in trying to set new parameters for U.S. aviation policy developments. He had recently seen John Slater, the president of Amex, to encourage him and explain that the award to Amex was fully in accord with his long-term plans for international routes, but Pan American was now endangering the possibility of this. Rowe urged the president to take vigorous action.

> Sam Rayburn [Democratic majority leader in the House] says unless you send word to the Appropriations Committee, this appropriation will be defeated and American Export will collapse. This will leave Pan American as a virtual world monopoly and your plan for government-controlled airlines to foreign countries would also end.[52]

A week later Roosevelt wrote to Congressman Taylor of the Appropriations Committee:

> I do hope the Appropriations Committee can put in the Post Office subsidy for the American Export Line to Lisbon. It is my thought that when peace comes, the Pan American should have the northern European line and the Export Line have the Mediterranean trade. In the meantime, we can well use more equipment in the only connecting link we have with Europe.[53]

Despite the president's efforts the situation remained intractable. By March Rowe was beginning to panic about the now likely outcome. He wrote the president: "Juan Trippe will be left alone in the aeronautics field and in foreign relations with South America and will be more powerful than the government of the United States. I use these words advisedly." Roosevelt decided to call in his closest aide and scrawled in longhand on the memorandum: "Dear Harry, Will you handle this quick?"[54] But it was to no avail. Even the president's chief fixer Harry Hopkins could not mend this situation. The subsidy was never forthcoming, but in the end it was the need for a stronger connecting link with Europe in time of war that eventually worked in Amex's favor, and from 1942 it did fly the Atlantic on routes to Portugal and Britain for the Naval Air Transport Service. Pan American could not prevent Amex and U.S. domestic airlines being drawn into wartime overseas operations. Such operations would well place them for postwar commercial service. However, regarding Amex, Pan American had a final say of sorts.

Amex eventually morphed with American Overseas Airlines after the war and later in 1950 it was ironically taken over by Pan American, but by then TWA was also fully operational on the Atlantic as well, and so Roosevelt's idea of at least two airlines operating to Europe serving different market segments had come to pass.[55]

Part of Pan American's strategy to block Amex was to challenge the route award in the courts in order to revoke Amex's right to fly to Lisbon. This court action, however, had far wider ramifications than simply Amex's future: it intended to challenge the very principle of the president's authority over the award of overseas route licenses. The outcome of the case was much more clear-cut than the saga of subsidy funding. On February 21, 1941, the Second Circuit Court of Appeals handed down its judgment on *Pan American Airways Co-Petitioner versus the CAB and American Export Lines Inc. Respondents*. The court ruled that in such cases the CAB is simply an adviser to the president and that he has sole power of decision, a power that was thus not challengeable in law. In Rowe's view the president could make his decision if he wanted on the basis of disliking "the color of the pilot's hair,", but on a more serious note, while there was no requirement for the president to give his reasons for approving or disapproving route awards, it was expected that his decisions should be based on considerations of "foreign policy and national defense."[56] General counsel in the CAB and soon to become its chairman and a key figure in policy development, Lloyd Welch Pogue, was ecstatic at the result. "The decision supported our position with respect to the paramount position of the President and gave us a clean bill of health in that regard."[57] Unwittingly, Pan American had done President Roosevelt significant service in prompting a judicial clarification of his powers over American international aviation.

Amex had to wait till 1942 before it could fly the Atlantic, but in the meantime it was not just Amex and the administration that continued to be angry and concerned. On April 14, 1941, Cornelius Vanderbilt Whitney, chairman of the board at Pan American, wrote to Roosevelt complaining of Amex and its ambition to fly the Atlantic. The president replied nine days later saying that he was not "unmindful of the pioneering efforts of Pan American Airways System in developing with substantial assistance from the Government, American flag foreign air service." However, after consideration by several federal agencies, it was "found that the existing service may well be supplemented and extended at this time by another company, with resultant great benefit to the nation, and that it si [*sic*] contrary to the public interest to continue indefinitely unrestricted monopoly in this field. Certificate of Convenience and Necessity for the American Export Lines was granted by the Civil Aeronautics Board after extended hearings, as all

Departments concerned feel that there is need of two tans [*sic*] – Atlantic air lines to Europe."[58]

The president was unhappy and concerned about the fate of Amex and expressed such views on more than one occasion. More importantly, the Amex saga made Roosevelt realize that more time, thought, and effort needed to be devoted to civil aviation, particularly in its international context. He and other key players had always kept an eye on the future. Even in the dark days after the Nazi onslaught on France and the Low Countries, they were never entirely distracted from longer-term issues of civil aviation's development. Now Roosevelt explicitly stated that "neither our short term or long term policy should be neglected at this time," and he asked the "several interdepartmental committees working at one time or another on the problem of this government's policy toward American airlines operating in the foreign transportation field" to assemble as an informal committee to advise on any steps in the near future that this government should be prepared to take and what role, if any, American Export Lines should play. He added, rather pointedly, that they should also "examine the position of Pan American Airways and its relationship to the government."[59] In fact, it was some time before an effective working committee was formed.

WAR

Franklin Roosevelt knew it was coming. But what happened on December 7, 1941,—the "day of infamy"—still shocked him. The next day the president spoke to Congress in a grimly angry but determined mode and a state of war was duly declared to exist with the empire of Japan. Pearl Harbor was the first of many victories for the Japanese, but they meant different things to different people. Those driven by the fancies of their own arrogance and barbarous warmongering rejoiced. Carried away with his victories against the Soviets and delighted by the entry of Japan into what was now truly a global war, Hitler tipped his hand against the United States, and in an act of ultimate strategic folly, declared war on December 11. Wiser minds read the writing on the wall as well, but what they saw was very different. Churchill thought that ultimate victory against the Nazis and their consorts in crime was now guaranteed. They could not prevail against the combined might of the British Empire, the Soviet Union, and most importantly of all the United States. There is no evidence to suggest that Roosevelt ever thought differently either. And an important part in ultimate victory would be airpower.

By the outbreak of war, U.S. civil aviation had arrived at an important stage in terms of its institutional arrangements and powers and policies that had been developed to enable it to contribute to defense. It had taken time and had been a struggle complicated by the more general objective of government reorganization, but the regulatory structure in the shape of the CAB and the principles that would determine how the civil aviation industry would operate, at least in the domestic sphere, were now in place. There was a clearer understanding of the remits for quasi-judicial and quasi-legislative authorities and of the administrative prerogatives of the Executive Branch. In particular the court case brought against the government by Pan American to try to overturn the granting of transatlantic operating rights to Amex had made it crystal clear that it was the president's word that determined who got what on overseas routes. For the time being this had little effect on Pan American, and, as we have seen, the exigencies of the approach to war delivered it more routes and more government support as it expanded its empire and simultaneously developed strategically important bases and international routes that would be vitally important to the military. At the same time, although questions still remained about precisely what the international side of U.S. civil aviation policy would be, both the positioning of key people in the administration and preparations for war heralded that policy changes were likely to come and changes that would break Pan American's monopoly.

Pan American's contribution to the preparation for war was unquestionable and of huge importance and was recognized as such by the president and others; nevertheless, people in key positions in the administration were not well disposed to Trippe's long-term ambition to uphold Pan American's exclusive hold on U.S. overseas routes. In addition there was an important development fostered by Edgar Gorrell, which impacted on policy and helped to push several American airlines into overseas operations when war came. This brought them invaluable international experience that they could exploit later when peace returned. We may recall that after the fiasco of the cancellation of airmail contracts in 1934 and Gorrell's contributions to the Baker Report, a group of airline executives persuaded him to take on the presidency of the Air Transport Association. He agreed and pursued with gusto an agenda as much of his own making as that of the leading airline corporate figures of the time. He was fully committed to promoting U.S. civil aviation, and he had considerable influence on the shape and content of the 1938 Civil Aeronautics Act. In addition Gorrell suggested in 1936 something that eventually grew into the Civil Reserve Air Fleet in 1951–52. That still lay in the future, but in 1938 in the aftermath of terrible storms that wreaked havoc in and around Boston, four of the big domestic carriers were used for federal relief work. Such a role for civil aviation seems rather obvious now, but it was novel at the time. Given further impetus by the effectiveness of this relief effort, Gorrell continued to work on plans that would enable civil airlines to retain their corporate status and play a key part if war were to come. In 1940 he sought and received help in finessing his plans, and in December 1941 he was all set to implement them if the president would approve.[60] It was largely on the basis of Gorrell's plans that other American airlines encroached on what had previously been Pan American's preserve.

Within days of Pearl Harbor, Gorrell and General Arnold were summoned to the White House.

> On FDR's desk, dated December 13, 1941 and already bearing his signature, was the executive order issued "pursuant to Title 10, U.S.C. sec. 1361", authorizing the President through the Secretary of War to take possession or assume control of any transportation system or part thereof.[61]

Gorrell was horrified at the idea of nationalizing the airlines, especially as he had put so much effort into devising a scheme whereby they could operate in an emergency to support the armed services whilst retaining their private status. He was ideologically strongly against government aggrandizement unless it was absolutely necessary. He argued his case with the president, asking what purpose it would serve to nationalize an industry that was at that very moment fully cooperating with the Army and Navy in an efficient all-out war effort. Roosevelt turned to Arnold for advice: he supported Gorrell. Remembering no doubt the problems the Army Air Corps experienced in 1934, Arnold observed: "Only the airlines...had the equipment and the skilled manpower to run a global air transportation system, as a civil adjunct to the military, but under military orders."[62] Roosevelt was convinced, and wearing his famous smile he tore up the executive order. From this emerged the Air Transport Command in charge of transport to all war zones. It was under the command of Colonel Harold Lee George, but with effective management coming from Cyrus Smith of American Airlines, who was given the post of deputy commander.

Trippe was furious. The idea of American domestic airlines being drawn into international operations was anathema to him and he tried to persuade Arnold that Pan American alone should take care of overseas transport. With typical arrogance he expected this to be without direct military supervision. While Arnold was not exactly pleased and would have nothing to do with such exclusivity claims for Pan American, he was still gracious enough to make a counter offer: Trippe could be a brigadier general in Air Transport Command. Trippe left the offer on the table and the meeting ended with ill-feeling on both sides. As one commentator put it:

> Even some of his greatest admirers felt that Trippe may have been his own worst enemy with his almost blind obsession to protect Pan Am from any

competition, even in wartime. Rightly or wrongly, it was an attitude that made him *persona non grata* in official Washington, and there is no doubt he got on the wrong side of too many top government officials—including the White House and Civil Aeronautics Board—to such an extent that it hurt his own airline.[63]

A variety of circumstances were conspiring to create the potential to undermine Pan American's dominant position on U.S. international routes in the future at the very moment when its ascendancy over foreign routes was absolute and its value to the U.S. Government was higher than at any time previously. This was bitterly ironic, but was always likely as American international aviation policy under Roosevelt developed. Competition was after all "the American way," and laws governing aviation always pointed in that direction even if never fully implemented in the 1930s. Four things were now coming together that would move things along toward a more competitive multiairline policy: the demands of war; the determination of key personnel within government; the requirements of long-term international civil aviation policy; and the ideas and determination of Franklin D. Roosevelt. And not only was the president fashioning his own ideas and becoming more determined about the need to develop policy, he also had decisive power to influence policy development. As a memorandum for Harry Hopkins indicated in March 1941, the CAB decides on all matters to do with domestic airline routes, and so the President has *"nothing"* to do with those decisions, however:

> The CAB also grants certificates to airlines flying into *foreign* countries. The President must approve or disapprove these decisions before they are made public, the theory being the President should have some sort of review because secret matters of foreign policy or national defense should also be considered.[64]

The president was thus in a strong position to craft international policy, and Trippe's position was weakening. Even so, there remained a great deal to be done and much to play for. Pan American was essential to the war effort and had massive experience and a fund of skills and capabilities, and Trippe remained a powerful influence in the U.S. Congress. Roosevelt was still feeling his way toward a suitable policy, and there were divisions and differences within his administration as to how policy should be crafted and what its substance should be. Also there were now other airlines that would demand a say in formulating international policy that would bear on their own fortunes as they too began to look to develop international operations. And finally how all these policy influences would engage with foreign actors and their ambitions and policies for an international aviation regime remained to be seen. By 1941 the Roosevelt administration had accomplished much in the domestic civil aviation sphere. The main challenge now lay abroad. What regime would apply there? The answer to that question and the formulation of international civil aviation policy lay primarily in the hands of powerful key figures within the administration.

CHAPTER 7

FORMING U.S. INTERNATIONAL AVIATION POLICY— DECEMBER 1941– MAY 1943

> "Land carriage, always restricted and, therefore, always slow, toils enviously but hopelessly behind vainly seeking to replace and supplant the Royal Highway of nature's own making." This quotation comes from none other than Admiral Mahan the number one naval strategist and, of course, the Royal Highway he is speaking of is the sea. But may he not turn over in his grave when I point out that his judgment is entirely correct—only the Royal Highway happens to be the air.[1]

WITH ENTRY INTO WAR, overseas U.S. air routes and a growing series of air bases proliferated in response to strategic demands. They were under military wartime management, but their potential for future peacetime use was never overlooked, and eventually, they prompted thoughts about postwar civil aviation. On the domestic front, the system was frozen in place with a CAB announcement on December 12, 1941, that it would not consider applications for new certificates of convenience and necessity. The existing system continued to operate smoothly within the well-established framework established by the 1938 Aeronautics Act, though now subject to overall direction by the secretary of state for war.[2] In the war years, the only issues arising for the domestic airlines concerned their possible entry into international air commerce. However, following Pearl Harbor, all civil aviation policy issues were pushed aside. It was not until 1943 that they again came into high-level focus, and then international policy monopolized attention, though to imagine that what began to take shape was policy in the singular would be to ignore the fact that several positions vied for dominance. The problem was that this was largely virgin territory. Past and present practice did not provide adequate guidelines for the future, and conflicting arguments emerged from key figures within the administration, from Congress, and from influential opinion formers about what to do. At the end of the day some accommodation would also have to be reached with foreign governments. Most policy-makers thus felt their way forward gingerly because important issues were involved that did not sit comfortably together.

Extreme nationalists, however, informed by manifest destiny and realist doctrine with its overriding emphasis on state power and security, were clear and determined: they wanted the United States to completely dominate postwar skies militarily and commercially. They were a distinct minority, but had impact and complicated the problem of dealing with other nations, which came to fear the prospect of American aviation imperialism. In stark contrast, idealists wanted to internationalize civil aviation to take it out of the state power equation altogether. The leading American proponent of these views was Vice President Henry Wallace, and there is evidence to indicate that President Roosevelt was happy to see Wallace moot these ideas in public and that he was sympathetically disposed to them. That does not mean that he ever intended to implement them in the real world, but it sets him well away in terms of disposition from the extreme nationalists. The majority view held a middle ground that nevertheless encompassed many important differences about policies and how they might be implemented. In this middle ground there was general agreement that the United States must have the leading position in air commerce because of security concerns, but "leading" for this group did not entail the kind of dominance sought by the extreme nationalists. Widespread agreement also emerged on the need for opening the skies for transit and technical stop and on a worldwide American presence for both security and commercial reasons, for controls on subsidies and pricing, for more freedom for frequencies and capacity, for the immediate start of operations after the war so that American airlines could seize the opportunities that beckoned, and for avoiding the establishment of a powerful international regulatory authority. The differences within the American policy-making process were not just about objectives but also about how to pursue them. And most of that debate took place within the middle ground and not between it and the internationalists or the realist nationalists. No universally agreed policy ever emerged, instead there were always factions at play aiming to alter at least some aspect of whatever happened to be in the ascendancy at a particular moment in time.

Of the officials engaged with civil aviation none were more important than Adolf Berle, Welch Pogue, Harry Hopkins, and Robert Lovett.

Berle was an assistant secretary of state and in overall charge of international aviation policy. He was intellectually incisive and naturally inclined to internationalism, but domestic commercial pressures and his commitment to safeguarding American national interests, particularly against the British whom he did not trust, injected a strong measure of pragmatism into his policy considerations. He had no time for fools, could be abrasive, and lacked a certain ability to get on with people, but there was no question about his intellectual ability. Possibly an even more important figure was Pogue. Appointed to the CAA in September 1938, he soon became its assistant general counsel and then in 1939 general counsel before being appointed to the CAB as chairman in 1942, a position that he held until 1946. Pogue was immensely capable. He chaired the key interdepartmental working subcommittee on international aviation and he was dominant in the CAB. He was a very important player in determining U.S. policy, and significant in this respect, he was wary of internationalism except insofar as it was necessary to open up rights of transit and technical stop around the world for U.S. commercial aviation.

At important junctures in policy development, Pogue worked closely with Harry Hopkins to try to restrict the negotiation of commercial air rights to bilateral negotiations in which U.S. power and prestige could be used to best advantage. In this respect he was directly at odds with Roosevelt's preference for commercial multilateralism. Hopkins was Roosevelt's closest adviser for most of the war. He first became involved with civil aviation directly as secretary of commerce, to which he was appointed by Roosevelt in 1939. After the outbreak of war, he became immersed in matters of aircraft supply to the allies and with the competing claims of the U.S. service departments, so he had a grasp of the broad panorama of aviation matters, and this was important given the inextricable knot that tied together civil and military aviation. Hopkins was a vital force in the Roosevelt administration, and many conscious of that tried to use him as a conduit to the president. Pogue did just that. He and Hopkins were very different politically, but they were both New Dealers, were great patriots, and saw eye to eye on much of aviation policy; they also came from Iowa, something Pogue later recalled as providing a kind of bond between them.[3] Importantly, however, Pogue knew that if the president opposed views presented to him by Hopkins, in the end he, Hopkins, would always "line up with the President."[4] There were limits to what Pogue could achieve through Hopkins's good offices.

The close links between civil and military aviation also meant that Robert A. Lovett, assistant secretary of War for Air, and to a lesser extent General "Hap" Arnold had important inputs into determining policy. When Lovett arrived in the War Department in November 1940, he knew little about aviation of any sort, but under Arnold's mentorship, he soon learnt and became an effective spokesperson for the Army Air Corps. None of these key players, with the possible exception of Lovett, had good feelings toward Trippe and the Pan American monopoly. Beyond that, however, there were important differences between them concerning the development of America's international aviation. In particular there were disagreements over just how nationalist and unilateralist or internationalist and multilateralist American policy should be, and they also frequently had to tussle with conflicting views from within their own institutional bailiwicks. They were all extremely able men, and together they composed the group—bar one—that largely determined U.S. civil aviation. The other member of this group was, of course, Franklin Roosevelt himself.

Roosevelt's introduction to civil aviation as president had been a baptism of fire because of the airmail fiasco, but by 1941 he had traveled a long way with the industry. He no longer believed that a unified regulator for transport was imminently viable and had pushed forward first the CAA and then the CAB. The domestic industry was now heavily regulated with controls over market entry and pricing, and there had been progress in the international sphere, though here things were more difficult because by its very nature it was not subject to U.S. jurisdiction. Even so, presidential control over the award of rights to U.S. carriers for foreign routes had been firmly established. What the final overall shape of U.S. international aviation policy might be was still unclear, and Roosevelt was by no means constantly engaged in the policy debates that developed, but his actions at crucial points clearly demonstrate both how important he deemed civil aviation to be and his determination to dictate the essential contours of policy. For example, in October 1944, Berle told Secretary of State for War Henry Stimson: "As you are aware, the policy and general method of approach towards the air settlements have been at all times under the direction of the President."[5] While it was not until November 1943 that Roosevelt clearly spelled out his overall vision to senior officials on international aviation, he had previously made his position pretty clear on a number of important specific matters. Equally importantly, he had pronounced on broad economic and security principles, such as in the Atlantic Charter and in early 1942 with his Four Freedoms.

From those specific and general statements, it was widely acknowledged that Roosevelt favored much more freedom for international air commerce than had existed in the past. A natural corollary of that was some kind of international convention or agreement to enable such freedom, at the very least on technical and safety matters. On more specific issues he had repeatedly spoken of a multiairline policy for the United States and an end to Pan American's monopoly. He also at least toyed with the idea of partial government ownership of airlines. The rest, for the time being, remained unspoken or vague, but even the contours of policy he had already drawn suggested a complex mixture of regulation and free-market competition. Finally, looking beyond purely commercial matters, Roosevelt was acutely aware of the security aspect of civil aviation. No clear water existed between him and his military chiefs on that, but once essential bases and routes were secured, he was more sensitive to the danger of a preponderance of American power creating insecurity for others. As a result he was prepared to be adventurous in leaning toward liberal internationalism for civil aviation. Those views were not always congenial to his policy-makers, some of whom contrived to compromise the president's vision for international aviation in significant ways.

PAST PRACTICE; DEFENSE REQUIREMENTS; IDEALISM AND INTERNATIONALISM; AND THE WILL OF OTHERS

Part of the problem of formulating policy was that what existed in practice was incomplete or contradictory and did not provide a model for what to do in the future. Even guidelines for dealing with technical matters were only inadequately provided for by the Paris and Havana Conventions, and they would have to be reconciled as well as expanded in order to produce a comprehensive and uniform system that could be applied worldwide. That implied the need for some kind of international organization. So there were difficulties in determining a way ahead even on the largely uncontroversial technical front, but they paled to insignificance once one turned to economic regulation.

On the commercial front, Pan American dominated the picture, but there was no consistency or governing principles. Things were driven by whatever advantages Pan American could grasp. In the Atlantic, pragmatism might dictate a "fair deal" with Britain and Imperial Airways: no such thing applied for operations in Latin America or the Pacific. Pan American took whatever routes it could, sought whatever preferential and exclusive terms it could, grabbed whatever subsidies and mail rates it could, and imposed whatever charges it could. Apart from airmail contracts, there were no controls over pricing. There was often no regulation over capacity and frequencies in the Western Hemisphere, but European governments insisted on severe ones on transatlantic routes. Market entry overseas was not restricted by the U.S. government until 1938, but the viability of a route even after that depended upon subsidies and the award of mail contracts as was clearly demonstrated by the Amex saga. Apart from agreements with Colombia, Canada, and the UK, Pan American had largely made its own way in negotiations, but there was growing pressure for more government involvement and control. Much of this made the relationship between Pan American and the government complicated, even though Pan American was a de facto chosen instrument and recognized as such by other countries. At the Imperial Conference in London in 1937, a senior British official, Lord Swinton, who later played a key role in the 1944 Chicago International Civil Aviation Conference, acknowledged that reality of Pan American as a chosen instrument, but also the convenient legal vagueness shrouding it.

> Pan American Airways were the chosen instrument of the United States Government who, in effect, give them complete political and financial backing, although, when it suits their purpose, the Government puts forward the Company as an entirely independent commercial organisation.[6]

Although Pan American had a monopoly on U.S. overseas routes, it did not extend to the land border with Canada. There other airlines conducted international operations into the northern neighbor, a neighbor that came to prominence in aviation in the 1930s with negotiations for transatlantic services. In 1938 Canadian and American officials meeting in the United States reached agreement on technical and safety matters and then assembled again the following year in Ottawa to hammer out commercial arrangements. Things now became difficult. The United States argued for a reciprocal exchange of air rights that would allow them both to mount parallel operations on any agreed route. The Canadians refused. They argued it would not be commercially viable. In fact, they were wary of direct competition. Rather surprisingly, the Americans gave way and a system was established in which each side controlled its own operations and serviced separate routes.[7] They would not go head-to-head. The fact was America needed to come to terms with Canada. As Berle observed in 1943, "Canada's importance in post-war civil aviation was obvious to anyone who looked at the map."[8] U.S. air routes to Europe and over the North Pole to the Soviet Union and Asia all lay through Canada. What was true in 1943 held in 1939 and also in December 1945, when they made a new agreement. Again, it embodied the principle of reciprocity, but no parallel operations. Here in the United States' aviation relations with Canada lay a rather different model to that drawn by Pan American.

From these perspectives U.S. policy emerges as a hodgepodge of different practices dictated partly by Pan American, partly by the U.S. government, and everything complicated by opaque collusion between the two. While few denied that this had worked in the past, there was growing dissatisfaction. Absence of competition was contrary to the prescriptions of the 1938 Aeronautics Act, and that troubled many officials. Also Trippe had alienated important people in government through his arrogant behavior and grasping, self-serving tactics. Looking to the future, the central issue was how best to draw things together in a coherent policy to maximize U.S. aviation interests. With the potential looming to launch worldwide services, it might be better if Pan American were to be joined by other U.S. airlines. Whatever were decided, airlines would need more open skies, and if the market were to expand as Americans wanted it to, then there had to be less foreign restriction on the amount of services they could offer. These were two crucial issues and would have to be worked out in conjunction with other countries. How to consummate reform and the extent to which it should be taken posed puzzles, the solutions to which proved perennially elusive.

It is important to note the contrasting practices of U.S. aviation policy in 1941 because they help to demonstrate the range of possibilities. The relationship with Canada may seem surprisingly regulated to some, but that is at least partly because U.S. policy has been oversimplified, and the aggressive, competitive style, which developed after deregulation in 1977–78, read backwards into the historical record. "Liberal" and "competitive" are words often used to describe U.S. policy during the planning for postwar aviation, but they were not the kind of liberalism and competitiveness of postderegulation America. The aviation policies that came to prominence between 1943 and 1945 were not so much driven by a simple conflict between regulation and free competition, but by where to strike the balance between them. No senior American official ever supported a free market for pricing or for free entry of U.S. airlines onto routes in direct competition with each other. Pragmatism and national interest constantly modified principles of commercial policy that officials might have pursued in their ideal world. The fact was that at the outset of the war the overwhelming majority of U.S. officials and politicians found neither the monopoly operations of Pan American nor the tightly controlled market with Canada very palatable. A more uniform and better system was their goal, but bringing it to birth would not be easy. Not only did American policy-makers lack a model to follow in crafting a postwar international civil aviation regime, they also had to contend with three major factors that vastly complicated the design process: security; proposals for internationalization; and accommodating to the will of others.

Throughout the 1930s, civil aviation's link with military power had grown irresistibly in the minds of politicians and generals. The course of the Second World War confirmed and added further weight to those beliefs. Squaring commercial ambition and defense requirements in a way that would achieve American goals and be acceptable to other countries was quite a challenge. In September 1942, Berle wrote:

> I feel that aviation will have a greater influence on American foreign interests and American foreign policy than any other non-political consideration. It may well be determinative in certain territorial matters which have to do with

American defense, as well as with transportation matters affecting American commerce, in a degree comparable to that which sea power has had on our interests and policy.[9]

To acknowledge the security importance of civil aviation was one thing, providing an answer for dealing with it was another. However, in Washington, widely held convictions leaned to cautious realism, dictating that until there were strong guarantees of a prolonged and secure peace, the United States must unilaterally ensure its own security. While America felt powerful enough to do this, many of its allies did not, and countries even as powerful as Britain looked to international regulation of commercial aviation partly as a safeguard for their future security. This divergence of views would cause trouble in trying to negotiate a new regime for international aviation. For the United States the unilateral pursuit of security had important implications for civil aviation. The first U.S. official civil aviation planning report, by a committee chaired and much influenced by Pogue, put the matter thus in March 1943:

> As time goes on, our margin of competitive advantage [in postwar international civil aviation] is likely to be reduced....It is not impossible that our situation would remain favorable, but to act on that assumption would involve substantial risks if successful participation in international air commerce is essential to our military security.
> The Subcommittee does not believe that we could afford to take those risks unless and until the situation with respect to military security in the post-war period is greatly clarified.[10]

Those of this frame of mind, and there were many in Washington, did not fully appreciate the paradox within: a paradox that troubled Franklin Roosevelt. One state's security poses a potential threat to other states and becomes their source of insecurity: this is the security dilemma. Fear that long-term peace might prove elusive was pushing U.S. policy-makers into seeking dominance in international civil aviation, partly because it was a crucial aspect of their security, but this could be perceived as threatening by others. The United States with its preponderance of power might be able to achieve security through such means at the end of the war, but the question was either for how long would foreigners place a great deal of faith in America not to misuse its power, or when would U.S. dominance provide an incentive for them to struggle to improve their own positions. International civil aviation was in danger of becoming further embedded in the perennial arms race. This was a gloomy scenario given the continuing ideological and security differences that existed in the world. Even among those nations with similar politics and values to the United States, there was a danger that American actions would provoke protectionist retaliation that would close off much of the world to U.S. airlines. That might not immediately lead to security competition and military conflict, but there was a well-established conviction in Washington that economic friction in the interwar period had been a major cause of war and could very well be a causal factor in starting future ones. Clearly a difficult and delicate line would have to be trodden if the United States were to realize its main ambitions of a secure peace and a prosperous and worldwide flourishing of U.S. airlines. By the autumn of 1943 President Roosevelt was highly sensitized to such difficulties and dangers, and he was more willing to take risks with the defense dilemma than Pogue and his committee. He set the parameters of U.S. policy accordingly.

A deeper understanding of the problem that arose when international civil aviation was subsumed by national security priorities is revealed by internationalist arguments, and these also connected with the most important "other" that the United States would have to deal with, Great Britain. Internationalists too recognized the problem of civil aviation and security. Their solution was not for a benign superpower to dominate aviation, but for it to be taken out of the interstate power equation by internationalization. They saw this as one of the necessary prerequisites for the development of United Nations' (UN's) collective security. And, for them, if collective security were not effectively established, then a future and greater war would inevitably come and be the end of all things. In other words, if they could not get it right for civil aviation, they feared that they would be unable to get general provisions for the peace right. Postwar international civil aviation was for them a kind of test case. Perhaps the most impressive idealistic statements in this vein came from Canadian sources in the form of Escott Reid of the External Affairs Department. For him: "What was at stake is the very future of our civilization." "Our twentieth century civilisation has created a Frankenstein monster of the air."

> The problems of air transport are not predominantly commercial problems but are predominantly political and security problems. The starting point in any international discussions of the subject should be affirmation that air transport must be made subject to the principles of international collaboration which we also hope to see applied to the related problems of the world system of security and post-war economic reorganization.[11]

The preferred idealist solution was a single international airline owned and operated by the nations of the world, which would service all routes, including domestic ones. Such schemes did not remain the preserve of woolly headed policy idealists. Variations on the theme were put forward by the

Australian and New Zealand governments. The power of idealism, however, never triumphed in such a way in Britain, which, after the United States, would be the other key player in postwar civil aviation, but it had important impact and left a legacy that had significant consequences for American policy-makers.

The Atlantic Charter in 1941 and Anglo-American discussions about appropriate consideration for U.S. lend-lease supplies to Britain committed both sides to certain principles—including equal access and freer trade—and to cooperate in constructing a new postwar economic order.[12] There was vagueness, but also sufficient substance in all this for the British to appoint a Committee on Reconstruction Problems under the Minister Without Portfolio Arthur Greenwood, in July 1941. Its brief was to think about the postwar economy. This set in train a succession of committees one of which looked at international aviation and produced the Shelmerdine, Finlay, and Barlow reports of April and December 1942 and June 1943, respectively.[13] All three reports looked with much favor on the kind of internationalization of the industry later promoted by Australia and New Zealand, but there were those who doubted its practicalities and likelihood of acceptance by either the United States or the Soviet Union. Most notably and vocally from this camp arose the voice of Leo Amery, secretary of state for India.

> Every major nation, at any rate, is henceforward bound to consider the devel-
> opment of its civil air transport as an essential and inseparable part of its
> defence policy.
>   If that is the case, then clearly no major nation is likely even to look at any
> scheme of internationalisation which is going to deprive it of exclusive control
> of any aspect of its own civil aviation or in any way limit its efforts to expand
> that civil aviation by the reservation of its internal services, by subsidies or
> special arrangements with particular nations whose alliances or friendships it
> may wish to cultivate.[14]

Amery had in fact succinctly summarized the kind of reasoning that was driving most American policy-makers.

As a result of such skepticism, modified versions of internationalization soon emerged. In particular, the form favored in London was intended to restrain what was expected to be the vastly dominant position of the United States in equipment and experienced and efficient airlines at the end of the war.

> ... the choice before the world lies between Americanisation and internation-
> alisation. If this is correct, it is difficult to doubt that it is under the latter
> system that British interests will best be served.[15]

Clearly, problems and arguments were emerging in London about post-war aviation, and policy-makers were increasingly troubled by the likely prospects for Britain. Those concerns were deepened by various pronouncements in the United States, most notably, as we shall soon see, by the maiden speech in Congress of Representative Clare Booth Luce in February 1943. She stirred up a veritable hornet's nest with extreme nationalist aviation sentiments. Soon after this, Prime Minister Winston Churchill made a decisive intervention for British policy. In June he circulated a paper expressing his views and calling for preliminary understandings with the commonwealth and the United States before moving forward on a broader front. Crucially, for the internationalists, Churchill stated:

> Our two earliest studies of post-war civil aviation have recommended complete internationalisation. If by this is meant a kind of Volapuk Esperanto cosmopolitan organisation managed and staffed by committees of all peoples great and small with pilots of every country from Peru to China (especially China), flying every kind of machine in every direction, many people will feel that this is at present an unattainable ideal. It is unnecessary, however, now to consider the argument for and against this and kindred proposals, since they are clearly unacceptable to the United States, the Dominions and probably Russia [*sic*]. We must agree upon some less high-spirited line of approach to guide us in the forthcoming international discussions.[16]

Churchill was actually wrong about the views of the Dominions. Even so, his views doused the ardor of British and Dominion internationalists generally, but this was not the end for them. The idealism behind original arguments for internationalization was now tempered by realism in the manner recommended by Finlay: the goal was internationalization rather than Americanization. The main policy thrust was for a powerful international authority that would wield wide-ranging economic regulatory power as well as take charge of technical matters essential to the proper running of the system. Most crucially, the authority should reserve and apportion segments of the market to the main players avoiding the danger of an American monopoly. Ironically, internationalization, initially seen as an idealist solution to the general problem of aviation, was now to be employed in a real-politik manner to counter American power and protect British and other countries' interests. It was variations on this theme that American policy-makers would primarily have to tussle with in the international arena as well as unilateral moves by Britain to try to protect its aviation market. They could not escape these tussles, for no nation, not even one as powerful as the United States, could play the international civil aviation game alone. Among the other players with whom it would have to treat, none were more important to the game than Great Britain.

Britain was the key that could either open or close the door on the world to U.S. airlines: it was the most important "other" whose will the United States would have to cope with. How to turn the key thus became of central concern to U.S. policy-makers. This was a fraught and difficult issue and had much impact on U.S. policy and on Roosevelt's own thinking. Before the war Britain had slipped further and further behind American technical capabilities in civil airliners. Then the prospect of war forced the government to pour virtually all available resources into developing military planes. What was available for civilian use produced planes that fell far short of their American counterparts. Britain's equipment deficit was then pushed much further into the red with agreements developed as a result of ongoing discussions between Britain and the United States for a division of war production. It was agreed that Britain should concentrate on fighter aircraft and night bomber production, whilst, among other things, the United States would produce transports. Transports of course involved the kind of technology for, and were easily converted into, civilian airplanes. During the war Britain produced no large custom-made transports.[17]

The picture for Britain's postwar international civil aviation thus looked bleak. It would not have the equipment to compete with the Americans. On the other hand, the British still held a trump card: the ability to exclude U.S. airlines from the British Commonwealth and Empire and client states. However, matters here soon took a turn for the worse with wartime developments that enhanced the American position from which to launch international services and sweep all other competitors from the skies. Prior to the war Imperial Airways, renamed British Overseas Airways Corporation (BOAC) in 1940, had satisfactory understandings with Pan American for the Atlantic. Things were less amicable in the Pacific, where Pan American dominated as it also did throughout the Western Hemisphere. Counterbalancing that, Trippe's airline only had limited access to Europe and was effectively excluded from the Middle East, Africa, and India. Worryingly for London, the war began to change this balance of power and collapse the spheres of influence. Pan American entered routes that positioned it for worldwide and round-the-world operations once peace came. Nowhere did this seem to the British more obvious and ominous than on the Takoradi route in Africa developed by Pan American in the summer of 1940.

Within months of the start of Pan American's operations in Africa, British air vice marshal Sir Arthur Tedder observed: "The cloven hoof of Pan American now well to fore." Tedder and others were convinced that Pan American was concentrating just as much on developing commercial opportunities now and for the future as on military support operations; they were right. This would amount to commercial penetration into one of BOAC's strongholds. Tedder later recorded that in a meeting with the chief

Pan American official in Africa in February 1941, he "proclaimed openly that it was his company's intention to operate commercially east of Cairo on the grounds that 'naturally Uncle Sam must try to get some return on the expenditure he is currently incurring in operating an air service to the Far East for military purposes.'"[18] The morphing of Pan American with the U.S. Government echoed Lord Swinton's 1937 remarks about the ambiguous standing of company to government.

These shenanigans rumbled on for months, but after America's entry into the war, matters were resolved by a series of diplomatic exchanges. After considerable argument, it was agreed that Pan American's operations should be conducted on a purely military basis and that if commercial advantages were to be sought they should be discussed after the war. This resonated much more widely than the Takoradi route. The U.S. spent huge amounts of money building air bases abroad during the war and this occasioned much clamor in Congress and the press and from public opinion about the need for postwar access for U.S. airlines to those bases. They wanted something tangible back for their money. This became another feature in developing U.S. postwar policy. But, returning to the resolution of the specific problems that arose from the Takoradi route, while the United States acquiesced to the British proposals, it also sought to preempt the possibility of them obstructing America gaining foreign air rights. On May 27, 1942, the State Department wrote to the British Embassy in Washington expressing the hope that "no attempt will be made by either Government, or by companies acting for either Government, to set up arrangements which would exclude air transport lines of the other." There should also be Anglo-American consultations about the development of future policy for international aviation. On July 28 the embassy replied, agreeing and suggesting that the proposals should apply worldwide. Matters were concluded on that basis, and this became known as the Halifax Agreement after the British ambassador to Washington.[19] It was a standoff between the two aviation rivals that kept things under control for several months.

These three issues—security, internationalization, and the will of others—were all part of the complex problem of designing American policy. Importantly all three emphasized the fact that international aviation could not be treated simply as a commercial matter. It was in this context that policy-makers had to address a series of key questions that would determine the character of the postwar international aviation regime. These questions neatly divided into two categories. The first concerned what might loosely be termed technical matters and did not cause any great difficulties: safety, technical and operating standards, meteorological and navigational provisions, and the international infrastructure. Although these issues differed in character, they had one thing in common: they were not commercial and did not raise the question of possible economic regulation. The second category did and proved to be most problematic.

Should the airlines continue to negotiate for their own commercial rights or should this be taken over by the State Department and the CAB? Should there be a chosen American monopoly instrument, a series of regional monopoly instruments, or should there be more direct competition between U.S. airlines abroad? Should new international companies be formed to provide all international services or at least part of them, for example in ex-enemy countries? Should there be government ownership or part-ownership of U.S. airlines? Would foreign airlines be restricted to airports on the borders or be welcomed into the U.S. heartland? If the latter then what about militarily sensitive areas, should they be exclusion zones? Was cabotage a good idea, and if it were, should it extend to cover routes to U.S. dependencies such as Alaska and Hawaii, especially if that meant accepting imperial cabotage for the European powers for their colonies? What should be done about subsidies? Should there be quotas and/or protection of a nation's own generated traffic—an important issue as it was correctly expected that the United States would generate the vast majority of international passengers? Should sovereignty over airspace be modified in favor of universal rights of transit and technical stop? Commercial international route allocations according to the 1938 Aeronautics Act were to be decided by the president in conjunction with the CAB, but on the basis of what commercial principles? Should they be acquired by bilateral or multilateral agreements? Should there always be reciprocity? In general the United States in economic relations called for equal access and nondiscrimination, but in civil aviation granting nondiscriminatory and equal access to the U.S. aviation market would deliver huge opportunities to foreigners in exchange for very limited opportunities for U.S. airlines. This was a troubling issue especially as there were fears that America's immediate postwar competitive advantages—the best equipment, a huge pool of trained personnel, and experienced and efficient airlines—would gradually be eroded by lower foreign labor costs and subsidized state airlines. Should, therefore, subsidies and pricing be controlled and possibly capacity and frequencies as well? If there were to be such economic controls then who should apply them—operators' conferences as in the maritime industry or an international authority?

During 1942, only sporadic and hesitant moves were made to address these issues.

THE SEARCH FOR POLICY BEGINS: 1941 TO MAY 1943

Notwithstanding panic and chaos that followed Pearl Harbor, civil airlines were engaged in an orderly way in the war effort. Gorrell and Arnold ensured that America's privately owned airlines would not be nationalized, and President Roosevelt set in train Gorrell's plans. For a time this meant more prominence and expansion for Pan American. Even before U.S. entry into the war, Pan American's route system had mushroomed from 62,305 miles in 1939 to 98,582 miles in 1941. This was well over twice the size of BOAC's routes and larger than all the European airlines' route systems added together.[20] Pan American was a key strategic asset for the U.S. government, but some were speaking more and more clearly about how such a claim had been overexaggerated and new questions began to arise about the company's performance. On December 22, 1941, Robert Hinckley, now assistant secretary in the Commerce Department, criticized Pan American in a vein that resonated with the vehemently partisan comments often made by Grover Loening.

> Despite the millions of dollars which this government has poured into Pan American's Latin American operations in the theory that this carrier was voluntarily and efficiently promoting our national objectives, the lack of such promotion is clearly apparent now that it has become so urgently desirable.... [Pan American] demonstrably subordinated to its own self interest in profit and private power when those interests have come into conflict with the interests of its government.[21]

Hinckley was one of many now expressing concerns about Pan American. Harry Hopkins for example grumbled: "I have never liked the idea of Pan American having a world monopoly of our airlines."[22] The fact was that U.S. domestic airlines, which had developed in a more competitive environment, were generally more efficient and effective. Nevertheless, route developments for war purposes continued to be assigned to Pan American, but gradually the domestic airlines began to move out as well. TWA and Amex joined Pan American on the Atlantic routes, United Airlines entered the Pacific and Indian Oceans, Eastern and Braniff moved into Central and South America, and Northwest Airlines took the route to Alaska.[23] But these were wartime operations, and the controversy generated by the prospect of a peacetime return to Pan American's civilian monopoly rumbled on for much of the war.

In the midst of all this and with the problems of war pressing closely in upon him, the president was posed with an administrative problem. Since Hinckley's move to the Commerce Department, the CAB had lacked strong leadership, largely because the new chairman, Harllee Branch, suffered from chronic ill-health. After one tour of duty Branch was more than willing to stand down from the chairmanship, and in late December 1941 opportunity arose to ring the changes. Roosevelt was presented with the possibility of appointing a new member of the CAB because of vocal opposition to reappointing Grant Mason expressed by close advisers and senior officials such as the Secretary of Commerce Jesse Jones. James Rowe, however, advised Roosevelt that "this is a tough one."[24] He did so because he knew that the opposition to Mason arose from motives that were not unblemished. Even so, he acknowledged that elevating Welch Pogue from general counsel to a member of the CAB and at the same time promoting him to chairman to replace Branch would make sense as he was very capable. The president received this from Rowe on December 19, but he had probably already made up his mind. On December 5 Steve Early, his press secretary, had damned Mason as a friend of the anti–New Deal columnist Arthur Krock and, equally damaging, as someone who consorted with Pat McCarran. He questioned his loyalty. A week later, Hopkins wrote to the president that he saw no good reason for reappointing Mason, who was "mediocre." In comparison Pogue was "a good New Dealer" and capable of dealing with the industry and Congress.[25] Roosevelt concurred and appointed Pogue as chairman of the CAB as of January 14, 1942.[26] This was to have huge consequences. Pogue worked on a narrower canvass than Franklin Roosevelt, and largely as a consequence of that, differences were to arise over policy, but they were both agreed about the importance of opening up the skies for innocent passage and technical stop, and this was one of the few aviation policy positions publicly articulated in 1942 and early 1943.

In June 1942 Pogue observed: "Freedom of the air is one of the principles which seems to be called for by the Atlantic Charter."[27] Six months later, speaking to the Nebraska Bar Association in Omaha, he argued passionately for freedom of the air.

> Aviation can be a compelling force in stabilizing the political relationships of the world. The present fight for freedom will be lost to no small degree if we miss the opportunity to accelerate this force by making the great international highways open to all nations.[28]

This was the start of Pogue's campaign, fully supported by Franklin Roosevelt, for opening up "the Royal Highway of the air." Pogue presented his fully developed thesis in an Aviation Day speech in Minneapolis St. Paul in April 1943.

> Our own enlightened self-interest, and that of all other nations, requires that, as a part of aviation's future international arrangements, a world charter be given aviation now, by granting generally this right of Commercial Air Transit.[29]

As Pogue claimed later:

> I conceived and proposed in [that]…speech that there should be a treaty among civilized nations permitting peaceful airline flights of civil aircraft of adhering nations on the way to traffic points beyond without the necessity of making costly separate bilateral agreements with each nation through whose airspace the operator had to fly.[30]

Pogue's assertion of sole responsibility for composing and promoting this policy should not obscure the fact it happened to be Franklin Roosevelt's position as well and he had spoken on it well before April 1943. Late in 1942 at a session of the Pacific War Council in Washington, the president said there "should be free access to the airports of the world for non-military planes and for the military planes of what he called the 'policemen' powers; that there should be freedom of the air resembling freedom of the seas." When he was challenged with the fact that the United States had refused to open up Hawaii to other countries' airlines before the war, he said "that problem would not arise after the war…all international air routes would be available for aircraft generally, subject to such conditions as were agreed upon, while local routes would be reserved for national undertakings."[31] Roosevelt did not use the kind of jargon that Pogue did, but it amounted to the same thing: widespread rights to transit and technical stop. Pogue had been right in June 1942; freedom of the air did indeed seem to be required by the principles of the Atlantic Charter: Roosevelt was consistent on some things. For the president this was partly an idealistic vision of freedom to travel worldwide as well as to open opportunities for American commercial airlines. Those beliefs were shared by Pogue as well, but emphasis was subtly different. Pogue placed more emphasis on the commercial value for U.S. airlines. He saw an opportunity for American airlines to consolidate and expand their world leadership in the air, and the first prerequisite for that to be consummated was to open up the skies with the multilateral granting of transit and technical stop.

While Pogue's views about rights to transit and stop were well formulated, like other American officials, though, he fluctuated between unconditional granting of rights to transit and stop and making them conditional on reaching a satisfactory commercial agreement.On the commercial front Pogue faced a dilemma that made him unsure of how to proceed. He wanted to seize the opportunities afforded by U.S. superiority in civil aviation, though not at the expense of endangering U.S. airlines in the longer term. The question was precisely how to do that.

> In view of the technical and business proficiency of the United States, supremacy in the field of international air transport can surely be gained by

it. In the light of the concrete experience of the past, however, it is apparent
that, if development in the field must be carried forward within the confines
of such diplomatic maneuvering as the regulations of bi-lateral agreements
with other countries for specific services, our advantages in ability will largely
disappear as a factor and our accomplishments will be geared rather to such
controlling factors as the abilities of the other countries to operate corre-
sponding service.[32]

This was clearly a reference to the kind of agreement Pan American and
Imperial Airways had made before the war not to start operations on the
Atlantic until both were ready. An obvious lesson to draw from this was to
depart from bilateralism in favor of multilateralism, but it was never quite
as simple as that. In the prewar regime both transit and commercial rights
were too politicized and that was largely because they had to be negotiated bilaterally. To overcome the problem of transit rights Pogue's favored
solution was multilateral agreement by which all signatories granted those
rights. However, he was aware that a multilateral exchange of commercial
rights might open up the United States to too much competition from
cheaper-run foreign airlines. Also, they would gain access to the huge
American market, in exchange for which U.S. airlines would only gain
access to their small ones. On the other hand, sticking with prewar bilateralism would not open up the market in a way that the U.S. wanted. The
trick for Pogue was to open up the world market for American airlines as
soon as hostilities ceased in such a way that they could maximize their
then-existing competitive advantages and exploit it, without endangering
the health and welfare of U.S. airlines in the longer run. In the end Pogue
opted for a modified form of bilateralism to achieve this, but it was not
what Roosevelt ideally wanted, as we shall see, and not what Pogue appears
to have implied in June 1942.

While Pogue edged his way toward clearer policy, Berle tussled with
administrative shortcomings and frustration in the State Department.
He received the departmental brief on aviation in February 1941, but by
September 1942 he had failed to persuade the department to accept what he
thought were appropriate structures for developing policy. He felt so frustrated and dismayed with lack of progress that he suggested to Secretary
Hull that the aviation brief be reassigned. That was not done, and over the
next six months Berle managed to move things along, largely because of the
press of developments in Britain.

The British seem to have formulated some air proposals relating to distribution of civil air transport after the war. Thanks to the dunderheadedness of
this Department in not arranging a setup that had an effective air man in it,
we are pretty helpless.[33]

Berle alerted Hull to what the British were doing, and finally he achieved movement. Hull wrote to the U.S. ambassador in London, John Winant, asking for more information on British aviation planning, and things began to develop: civil aviation's profile was finally being resurrected in Washington.[34]

Matters gathered pace in Washington, and momentum was sustained by the visit of British foreign secretary Anthony Eden in March. His agenda was postwar planning, and it included civil aviation. In talks with Roosevelt it was acknowledged that policy development still had some way to go but that Anglo-American consultations might take place later that summer. In the meantime neither side should commit itself publicly to an international aviation policy. That provided sufficient urgency to formalize U.S. planning.[35] Berle had already drawn together, with Hull's approval, an informal committee to explore aviation policy, and on March 29, 1943, President Roosevelt approved those moves, and the committee was officially recognized as the Interdepartmental Committee on International Aviation. Berle was chairman, and its key members were Robert Lovett, Ralph A. Bard (soon replaced by Artemus Gates, Assistant Secretary of the Navy), Wayne Taylor, undersecretary of Commerce, and Pogue. The committee's working subcommittee was chaired by Pogue, and he was its dominant influence.[36] In the absence of a specialist appointment in civil aviation of a kind Berle had urged the State Department to go in for in 1942, ideas about civil aviation passed largely by default to the chairman of the CAB. It was widely recognized that Pogue was at the center of formulating policy. He was the dominant figure in the CAB not just because he was very able but also because, for a variety of circumstances, none of the other members were either available or capable of rendering him much help. In considering a possible new appointment to the CAB in September 1942, Rowe explained to the president that "the young and able Chairman, Welch Pogue, has a tough job and needs A-1 help very badly."[37] In fact it did not materialize. Pogue soldiered on more or less alone, determining policy proposals emanating from the CAB as well as exerting a major influence in the working subcommittee that he chaired. Regarding the work of that subcommittee in January 1943, Secretary of State Hull described Pogue as "taking the laboring oar," and two months later Berle told the president that Pogue was doing all the "heavy drafting."[38]

Pogue had already instigated policy developments and was able to forward to Wayne Taylor on January 7 preliminary proposals drawn up by the CAB. They called for the expansion of U.S. civil aviation "as rapidly as possible and over all routes economically viable." For Pogue this was to become an obsession. He feared that if the United States did not seize the moment, it would gradually be excluded by other countries from operating worldwide, and then the competitive advantage of U.S. airlines would be eroded by cheaper foreign labor costs and government subsidies. To secure its rightful place Pogue wanted the government to move the airlines, namely, Pan American, out of the diplomacy game and take charge of negotiating air rights. Limited competition ought to be nurtured to ensure the continuing dynamism in the U.S. airlines industry, but never to the point of it becoming damaging: it had to be carefully regulated. A further measure to ensure against possible dangers to U.S. airlines was that any disposal of surplus postwar lend-lease aircraft should be carefully controlled. Pogue did not want foreign airlines to benefit from U.S. generosity with aircraft that could be used in the commercial marketplace before he had secured an international regime that would ensure U.S. civil aviation could flourish.[39]

As the bureaucratic machinery in Washington finally cranked up, further pressures arose in the public domain, which raised searching questions about the future of international and U.S. civil aviation in particular. These sparked off heated public debate and congressional concerns. There were developments on both sides of the Atlantic. In London controversy and disagreements were becoming commonplace about future aviation developments. Concern about Britain's lack of suitable aircraft for postwar use had prompted the appointment of the Brabazon Committee in December 1942. There were also heated discussions in the House of Lords about Britain's equipment deficit and the need to strengthen competitiveness and secure Britain's "due share" in the postwar world.[40] These developments stirred thoughts in Washington as well, and it was here that the most controversial issues emerged, and they did so from entirely opposite ends of the spectrum of possible opinion.

Vice President Henry Wallace was a well-known idealist progressive whose internationalist ideas went far beyond the conventional wisdom of the State Department internationalists, even those considered to have troublingly radical views, such as Sumner Welles, who was the undersecretary of state and a close friend of the president. Wallace and Hull had expressed rather different ideas about the possibilities for the postwar regime in 1942, but in 1943 Wallace tried to promote an even more radical agenda. He urged the president to promote an active world organization that would do much in the postwar world including controlling cartels and running international airports.[41] Later, in March, he wrote:

> The establishment of a network of globe-girdling airways ought to be the first order of business. The airways I visualize would have as their primary justification the safeguarding of world peace. They would be operated by the air arm of the United Nations peace force.[42]

Wallace's idea of globe-girdling airways resonated with both internationalists and America's extreme nationalists because it connected with the possible future use of the vast number of air bases that the United States had constructed for war purposes around the world. By 1943 these amounted to 207 with military and potential commercial use and a further 66 solely for military use. There was much concern that the United States should receive some reward for this vast expenditure and move to make agreements with the host countries while its negotiating hand was strong about postwar security and commercial aviation rights. The internationalists wanted the bases handed over for UN use, the extreme nationalists to employ them in perpetuity for America's own military security and commercial air advantage. In the middle stood more moderate opinion that saw the bases as a possible bargaining counter to extract "equitable" commercial rights for the United States and military use rights for the UN, or failing that for sufficient U.S. military use to provide adequate security.[43]

Wallace's idea of taking civil aviation out of the hands of private companies and internationalizing it was just about as radical as one could get, and he promoted these ideas widely in newspaper and magazine articles.[44] They were anathema to Trippe and his extreme nationalist allies such as Henry Luce, who popularized "the American Century" in 1941 as a way of encapsulating the contemporary and hegemonic destiny of the United States. Luce was a powerful and influential man through his ownership of *Time, Life,* and *Fortune* magazines. In the elections of 1942 his wife Clare Booth Luce was elected to Congress for Fairfield County Connecticut. Groomed by Trippe's lieutenant Sam Pryor, she delivered her maiden speech on February 9, 1943. Entitled "America's Destiny in the Air," her target was Wallace and internationalization and her promotion the American Century in the air.

> But much of what Mr. Wallace calls his global thinking is, no matter how you slice it, globaloney. Mr. Wallace's warp of sense and his woof of nonsense is very tricky cloth of which to cut the pattern of a post-war world.[45]

She spoke of the need for U.S. airlines to fly everywhere in the postwar world and as American airlines, not as part of some crackpot scheme of internationalization. With a single word "globaloney," she gained immediate celebrity status and sparked an international controversy about U.S. intentions for postwar aviation. Internationalization of a kind proposed by Wallace was always highly unlikely of acceptance in Washington, and it was soon seen as such in London as well, but the damage done by Clare Luce was to undermine the credibility of internationalization in general, not just in its most extreme form. "Globaloney" was a pretty undiscriminating term of abuse. Any idea of subjecting U.S. airlines to regulation by an international authority over anything other than technical matters was even more unlikely in the aftermath of Luce's speech and the nationalist ambitions it encouraged. There was little strength of opinion in Congress for "giving away" American commercial advantage in civil aviation to an authority run by foreigners, and Trippe and his allies in the Congress would hammer out these arguments again and again over the next three years with telling results. Knowledge of such congressional views had impact on policy-makers in the administration and on their estimates of the kind of policy it might be possible to achieve. But before returning to examine further policy developments, another development initiated by Trippe demands attention.

In May 1943 Trippe courted public support by laying out plans for cheap postwar air travel for the "average man" and welcomed competition, at least of a kind. He proposed that the United States should offer to supply air transports after the war to BOAC until Britain could produce her own airplanes. Trippe had not disclosed his hand entirely here, but it was a clever move and one that won him considerable support. To fully appreciate his position, there are three other aspects that need to be considered. First, it was no accident that he had mentioned BOAC. Like Pogue, Berle, and others, he knew that coming to terms with Britain was a sine qua non of any successful postwar aviation regime. But his intention was not so much to compete as to collude with BOAC in carving up the world between the two airlines.[46] From one perspective this might be seen as a form of realpolitik internationalization, but certainly so far as the bona fide thing was concerned that remained totally anathema to Trippe. On July 1 he lunched with the president's chief of staff, Admiral Leahy, and "spent the hour expressing an opinion that any internationalization of air routes and air facilities would practically destroy American commercial aviation because of our higher production and operation costs."[47] However, notwithstanding all his powers of persuasion and skill in mobilizing lobby power, the situation gradually slipped away from Trippe and his company. But, while he ultimately failed in his ambitions to perpetuate Pan American's monopoly on overseas routes and to cartelize the international regime in the hands of Pan American and BOAC, his efforts still affected policy outcomes in that they made a case for and strengthened the more nationalistic positions advocated by influential members of Congress and some important members of the administration. Furthermore, his vigorous lobbying kept the idea of monopoly alive as a possibility that demanded time and attention and complicated policy-making throughout 1943 and 1944.

A direct consequence of the flurry of publicity given to aviation by Luce's globaloney speech was a meeting between Berle and Roosevelt on February 18, 1943. The president had been thinking about postwar civil aviation but claimed that "there was no point in going too far at this time, even if Mrs. Luce did make speeches." However, he thought that if the British wanted to run a line from Canada to Brazil, they ought to have rights of innocent passage and to discharge passengers in the United States. The president also mentioned the possibility of allowing foreign crews to be based in the United States and vice versa. All this was rather typically vague—"off the bat," as Berle put it, and he, the president, "obviously had not had time to go into all of the implications."[48] Even so, Berle surmised that the president envisaged nations signing an agreement that exchanged rights for innocent passage and technical stop—later known as Freedoms 1 and 2, and rights to take passengers from its country of origin and disembark in a foreign country and then pick up passengers for the return journey—Freedoms 3 and 4. (The language of the Freedoms was often used interchangeably with Rights, and they both entered the vocabulary of negotiations gradually, but for the sake of brevity and clarity, such language will be used in this narrative from now on.) This would also involve nations designating airports for international traffic and an international authority to oversee safety and technical matters, though Berle commented that the president had made no mention of an international committee or authority. Berle thought that policy was still fluid as he remarked:

> I do not consider that we have an instruction along this line and any suggestion should be looked at with care. I believe that we are certainly coming to something like this before too long.[49]

A few days later some clarification was forthcoming with a preliminary report from Pogue's subcommittee. In a covering note, Pogue addressed two of the immediate driving factors behind developments. These were obtaining agreements from foreign countries for military and possibly commercial air rights in bases built by the United States for war purposes overseas and the postwar fate of transport aircraft supplied to foreign countries through lend-lease. Over the following months there was much domestic controversy in the United States over these matters. Nationalists in particular wanted to use them as bargaining counters to extract favorable commercial and military air rights, though Berle had indicated in hearings before Congress on lend-lease that any rights would have to be subject to negotiation with the host country and agreed taking into account the broader picture, which required the "fair exchange of legitimate interests" on an "equitable basis." This conciliatory line was appreciated in Britain and Canada,[50] and these more moderate ideas were given much consideration by the interdepartmental committee. While the bases and fate of lend-lease transport aircraft continued to have sporadic impact, they only marginally affected the actual substance of postwar U.S. international civil aviation policy.

Pogue's opening remarks on the preliminary report dealt specifically with the bases issue in the context of the imperative of reaching agreement with Britain. He reported two assumptions made by the subcommittee: first that negotiations were especially urgent with those countries in which the U.S. had constructed air bases, and the British Commonwealth was at the head of that list; and second that the committee understood that early negotiations with Britain were expected. Following on from this Pogue emphasized that the British saw "post-war commercial rights as the essence of the problem." He hastened to add that the subcommittee did as well and that a crucial distinction should be made between Freedoms 1 and 2, on the one hand, and 3 and 4 on the other. Pogue argued it would not be in America's interest to grant 1 and 2 unless and until 3 and 4 covering commercial opportunities had been agreed upon for all the units of the British Commonwealth. As to the substance of an agreement with the British Commonwealth, there should be a reciprocal exchange throughout each others territories of Rights 1–4, with commercial operations to be "divided approximately equally" between the United States and Britain providing that there was a minimum for each side of two schedules a week. This was an important recommendation.[51]

If such provisions were to be applied generally in a multilateral agreement, then the United States would be accepting at least an initial division of traffic and automatic and reciprocal exchange of commercial rights for two schedules a week with further frequency subject to negotiation with any country that signed up to the agreement. Whether Pogue was fully committed to this is difficult to say, and there was some ambiguity and a degree of uncertainty in the substance of the report that makes analysis of his position difficult. In the lengthy discussion section of the report, two extreme possibilities were proposed: one consisting of traditional bilateral negotiations on the basis of reciprocity; the other adoption of a free competitive system in which "United States carriers would be legally permitted to engage in international air commerce in any part of the world without restriction by international agreements controlling the international air commerce of particular routes and world regions."[52] The problem with this, observed the subcommittee, was that success for U.S. airlines would depend on their competitiveness and that could very well diminish in the face of cheaper foreign labor and operating costs. Thus, while the world remained insecure and the relationship between military and civilian aviation a vital national security interest, America could not gamble. This approach should not be adopted. Instead some middle way should be sought, but exactly what was not entirely clear.

At various points, for example in dealing with Britain, bilateral talks for an exchange of tightly regulated reciprocal rights were proposed. In other places there were recommendations that the kind of controls that had originally been incorporated in the Anglo-American 1937 understandings regarding the simultaneous start of transatlantic services and rigid controls over frequency and capacity should be avoided. In other words creating tightly regulated and strictly divided markets should be avoided. There seemed to be a general conviction that bilateral negotiations were preferable, certainly in the immediate future, and yet it was also "desirable to begin multi-lateral discussion of general questions of freedom of transit, landing rights for technical purposes, and commercial rights."[53] However, even with transit and technical stop, the subcommittee was not happy to see a general multilateral agreement on this until satisfactory commercial rights had been achieved with the British Commonwealth. Notwithstanding this caveat, there was a general appreciation that there would have to be an international agreement of some sort to cover technical and safety matters of the kind covered by the Paris and Havana Conventions. The report was a start, but different parts of it were difficult to reconcile one with another, and at the end of the day, it left many issues muddled and unresolved.

As for Pogue, he may have been happy with the content of the recommendation for proceeding with the British Commonwealth because he knew they controlled so many important transit and commercial outlets. Agreement had to be reached with Britain if ambitions for postwar American civil aviation were to be realized. In this case, reciprocity and division of traffic made sense to him. It was a repeat of the need to reach agreement with Canada in 1939–40. It is doubtful, however, that he ever wanted this to be applied universally. Certainly he was soon strongly to question the wisdom of automatically exchanging rights for commercial entry, imposing rigid divisions of traffic, and achieving reciprocity in all markets.

On March 12, Berle made the best he could of the report for the president, summarizing it briefly as recommending an international agreement for rights of transit and technical stop with reasonable conditions applied and the right to block off security areas; two commercial landings a week for all signatories with more possible by agreement; a limited right to maintain service crews abroad; and no entry into cabotage except by special agreement. Matters were to be progressed by early talks with the British, followed by broader discussions leading to a UN conference.[54]

Consideration of policy continued throughout March and April 1943, and once again the issue of whether Pan American should continue to have a peacetime monopoly over U.S. routes arose. At a meeting of the interdepartmental committee on March 11, Robert Lovett presented a memorandum "to the effect that the interests of the United States might be best secured by consolidating the foreign air commerce of the United States in a single corporation."[55] It would be easy to see the hand of Trippe in this. He was certainly busy disseminating his views among the military. At Pan

American's corporate hospitality centre on F Street in Washington, DC, Pogue recalled a dinner there with General George C. Marshall speaking about postwar aviation, and he later "realized that Marshall's pronouncements were verbatim statements of what he had heard from Juan Trippe."[56] At the same time the military were much indebted to what Pan American was doing to help the war effort, and from the military point of view the link between security and civil aviation was the overriding one, and a single, large, powerful U.S. airline that could take on the rest of the world naturally had appeal. Whatever the mixture of motives behind this might have been the fact was that Pogue's working subcommittee now undertook to examine the issue in detail.

Berle's own views and understanding continued to develop, and he sought to clarify America's basic interests in aviation. To that end his executive assistant, Robert G. Hooker, prepared a lot of material that Berle later incorporated into a paper simply entitled "Aviation Policy." Interestingly, given the lack of clarity in the subcommittee's preliminary report, Berle said to Hooker that the paper might be handed to "Mr. Pogue as a suggestion."[57] The paper laid out priorities under which details could more easily fall into place. It discloses just how pragmatic Berle was prepared to be to attain those priorities. The starting point for him as with all other officials was "the primary interest of the United States must always be its military security." And that, as with most others, tempered his idealism. Securing the maximum access for U.S. civil aviation across the world and securing continuing access to bases necessary for U.S. defense were the priorities, and whatever "development of air navigation rights...achieves, this is in the best interest of the United States."[58] Questions of competition or monopoly or some middle way would all have to be decided on the basis of which was most likely to deliver what the United States needed.

By the end of April 1943 the interdepartmental committee had also moved forward and agreed on "the essentials" for its first report. For the time being at least, it looked as if much of the ambiguity and uncertainty that had plagued the provisional report had been dispelled. However, neither the question of monopoly nor whether it would be better to negotiate bilaterally or multilaterally for commercial rights had been laid to rest. In conversations with Canadian officials in February and March 1943, Berle seemed resolved that "internationalization" was impossible and that neither air sovereignty nor freedom of the air were desirable, but he remained vague as to where the balance between them should be struck and on the important issue of negotiating procedures he equivocated: "Bi-lateral, or better still multi-lateral arrangements between governments" should be sought.[59] This question of bilateral or multilateral exchange of commercial rights and the accompanying issue of reciprocity were to cause difficulties within the American policy-making process.

Berle reported to Secretary Hull on April 30 on the committee's proposals and set them in context. He explained that Luce and her ilk had created a serious problem for commercial international aviation with "the idea that Americans could go anywhere and sell anything; but that other countries must be excluded not only from the American market but from any market in which the United States can gain dominance."[60] This had angered and worried other countries and set in motion ideas about excluding U.S. airlines from overseas routes as a means of protection. Those ideas had not as yet resulted in clear or concerted action, but this danger had to be nipped in the bud. The committee wanted to talk as soon as possible "looking towards a generalized settlement of the problems of air navigation rights on an equitable basis."[61] Fearing that if the United States were to "start a process of exclusion, the British can exclude quite as well as we can," the committee with substantial unanimity concluded it would be best to aim for a general international agreement using America's chief bargaining chip to achieve that, namely, access to her market. In the interwar period the United States had generated the overwhelming proportion of and its airlines had carried over 80 percent of international passengers. There should be rights of innocent passage and technical stop for all signatories, subject to commonsense restrictions. Crucially the committee proposed:

> To avoid smothering the traffic with an infinity of landings, the experts suggest that there be an offer of a general agreement; that each signatory to the agreement shall have as of right a limited number of landings in the territory of each signatory to the agreement: it is tentatively suggested that there be two landings a week, as of right—and that further landings shall be matter of negotiation.[62]

To avoid destructive competition there should be a regular users' conference to set rates as in the maritime industry. The subcommittee had specifically looked at the issue of Pan American's monopoly and with one dissenting voice had agreed on a multiairline policy in which each airline would be assigned separate operational zones, though it was recognized that powerful political forces existed that could still cause problems here. The U.S. government should take charge of negotiating the new regime and would thus take responsibility for representing and protecting the interests of U.S. airlines abroad. Berle was very much in favor of the multiairline policy and the key negotiating role for the U.S. government. If these proposals were formally accepted, then he envisaged proceeding with talks with Britain and other key powers before moving to a general conference. But, as he put it: "The heart of a general navigation agreement would have to rest on agreement between the United States and the British Empire and Commonwealth of Nations...."[63]

Four weeks later in a meeting with Hull, from what Pogue said it was clear that there were continuing problems and that there had been further developments. It seemed there were still more pages to turn on the saga of Pan American's monopoly, but the most important matter was an emerging clearer distinction about how rights to transit and technical stop and commercial rights were to be dealt with. Pogue reported that it was the view of the committee that "it was to the advantage of the United States to have wide rights of 'innocent passage' through the air over other countries with the right to refuel and overhaul, and take refuge in storm. This did not include the right of commercial outlet."[64] Commercial outlet he explained should be on a bilateral basis "determined by circumstances in each case."[65] With Britain and its Dominions this would probably require reciprocity, with others, however, maybe not.

This view on bilateralism seemed to be somewhat at odds with the views Pogue had expressed only a year earlier when he wrote: "If development in the field must be carried forward within the confines of such diplomatic maneuvering as the regulations of bi-lateral agreements with other countries for specific services, our advantages...will largely disappear...."[66] So what was Pogue's thinking? He did not want to return to the prewar regime. The clearest difference between his current thinking and what went on then was the call for "freedom of the skies," namely, for transit and technical stop. That would be a major transformation of the old regime, and it should be done multilaterally by all signatories to an international agreement. On this Roosevelt was in full accord. The other difference was that bilateralism would not be as of old because the United States would be in such a powerful and dominant position in civil aviation. It would have a monopoly of effective modern equipment; it would have huge efficient and experienced airlines; it would have a string of bases around the world constructed at its expense during the war and with some moral claim upon them for postwar use; it would have the largest potential market to which others would want access; and it would have a wealth of prestige from the war that it could deploy to achieve its objectives. These assets would enable the United States to avoid the chaos of interwar bilateralism. The United States would be able to impose a more structured and uniform system based on certain principles, but with the flexibility to safeguard its interests when necessary. The rest of the world would have to buy into this or else they would be left on the periphery of civil aviation. These ideas were not entirely consistent with the position of Franklin Roosevelt, but Pogue had influential allies and the majority of the airlines on his side. What the outcome of this might be was difficult to predict.

CHAPTER 8

OF SUBORDINATES AND THE PRESIDENT

> One hazard that must always be borne in mind in attempting to project the line that the United States will follow with regard to post-war international aviation is that the views held by subordinates in the United States government, however distinguished, may not turn out to be United States policy.[1]

THE THREADS OF U.S. AVIATION POLICY ENTANGLED and became ever more difficult to straighten out as 1943 went by. Already by April significant differences had emerged among the main policy-makers in Washington, then two dynamics came more forcefully into play to make things even more difficult. These were inputs from the domestic airlines and international challenges. They both overlapped in the concerns they raised, but the former focused more on Pan American's monopoly and the optimum environment for U.S. postwar airline operations, including the possible use of American-built bases overseas, and the latter on transit, commercial rights, and the problem posed by Britain if it obstructed entry of U.S. airlines on international routes. For many it would be a bitter pill to swallow indeed if America had virtually nowhere to land abroad after the war given both the foreign air bases that it had built and the potential for civil aviation that it possessed. In particular these fears were informed by suspicions of the British. Notwithstanding the Halifax Agreement, the Americans became convinced that the British were making moves to sew up much of the world and exclude U.S. airlines. Unfortunately such feelings were reciprocated in London, making for a difficult and confrontational situation, which determined much of what unfolded at the 1944 Chicago International Civil Aviation Conference. For U.S. policy-makers the danger of exclusion challenged American national interests and encouraged more unilateralist and nationalist thoughts about securing commercial and transit rights for U.S. airlines by whatever means available. It also propelled matters forward toward international negotiations, but then procedural matters arose that had direct implications for what the U.S. might be able to secure for itself. Should it pursue air rights bilaterally, multilaterally, or by both means? As the allies liberated areas in North Africa and progress was made in Europe, both the British and the Americans were aware of the pressing need to restart civilian services, and that foregrounded the importance of bilateral talks in the absence of an international agreement. This had important consequences for Roosevelt's commitment to liberal multilateralism. And just to make matters even more complicated in Washington, aviation policy continued to be such a difficult issue in Congress that it was impossible to declare a full and clear position, and on both counts of policy and procedure, differences emerged between the president and his subordinates.

THE DOMESTIC AIRLINES AND FURTHER POLICY
DEVELOPMENTS

Pan American's monopoly, and its corollary what to do after the war, with U.S. domestic airlines operating abroad under the auspices of the military Air Transport Command, troubled Pogue and General Arnold, and in the late spring and early summer of 1943 they took action to try to bring matters to a head. There were sound reasons for doing so. Pan American's enormously influential lobbying in Congress and its skill in public self-promotion needed counterbalancing, and Pogue saw the potential of the domestic airlines to do that. They too now had vested interests, namely, they ran overseas routes in the wartime and were eager to operate them on a civilian basis after the war. Aeronautical manufacturers also saw benefits for themselves if Pan American's monopoly could be broken, as they would then no longer be solely dependent on one airline for orders for large transoceanic planes. In addition, Pogue was keen to energize policy-making and action on the international front. Making postwar civil aviation into a media issue was one way of forcing things along.

On May 4, 1943, the CAB, after consultations with the interdepartmental committee, published a list of questions about postwar policy and invited the airlines and aeronautical manufacturers to reply by June 1. The responses were prompt. The manufacturers and the overwhelming majority of "domestic" airlines returned collective responses followed in the case of the airlines with supplementary remarks on July 15.[2] Only United Airlines, Amex, and Pan American refused to join the airline collective, though some months later Amex changed its mind. Trippe responded to the CAB separately on behalf of Pan American on May 31. His position was predictable.

He wanted nothing to do with granting general rights and automatic reciprocity, and he feared that the benefits of a general exchange of transit and technical stop were more apparent than real.[3]

> ...we should keep ourselves free of any general commitments in favor of reciprocity, that we should seek landing rights without offering them, that we should handle requests for landing rights from countries that have granted them to us, on their merits, that in practice...we should successfully, and without jeopardizing our own position abroad, find plausible reasons to deny most requests and keep our concessions to a minimum.[4]

A better statement of the American imperial aviation position one would be hard-pressed to find and one that clearly demonstrated that there was reciprocity and then there was *reciprocity*. No senior official in government, not even Lovett or Pogue, wanted to go to this extreme. But, more moderate aspects of this position did appeal to them, and most helpfully for Pogue they were generally reflected in the collective responses from the domestic airlines and the manufacturers.

Both groups emphasized the importance of the greatest possible expansion of U.S. aviation by free enterprise without government ownership or any form of internationalization of operations. In its supplementary response the airlines spoke even more forcefully, calling for "free and open competition—world wide" subject to appropriate government regulation. There was slight deference to foreign sensibilities in that emphasis was given to flying the most direct routes to and from the United States. In other words U.S. airlines would not be like tramp steamers scooping up "local" trade wherever it might be. The groups also both looked to equal access and nondiscrimination as principles for practice, but cautioned against the unrestricted sale of aircraft abroad after the war. They opposed reciprocal concessions on cabotage and advised that international gateways should be designated largely on or near the U.S. border so as not to damage domestic services. The airlines came out firmly in favor of the widest possible agreements for transit and stop—a "keystone" of the international system. Such rights would be subject simply to common-sense restrictions and possible security exclusion zones. There should be no barriers between the domestic and international spheres, thus allowing the domestic airlines to move out internationally. The responses did not specifically call for the demise of Pan American's monopoly, but for policy consistent with the competitive prescriptions of the 1938 Aeronautics Act. It amounted to the same thing. Looking to the opening of new routes, they favored the continuation of airlines negotiating for air rights, but with government supervision, and recommended new production of civil airliners be set in train as soon as national security considerations permitted.[5] The airlines were already thinking of the details of postwar operations and went on to identify desirable international routes in their supplementary response. That same month "Hap" Arnold called a meeting in Washington of airline representatives and told them that Air Transport Command would withdraw as soon as possible from international operations and that they should consider where they would like to fly after the war.[6] The airlines were soon busy filing for overseas routes, and Pogue moved in the summer of 1943 to melt the CAB freeze on issuing new certificates of necessity and convenience. This sounded a warning note to other countries and especially Britain that the Americans intended to move out onto international routes as soon as conditions allowed. It all added to the paranoia about U.S. aviation imperialism, but it helped to get things moving and so far as Pogue was concerned well positioned U.S. airlines for exploiting the opportunities of the international marketplace.

On the key issues of economic regulation and the acquisition of commercial international aviation rights, the airlines favored case-by-case assessments of routes, a reciprocal exchange of rights for those that were viable, though without restrictions on frequency and capacity, and as much freedom for the airlines as possible within a safeguarding regulatory framework.

> It is clear that some uniform "rules of the road" for the airways must from time to time be established through international agreement. To the fullest extent possible, however, air carriers should be permitted to deal with the problems discussed under this question through private understandings reached among themselves subject to appropriate Government supervision. Many of the problems suggested by this question will not be of immediate concern after the war and solutions should be permitted to develop gradually in the light of existing circumstances.[7]

The *New York Times* summarized the outcome of all this as U.S. airlines favor "free competition and world-wide freedom of transit."[8] That did not quite capture the complexity of the situation, but one clear message was that Pan American's monopoly was now endangered. However, it still remained a difficult issue. Even with pressure mounting for a more competitive international policy, Berle could not see how Pan American could be legally ousted from its de facto position of dominance. Furthermore, there was a clear focus for Pan American influence in the Senate Commerce Committee chaired by Josiah Bailey and the Commerce Subcommittee on Aviation chaired by Bennett Champ Clark: in both Trippe had allies. The subcommittee work on aviation dragged on interminably examining among other things the issue of monopoly. That inclined senior officials, including Berle, to leave monopoly to the legislators to sort out, but it would continue to trouble policy-making for some months to come.[9]

Pogue's engagement of the domestic airlines in policy formulation had long-run consequences that impacted on matters, which actually turned out to be more important than the monopoly issue. First, there was the matter of competition and adequate operating freedom for the airlines. This was not just a matter of breaking Pan American's monopoly, nor in any sense a play for a free market. However, the airlines did not want the potential for their operations strangled by predetermined restrictions on frequencies and capacity unrelated to market demand, or potential market development. This principle was the key to rapid expansion of U.S. airlines. The second and third factors were closely related to this. The airlines favored the widest possible grant of rights to transit and technical stop to open up opportunities, but they did not then wish them to be closed down by commercial restrictions imposed by any kind of international governing body acting prematurely before the nature and size of the market emerged. At least that was the publicly spoken justification for arguing for an interim international agency to coordinate safety and technical matters with only research, advisory, and consultative powers: the unspoken reason was that U.S. airlines should not be politically prevented from seizing opportunities offered by their predominant position. Fourth, the widespread consensus on the need for some kind of pricing control was now focused by the airlines very clearly on the idea of an operators' conference setting rates subject to government approval. And finally, the airlines did not favor a multilateral agreement on commercial rights. In a paper trying to bring together what he believed would be proposals that would "command general assent," Berle noted that "commercial interests [i.e., the airlines] seem to fear any unlimited generalized system" and instead preferred reciprocity worked out as appropriate in each individual case.[10] In short these views, expressed by the airlines, reinforced Pogue's wish to open up the international market through widespread rights of transit and stop, but then commercially to exploit it through a robust form of bilateral negotiations that would not always provide reciprocal or equal opportunities for partners. This bilateralism was also, of course, favored by the extreme nationalists, by Pan American and its powerful supporters in the Congress, and by a more moderate faction including Lovett and the War Department. It was not Berle's first choice, but he was being swayed by events and powers beyond his control. Most significantly, it ran directly contrary to what the president desired. Eleanor Roosevelt was overheard saying in early 1943 that her husband thought that the whole "matter seemed 'quite simple' in that there should be free use of airports throughout the world for all nations to operate air services" except for cabotage. General Arnold also testified that on civil aviation: "President Roosevelt and I had talked it over many times. The President was firm on the point that foreign lines should be able to cross the United States, picking up passengers in New

York and San Francisco bound for foreign countries, but not picking up passengers in New York for San Francisco, or local points. These were the same principles that applied to steamship lines."[11]

For the rest of June, through July and for the most of August, Pogue's subcommittee and the full interdepartmental committee struggled to work out policy recommendations that would in Berle's phrase command general assent. As they did so the need for robust action became more imperative as a result of growing awareness of dangers posed by Britain. Matters had waxed confrontational originally with British fears of American aviation imperialism generated by Pan American's behavior in Africa and its taking over of the Takoradi route. Those fears had waned in 1942 because of the militarization of the route and the consummation of the Halifax Agreement in the summer of that year, but they never went away completely.[12] In 1943 a combination of aggressive American capitalism, talk of "the American Century" and aviation ambitions, and Britain's enfeebled position in transport equipment prompted much concern in London and raised the voice of protectionism. Berle was alert to this and that the British might take action detrimental to the interests of U.S. airlines. Troubled deeply he wrote to Secretary of State Hull: "If the situation deteriorates, both he [FDR] and the Department will probably be subject to a great deal of criticism later on."[13] Berle explained that the problem arose largely from a nationalist minority in London who wanted a closed preferential system that would exclude U.S. airlines, and he mentioned recent British agreements with Ethiopia and the Soviet Union, their ambitions for the West Indies, opposition to U.S. links with Scandinavia, and their drive for aviation talks with the Dominions. While the Halifax Agreement was still in effect, he felt that negotiations on aviation should be pursued swiftly with the main players and looking eventually to a UN conference before the British established entrenched positions and an exclusionary regime.[14]

The ideas expressed by the domestic airlines and the urgency for negotiations were reflected in the revised proposals of the interdepartmental committee adopted on August 26, 1943. During the redrafting, Pogue's subcommittee again tussled with difficult issues. Thomas Burke from the State Department had repeatedly been the most outspoken on the subcommittee and was highly skeptical about the emphasis laid on competition and felt that some form of government ownership should not be entirely ruled out as it might be required for political or security reasons.[15] His views were embodied in a minority report, but everyone knew that they reflected ideas and concerns that were still widely held. Furthermore, in the final phase of work, the secretary of the subcommittee, P. T. David, commented to Berle: "From the standpoint of any general statement of commercial policy, the recommendations may seem restrictive and illiberal...."[16] They had certainly taken a turn in that direction over the preceding two months. After due consideration the full interdepartmental committee reaffirmed the importance of seeking rights to bases built abroad and to extensive rights of transit and stop, though subject to reaching satisfactory commercial rights first. Air rights should be bilaterally negotiated, at the same time as moving toward a UN conference. Exactly what the outcome of a conference should be was left vague, and it was never explained how bilateral negotiations might be reconciled with the multilateralism of a UN conference. What was clear was that the conference was to be mainly "educational and preparatory" and for establishing an interim commission to replace the International Commission on Aerial Navigation (Paris), but any regulatory powers vested in a new permanent authority should only be considered after further study. Pogue and Berle were determined that they should not play into British and other foreign hands by creating an international authority with power to assign routes and passenger quotas and control capacity and frequency. The committee noted that "regulated competition has been triumphantly successful" in the U.S. domestic sphere of aviation and the general idea was to create a similar system for the international. To do that action was needed before others established entrenched and exclusionary positions: "We have the transport airplanes, the existing organizations, and accumulated experience, while others have control of many strategic routes and certain centers of commerce. We are beginning to lose our lead in transport planes, organization and experience, without securing any countervailing increase in the availability of air rights." The Halifax Agreement provided some safeguards for American interests, but if a general agreement on civil aviation proved elusive, then the Americans feared that "this self-limiting commitment would probably come to an end, and the British would doubtless be able ... to negotiate agreements shutting us out of most of the countries from west Africa to Singapore."[17]

At the same time as the committee was coming to these conclusions, President Roosevelt met Prime Minister Winston Churchill at Quebec. Secretary of State Hull joined them there on August 20, 1943, and he had been briefed on civil aviation matters by Berle. The assistant secretary expressed concern to his boss about America's lack of preparedness and his deep suspicion of the British, but he advocated negotiations with them because nationalistic unilateralism—"a policy of 'grab'"—would serve British interests better than America's. At least that was his view at the time: it changed later. He advised Hull that prospects for talks should be held open, even though the United States was not yet ready to embark upon them. The excuse of having to consult Congress, Berle suggested, could always be invoked with the British to play for time.[18] Roosevelt and Churchill did indeed speak about postwar aviation at Quebec, though only in very general terms of freedom of the skies. The only specific matter to arise was Churchill's desire to have the president approve of a commonwealth get-together for preliminary discussions before Anglo-American talks took place. This had caused considerable difficulty between the British and the Canadians because the latter were wary of upsetting their powerful neighbor to the south by any appearance of ganging up with other commonwealth countries against it. The net effect of this Canadian caution had been delay, but when the matter was raised by Churchill, the president raised no objections, and the prime minister later robustly told the Canadians how things were going to proceed, whether they liked it or not. In fact this led to an important meeting of the Dominions and India in London in October 1943.[19] Broad agreement about policy was largely achieved, and this placed more pressure on officials in Washington to finalize some kind of negotiating position.[20]

A few weeks after the president's trip to Quebec, aviation matters were pushed into the public domain in a controversial way in Washington by the return of senators who had traveled abroad during the summer to inspect the results of U.S. war expenditures. One of the burning issues for many members of Congress was the use of U.S.-built air bases after the war. Bearing in mind the restricted access to airports and routes that the U.S. would confront after the war, unless something were done, Senator Brewster observed with characteristic hyperbole: "There isn't a spot outside of this hemisphere we can land after the war."[21] The same day that Brewster's comment was reported in the press, a journalist at a press conference at the White House summed things up in similar vein: "Six months after it's over [i.e., the war], it's over for us commercially too." It was this that prompted the president to expound his views on postwar aviation. He said that at Quebec he and Churchill had discussed postwar aviation in the general terms of the principle of free air and that he wanted the widest possible exchange of transit and stop and commercial outlets that allow airlines to take passengers and cargo from their country of origin to another country and pick up passengers and cargo from there for the return journey. He did not want government to get into the airline business though he thought that there may be very exceptional cases where operations had to be run by government or the UN. Roosevelt also explained that he would like all airports, including those built abroad by the United States, to be open for free commercial operations by all airlines. When asked if that might involve the United States exercising sovereignty over U.S.-built bases abroad, he responded that if the tables were turned, "How would we like that if they said that to us?" He was clear about reserving cabotage, but was not precise on several issues, including what became the thorny issue of the Fifth Freedom, the right to pick up in another country and carry passengers and cargo on to a third-party destination. When challenged by one reporter about the danger to

U.S. airlines of lower operating costs of foreign airlines, he suggested that the best method might be to bring them up to the same standard of living as Americans enjoyed.[22]

This was the first major public statement of U.S. policy. It did not answer everything by any means, but it signaled direction. That, so far as the president was concerned, led toward more freedom of the air, open opportunities for commercial entry, and sensitivity to the needs and feelings of others. His caustic comment about exercising sovereignty over U.S.-built airbases abroad indicated his concern not to alienate friends and allies. He felt that for his vision to work, confidence and cooperation had to be cultivated. His statement had important consequences. It raised the profile of aviation in public and congressional minds, and it accelerated preparations for talks about a new postwar regime, but it also generated widespread criticism over the wisdom of opening up U.S. airspace for transit and stop to all comers. This latter aspect was in due course to have substantive effect on U.S. policy.

On October 18 Lord Beaverbrook, Canadian press baron, close friend of Churchill's and recently appointed Lord Privy Seal with the brief of developing Britain's postwar civil aviation policy, wrote to Harry Hopkins reporting that talks with the Dominions and India had gone well and so how about some Anglo-American talks? This kept the momentum going and was in line with U.S. thinking on procedure, namely, talks with the British first and then on to a UN conference. Hopkins replied on October 27, however, that the United States was not yet quite ready, but everything would be done to move things along.[23] In fact, things were already in train. On October 15, in a joint statement, the CAB and the State Department announced that routes and rights were to be negotiated by the two agencies working in tandem. Pogue later claimed: "Thus the curtain for action by and between governments on the international stage was rung up in anticipation of the ending of the war."[24] At the same time, Berle, exasperated by Hull's failure to make decisions on civil aviation, purportedly because he was too busy with other matters, had again taken matters directly to the president.[25] On October 20 Roosevelt acted. He wrote to Undersecretary of State Edward Stettinius. "I am anxious to have a talk with you and the Secretary about it [i.e., postwar civil aviation] before our policies are too extensively developed." He did not want to slow down policy planning, but he neither wanted to "give other nations an improper notion as to what this government is going to pursue...."[26] This note set a series of developments in motion.

A MEETING—BUT NOT OF MINDS—AT THE WHITE HOUSE

The interdepartmental committee report of August 1943 resolved little. Compromised by the minority report and failing to resolve some key issues, most notably over Pan American's monopoly, it never officially saw the light of day though much of its content was leaked to the press. Pogue's subcommittee labored on gathering the views from interested departments and from the industry, and David produced a series of papers at the beginning of September on the more intractable problems, but the making of policy was beginning to shift into more senior hands.[27] The president had strong views on aviation, and it was clear at least in his own mind what he wanted. He always kept a close eye on developments and often took initiatives that would bear on postwar civil aviation without officials like Pogue being aware. A good example, which will be considered shortly, was the president's plans for the postwar Pacific. Roosevelt wanted an aviation regime as open as possible and was not obsessively worried about security to the point that it compromised his vision and led to policies that would alienate friendly countries through fear of U.S. aviation imperialism. But the president was not the only man with a vision, nor did he have a monopoly of influence on policy-making.

At some point, during the late summer or early autumn of 1943, Pogue began to cultivate a closer relationship with Harry Hopkins. When this precisely happened is unclear, but the fact of it having happened is not.[28] Pogue was disturbed at the slow pace of developments and by important aspects of policy. On some policy issues he remained fully in accord with the president's views. For example, in late September, he sent a paper to Hopkins making recommendations on "two overriding issues." These were about "transit and stop" and monopoly. On both he was in line with the president. Pogue made it clear that he thought that there would be huge opportunities for American airlines at the end of the war, and these were important to seize for commerce, employment, U.S. overseas commitments, and security.[29] To be able to exploit the potential, the airways had to be freed from the "shackles" that currently held them back: rights to transit and stop should be widely granted. Pogue was also in line with Roosevelt in his desire to see a multiairline policy with U.S. airlines assigned to different operational zones. He went so far as to speculate that if traffic warranted it, there could even be competition between U.S. airlines within the same zone and on the same route. But there were other things that troubled Pogue and on which he was not in agreement with the president.

Pogue appears to have been energized by the change of gear initiated by the president in October. At some point in the month he had a secret session with Hopkins, which he followed up with a long-hand note. Matters were taking on a highly personal and conspiratorial air.

Harry: Here is a draft of the memo. No one knows about it or our talk. I'll be with you whenever you want me if you would like to discuss anything further.[30]

What Pogue had enclosed was quite extraordinary. It was a draft presidential memorandum for circulation to Berle, Lovett, Gates, *and Pogue*—the members of the interdepartmental committee—charging them to draw up U.S. positions on important policy questions in accordance with general guidelines. Those guidelines were provided by Pogue in the memorandum. He proposed his now well-established views on transit and stop and on releasing the shackles that held back aviation including exclusive and discriminatory zonings, but he also added that ex-enemy countries should be denied airlines "for a long time." Careful consideration should be given to the postwar use of bases built abroad by the United States and whether they should be opened up to commercial traffic. There should be no monopoly over U.S. overseas routes, and with few possible exceptions, the airlines should be under private management. So far, there was nothing particularly controversial, at least in terms of departing from the president's views, but then came Pogue's views on commercial rights. In his covering note to Hopkins, he prefaced his comments on reciprocity by explaining that he intended to deal with it "in such a manner which will not stir up international egos, should the memorandum ever come to light." What he meant by this was that he had couched the proposal specifically to deflect possible criticisms that the United States aimed to scoop up all international traffic. The supposed safeguards against that were twofold. First the CAB intended to lay down for license only direct routes between the United States and foreign destinations—no "tramp" traffic. Second, and set out here in Pogue's draft proposal, demand would have to justify the inception of a route.

> The privilege of our international operators to discharge and take on traffic abroad, and of foreign operators to do the same here, should be arranged for between or with the approval of the governments concerned from time to time. We should base our discussion in each case upon the desirability of the route from our national point of view and not upon any automatic formula which might result in starting unjustified operations.[31]

The key positions expressed in this memorandum by Pogue, which departed from the president's views, were the concept of a restrictive form of reciprocity that the U.S. could extract from individual countries and the rejection of automatic or multilaterally agreed formulas for exchanging commercial rights in favor of bilateralism. Interestingly and clearly evidenced here, Pogue disliked the language of commercial air rights or freedoms altogether, much preferring the term "privilege". His general disposition regarding international aviation was thus somewhat different from that of the president, who repeatedly emphasized freedom.

Hopkins circulated Pogue's ideas round interested parties, and on November 3 Robert Lovett returned to Hopkins what he referred to as "the rough memorandum," commenting that it seemed adequate. He also enclosed a memorandum from the War Department entitled "Post-war Civil Aviation." It departed even further from the president's views, suggesting that while reciprocity might be appropriate for the big players such as Britain and the Soviet Union, it might be desirable to negotiate with others on a "basis other than reciprocal agreements."[32] The memorandum went on to add specifically that in exchanging commercial rights, "special agreements" might be necessary. Pogue in effect had cast Hopkins in the role of collating views for the president, but hardly in an impartial way. Pogue had set the agenda and indicated the basic contours of substantive policy ahead of the consultation process. These preparations were the preliminaries to a meeting at the White House over which Roosevelt presided on November 10, and it included Stettinius, Berle, Lovett, Pogue, and Hopkins. On the day Hopkins sent the president a summary commenting: "These are the kind of things about civil aviation that I gather you want to emphasize as indicating your policy in regard to the forthcoming negotiations."[33] Hopkins was largely correct, but he had not fully captured the picture of what the president wanted to say: and more to the point neither had Pogue.

Stettinius, Berle, Lovett, Pogue, and Hopkins met with the President at 2 p.m. Roosevelt explained that he had begun talks on aviation with Churchill at Quebec, and he would now indicate the policy he wanted followed. "Reading from a memorandum which he said he had himself prepared, he gave...oral directives."[34] What Roosevelt said largely followed the gist of Hopkins's memorandum, but there were important differences. It is also of note that Stettinius left the room for much of the discussion to meet Cordell Hull returning from the Moscow foreign ministers' conference. Stettinius was, of course, Trippe's brother-in-law. According to Pogue's later recollection, as soon as Stettinius was out of the door, the president adopted a low, confidential tone and declared that there would be no monopoly on U.S. overseas routes. Pan American might have the lion's share, but neither it nor any other company could have it all. The president said "he still felt that the plan he outlined to Mr. Pogue...two years ago, of various companies having "zones," still appealed to him."[35] He favored regulated competition with government ownership only playing a part if a route were of strategic importance but unviable commercially. However, as soon as it became viable, the government should withdraw. Similarly, regarding subsidies, they should only be sustained for as long as a strategically important route was unable to pay its way. There should be national legal ownership and control of internal aviation services, unless a country was too backward to make provision for itself. He made it clear that he did not want American airlines muscling in and taking over the domestic operations of other countries. However, for ex-enemy states, they should not be allowed to "fly anything larger than one of these toy planes that you wind up with an elastic."[36] It might be necessary to create some kind of international company to provide services for them. He wanted a multilateral exchange of rights to transit and stop, remarking that this "would dispose of any need for a United Nations Authority to manage airfields," though some internationally operated facilities might be necessary on routes that did not pay their way. Generally, apart from safety, weather reporting and technical matters, the president seemed to see little role for any international organization. The president thought that there should first be quiet talks with the British in preparation for a UN conference. None of this would cause much concern to the assembled officials, but the president's views on the granting of commercial rights did, at least for Pogue.

Hopkins's memorandum recommended rather conservatively that rights to transit and stop should be "secured on a reciprocal basis." In itself that might suggest a conservative attitude toward commercial rights as well, but in fact Hopkins remained vague, simply referring to existing statutory pro-visions and saying that they should continue to govern international policy. The president was neither conservative nor vague. He declared in favor of "a very free interchange. That is, he wanted arrangements by which planes of one country could enter any other country for the purpose of discharging traffic of foreign origin, and accepting foreign bound traffic." He knew what he was talking about. He clearly and precisely explained not only what later became commonly known as the Third and Fourth Freedoms, but also the Fifth Freedom. Regarding the latter he actually illustrated what he meant by explaining that a Canadian line operating to Jamaica should be allowed to pick up Fifth Freedom traffic in Buffalo for Jamaica, but not cabotage traffic for Miami. He was in fact drawing a picture of a general multilateral agreement that would automatically grant transit and stop and commercial outlets in terms of Third, Fourth, and Fifth Freedoms to all nations who entered into consort. This was the president's vision of freedom of the air: it was not Pogue's.

BILATERALISM, MULTILATERALISM, AND DIFFERENT KINDS OF RECIPROCITY

Whether Pogue had wind of what the president's views were before the meeting on November 10, 1943, is difficult to say, but on that same day he sent Hopkins a draft speech he was shortly to give in New York. Pogue indicated: "Unless I hear from you I will assume that you see no objection to this talk."[37] The speech touched on generally agreed policy about U.S. bases built overseas and their possible postwar use, on private enterprise and appropriate government regulation, and on the widespread granting of transit and stop. Pogue preached that international civil aviation was not just about commerce but was "the greatest potential force for world political and social advancement."[38] So far, so good, and all this was in tune with the president: then came commercial rights.

> With respect to the granting of "commercial outlets" the right of any foreign airline to discharge and take on passengers and traffic, each nation must decide where its best interest lies. It would be quite unrealistic, at this stage of the world's developments, to assume that such commercial outlets should be more or less automatically granted to all comers.[39]

From one point of view this might smack of downright insubordination. To anyone reading Berle's report of the meeting at the White House, it would have been clear that what Pogue was saying here was diametrically opposed to what the president had instructed. He did want "commercial outlets...more or less automatically granted to others." On September 26 Berle wrote to Hull and Stettinius: "The President's ideas appear to be running along the lines of a general air navigation agreement." There was not much scope to say anything else after November 10, but interestingly Berle added: "Though he might modify this on further consideration in favor of negotiating separate air navigation agreements between the United States and each individual country."[40] Berle was very aware of the strong institutional and political forces that preferred the bilateral approach, and he was also beginning to recognize that opportunities for inaugurating civil aviation services arising as areas were liberated might demand immediate action that could only be taken through bilateral agreements. Eventually the president too acknowledged this but remained strongly wedded to a UN conference that would produce multilaterally applicable commercial rights.

Pogue was clearly troubled and not content and again turned to Hopkins for help, sending him memoranda on November 21 and 26. In them Pogue tried to retrieve his preferred position. The first note was the more important. It dealt with commercial rights. Claiming rather implausibly that he was a "little confused" after the meeting with the president, and in particular "not clear as to whether the President thought that this right to pick up and discharge...traffic should automatically exist," he was keen to point out that his subcommittee "recommends that this government retain control in granting to foreigners of the right to discharge and take on traffic in international operations."[41] A few days later "another thought occurred," and Pogue, overly concerned about the dangers of foreign competition and the need to establish an embedded and dominant position for U.S. airlines immediately after the war, argued that subsidies might be more needed than the president had intimated. "I have some question as to how many of our international routes could be run entirely free from government subsidy. I believe that some day in the near future a good many of them can operate entirely free from subsidy but that result is dependent upon a good many factors which do not remain stable."[42]

Struggles over policy continued over the following months often to the frustration of the British and the Canadians who were now eager for talks, but who were also increasingly fearful of what U.S. policy might turn out to be. For some time they were unable to form a firm picture; however, in November and early December 1943, Canadian officials were led to believe that the United States would seek a multilateral exchange of transit and stop and commercial rights by bilateral negotiations.[43] In late December Berle reported to Hull that the question of reciprocity for landing rights was becoming "controversial." There were widespread concerns at the president's ideas for freely granting rights to transit and stop, and Pan American continued to lead the charge to obtain commercial rights from others without granting them in return. As Berle correctly observed, the "basic desire is to choke off competition," but he felt this had "distinct dangers," and in any case, "It should be possible, within the doctrine of general reciprocity, to establish the principle that there must be sufficient traffic existing or potential, or other public interest adequate to justify the maintenance of the airlines we are asked to accept."[44] It was also pretty clear to Berle that the president did not want to go down the route of reciprocal bilateralism. "We have every indication that the President does not favor a system of bilateralism of this kind and we have as yet no reason to assume that the Congress will require it."[45] And on the view that freedom of transit and stop would be of advantage to the United States, Berle again confirmed that "it is understood the President is of this view."[46]

Policy, notwithstanding the president's directives on November 10, continued in flux. In response to public and congressional criticisms, there was a shift once again on transit and stop, and it was decided to make those rights dependent upon a satisfactory prior agreement on commercial rights. But the really crucial questions were how commercial rights should be acquired and what they should actually be. Between December 1943 and April 1944, with one or two policy exceptions, there was a gradual slippage in the bureaucratic process away from the liberal position outlined by the president. One exception was a refreshingly relaxed view from the Army Air Corps on the question of transit and stop. Providing it was properly regulated, which meant government designation of routes and airports, then the benefits of a reciprocal exchange were deemed to "outweigh the military risks involved."[47] Much of the rest of the Army Air Force's position was either rather predictable, emphasizing civil aviation's bearing on national security through its adaptability for military use and its importance for developing the aeronautics industry generally, or rather vague platitudes about the "maximum encouragement of regulated competitive enterprise" and the reciprocal exchange of commercial rights "subject to reasonable controls" to cater for the national interest and avoid the abuses of harmful competition.[48] Once again it was the CAB and Pogue that provided a more detailed picture of policy, and they laid it out in a special report dated April 12, 1944. This was finalized at the very time that Berle and the Vice Chairman of the CAB Edward Warner were conducting talks with the British in London.

The picture that emerged from the CAB report of April 1944 was significantly at odds with what the president had said in November 1943 about commercial rights and subsidies. In brief it called for a broad granting of transit and stop, but with commercial rights only granted on a bilateral basis and when in the national interest. This, the report claimed, was probably the only effective way of controlling foreign competition: one might have added it would also secure dominance for U.S. airlines. Further safeguards against foreign competition were provided by the right of the U.S. to use subsidies to sustain routes. This went further than the president's comments had suggested. In order to facilitate the expansion of U.S. airline operations, there should be no politically prescribed limitations on capacity or frequency or over the inauguration of services, nor should quotas or routes be allocated by an international authority. U.S. airlines should be able to seize their opportunities at the end of the war. To ensure that was not hindered by an international authority, the proposals suggested that while there should be cooperation internationally to control rates, subsidies, and unfair or cutthroat competition, this should not be in the form of compulsion by a powerful international regulatory body. The CAB specifically called for legal changes in the United States that would empower the CAB to control rates for U.S. airlines on international routes, but otherwise matters should be left at the end of the war as fluid and free as possible.

> The United States should grant to foreign air carriers operating rights involving the taking on and discharge of traffic only where the extension of that privilege is required in order to permit the establishment of air services by United States carriers, the inauguration of which is required by our national interest. In determining the point in which the United States and a particular foreign air carrier shall be permitted to take on and discharge traffic there must be considered on the one hand, the desirability of avoiding the maximum extent possible diversion of traffic from our own domestic airlines, and, on the other hand, the desirability in some cases of authorizing such a commercial entry at a given point if necessary to obtain a valuable right for the United States elsewhere in the world.[49]

Even these kinds of principles should only be applied if general agreement with the British were accomplished. This kind of apprehension about Britain and how it might move also came out clearly in respect to the expressed need to oppose any kind of agreements regarding inter-European traffic that might be made to exclude U.S. carriers. There were serious difficulties in all this. On the one hand, the United States needed more freedom to infect the existing international regime; on the other, it could not tolerate a type of "chaos" in which U.S. competitive advantages might be eroded over time.

> In the light of these considerations, prudence and sound economics require that the right to pick up and discharge traffic continue to be granted by specific consent of the government whose territory is involved. Under this procedure the United States would retain the right to say what carriers should participate in traffic to and from points in its territories and compete with its own carriers. It does not follow, however, that we should support a similar policy with respect to non-stop passage and technical stops in commercial air transportation. We believe that a substantial liberalization of existing international procedures, relating to the latter rights is both feasible and desirable.[50]

Echoes can be seen in this paper of the views not only reported from the domestic airlines but also Trippe's and the more nationalistically minded groups. Pogue was not as extreme as the latter, but he overlapped with them on a number of issues. One obvious and stark difference, however, was that he was not prepared to countenance a Pan American monopoly. The rights he sought would be distributed among several U.S. airlines.

Things were closing down on the president's preferred position of a multilateral exchange of commercial rights, and it was in this vein that Berle and Warner held preliminary talks with the Canadians and British in late March and early April 1944.

MOVEMENT TOWARD TALKING WITH THE BRITISH

Because of difficulties in resolving differences about aviation policy and lack of progress in Congress, the United States had procrastinated with the British about preliminary talks, but in the end developments conspired to force its hand. The war progressed well in the autumn of 1943. The Battle of Kursk in July was a turning point on the eastern front, and it was followed by significant Soviet advances in September. That same month Anglo-American forces invaded Italy, and within weeks the Fascist regime collapsed and Italy changed sides and declared war on Germany. More attention was now given to the future. It was vital not to repeat the mistakes of 1918–19. Roosevelt, with "victory perceptibly in the air in October 1943...began in earnest to

make plans and formulate policies for the post-war domestic economy."[51]
It was in this context that increased fears of British moves in civil aviation prompted Berle to plead for the president to name his negotiating team
and start talks directly with them. The president, while not naïve about the
British, interestingly viewed civil aviation and security priorities in a more
relaxed way than either Berle or Pogue. He had already given considerable
attention to preliminary work on postwar planning and that included taking steps to secure America's postwar position in the Pacific. Because of
Pearl Harbor, this was the most sensitive of security areas, so Roosevelt's
views here are important indicators of just how he saw security and postwar
civil aviation. If he could be relaxed enough in this theatre to promote his
vision of air freedom, then it would be a very strong confirmation of just
how strongly and clearly he wanted a cooperative, liberal, and multilateral
postwar aviation regime generally.

As early as March 1943, Frank Knox, secretary of the Navy, exchanged
views with Roosevelt about the long-term fate of the Pacific and the importance of island bases for U.S. security. This was also of great concern to
General Arnold, who was determined that the United States should not be
caught unawares a second time. Roosevelt majestically took the whole issue
of the Pacific over himself, saying he thought that he had better discuss
matters with the British himself. His ambitions went far beyond U.S. sei-
zure of the Japanese-mandated islands. He also wanted to resolve disputes
with the British over ownership of several islands and to seek access to bases
held by them. He was supremely confident that he could achieve all this
and would not trust the Navy or anyone else to sort things out. In order to
have a detailed grasp, particularly of the needs of postwar U.S. civil aviation, he commissioned his old friend and Arctic explorer Admiral Richard
E. Byrd to survey the Pacific.[52] The survey began in September 1943, and
Byrd reported back to the president in April 1944. It will be examined in
due course; however, prior to starting out, Byrd wrote to Admiral William
Brown, the president's naval aide, asking if he should keep the survey quiet,
especially from the British. Brown entered for the record that he had:

> ... told Admiral Byrd that I had heard the President say repeatedly that except
> for air bases that may be required for national defense, in general his idea of
> post-war commercial aviation is that the islands of the Pacific should be open
> to commercial use by all nationalities and that, therefore, I believe there was
> no need for any secrecy about what we are doing. . . . [53]

Here is evidence from yet another source to indicate that Roosevelt was consistent about freedom, even when it involved the security-sensitive Pacific.
He wanted freedom to incorporate the rights of innocent passage and

technical stop and for commercial air rights to be exchanged multilaterally. He neither feared that the U.S. airlines would be crippled by cheaper-cost foreign airlines nor was prepared seriously to compromise his vision because of undue concerns about U.S. post-war security. Even the Pacific should be open to all.

Berle's concern by early 1944 was not so much about the level of U.S. liberalism in aviation as about Britain's possible protectionism and its ability to close down opportunities for U.S. airlines. Since the commonwealth aviation meeting in October 1943, suspicions had grown about British objectives. There was talk of the British establishing operations dominated by BOAC for the whole of Europe as a kind of counterweight to the huge domestic aviation market enjoyed by America. But matters did not rest there. The British were getting impatient with American delays in entering talks and ironically mirrored American fears of losing what they hoped would be their postwar aviation market. The British felt that American airlines, with at least tacit consent of the U.S. Government, were going "all out" for postwar supremacy and that they had to take "immediate counter-measures."[54] Both sides fed each other's paranoia. Reports had reached the British that American airlines were "seeking to establish themselves in numerous countries" and were within reach of establishing round-the-world routes. The British professed to the Canadians that they had until now restrained British aviation interests from participating in aviation developments in foreign countries, but in the face of this American threat they were now encouraging similar tactics and in particular sought to purchase an airline in Uruguay. It seemed to the British that "this show of activity may bring the United States Administration to a meeting earlier than would otherwise be the case."[55] It did.

Almost in panic mode, Berle explained to Hull: "The whole tempo of aviation affairs has speeded up in the last week. It is plain that the British, if talks are not forthcoming pretty soon, will proceed to organize their affairs on the theory that we are going to play a lone hand." In case of that contingency arising, the British were not only trying to devise an air bloc in Europe but were consulting with the Portuguese for joint operations to cover the Mediterranean, and British steamship companies and BOAC were trying to purchase airlines in South America. Berle ended the note: "I suggest the President name his negotiating team immediately."[56] Berle also tried to square things with the Congress, and he met with Senator Clark, whose Sub-Committee on Civil Aviation continued its work on how American airlines ought to operate abroad after the war. Clark expressed strong views against talks with the British unless the Soviets were involved. On February 14, 1944, responding to a note from Berle about the proposed talks with the British, the president affirmed that he would like to have the Soviets involved, but more significantly, he also emphasized the centrality of a future UN conference.

> I think this is a good way of going about the first Air Conference but it must be made clear that this is wholly preliminary to a United Nations' Air Conference to be held later in the year.[57]

This finally committed the Americans to conversations with the British, but there then followed a fiasco of proposal and counterproposal for talks involving an ever-expanding group of nations at ever-changing venues. In the end it was decided that it would be best for Berle and Edward Warner to travel as quietly as possible to London via Canada for preliminary talks with the Canadians and the British.[58] At the same time the United States embarked upon a series of separate talks with several countries, but the priority remained some kind of deal with the British for crafting a new international civil aviation regime. The talks in Canada and London raised the curtain on that drama; however, notwithstanding the president's emphasis on the importance of an international air conference, there was now an increasing danger of bilateral talks compromising a multilateral solution to postwar aviation matters.

AMERICAN TALKS WITH THE CANADIANS AND THE BRITISH—MARCH AND APRIL 1944

The exploratory talks with the Canadians did not bode well. The Canadians had drawn up a draft International Transport Convention, based largely on ideas developed in what was referred to as the Balfour Report that emerged as one of the results of the October 1943 Commonwealth Talks in London. The Canadians had added in their own perspective, especially reserving the relationships of contiguous states from the application of the convention, that is, U.S.-Canadian aviation relations. Another priority of the Canadians was that Freedoms 1 and 2 should only be granted subject to satisfactory agreement on commercial rights as transit rights were their main bargaining chip. In March 1944 this at least was fully in line with U.S. thinking. The main divisive issue was the Canadian commitment to creating a powerful regulatory body to oversee the postwar international aviation regime. This sounds similar to the British position, and it was, but there were nuanced differences. The Canadians wanted more freedom and competitive scope than the British because of high hopes for Trans-Canada Airlines, the protégé of the powerful supply minister C. D. Howe and his ally, Herbert Symington, head of the airline. There were also differences within the Canadian camp between idealists and the more pragmatic and commercially minded, which complicated relations with Britain and the United States alike, but this story has been related elsewhere.[59] The central points for our present concerns are that both the British and the Canadians insisted on a powerful international regulatory authority, and the Canadians, although in a less confrontational posture with the Americans than the British, still found Berle's proposals to reek of ruthless realpolitik. John Baldwin, assistant secretary to the Canadian Cabinet War Committee, put it like this:

> This policy would appear to be based upon the assumption that the U.S. because of its superior ability (both actual and potential), and greater traffic offering, would be able to dominate the international air transport scene without any effective international regulation being required.[60]

Symington, in reflective mode shortly after talking with Berle and Warner in Montreal, wrote to Howe: "The more I think of it, the more disturbed I am."[61] He was too much of a practical business man to want to defend the Canadian plan in its entirety, but he exclaimed that it was "at least, robust, courageous, and fair.... " The obvious implication being that the American position was none of those things. He was exasperated by Berle's refusal to contemplate a powerful international regulatory authority on the grounds that it would be unacceptable to the American people and Congress and bemoaned the situation that this left everyone in, namely, reliance on American "fairness." Even American attempts to offer a sop to the Canadians on the second day of the talks simply exasperated Symington further. The Americans suggested an interim period of about two years in which the International Convention would not wield regulatory power, but consult, collect information, and prepare reports. He caustically observed: "In the meantime, any nation, really only the United States, can put on all the frequencies on all the routes that it desires." Such operations would be unlikely to be dislodged later. Finally, switching away from pragmatic mode to an idealist flourish, he complained: "To me, the most regrettable feature is that it is symptomatic of a spirit which bodes ill for world peace."[62] One suspects that President Franklin D. Roosevelt might have been persuaded to draw a similar conclusion.

The talks in London were a rather curious affair. They appeared to go better than those in Montreal. Expressed levels of satisfaction on both sides were certainly higher, but an awful lot of fudging went on and later, not surprisingly, there was controversy over exactly what each side had meant. Berle led the small American delegation consisting of Edward Warner and Livingston Satterthwaite, shortly to be appointed U.S. civil aviation attaché in London. The British were led by Beaverbrook, who was primarily assisted by Harold Balfour and George Cribbett from the Air Ministry; Richard,

Law minister of state at the Foreign Office; and a handful of other officials. There was common ground over the need to create an international body to supervise technical matters and a full meeting of minds on cabotage, which should extend to possessions, but not self-governing dominions. Both sides also found agreement on transit and stop that should be widely granted, but only once "reasonable arrangements" were in place "for airport use and commercial outlet."[63] Also, very importantly, toward the end of the discussions, there was agreement to revisit and extend the Halifax Agreement in order to regulate any British or American international aviation agreements. So far, so good, but then the fudging began.

Maybe one should not read too much into verbal quibbles, but at the outset of considering commercial matters, the Americans specifically called for the abandonment of the term "freedom of the air": it had been too loosely used and was meaningless. The British agreed. One wonders, given his frequent use of freedom in regard to postwar civil aviation, whether Roosevelt would have gone along with that if he had been there. The meeting now considered commercial matters under the three headings of sovereignty; transit and stop; and commercial outlet. Little difficulty emerged over the first two, and Beaverbrook also reaffirmed something he had said in the House of Lords on January 19, 1944, namely, that Britain would open up bases it controlled round the world for commercial aviation traffic (though Britain did not have power to do this regarding airports in the Dominions). Berle reciprocated in a sense by indicating that the United States would make modern transports freely available to the UK for purchase after the war.[64] The problems arose, as expected, over the regime for commercial outlet.

The British wanted a system that would match traffic with capacity, ensure equitable participation by each state, and control subsidies. The Americans agreed with the first aim, thought the third was acceptable in principle but would be difficult to achieve in practice, and objected that the second aim involved an undesirable level of control. In each case the devil was in the detail. The Americans did not want to match traffic and capacity by predetermining frequency allocations as the British did, but for the market to decide by allowing airlines to offer the capacity and frequency they chose. At one point the British suggested that frequencies and capacity should be apportioned by an international authority on the basis of traffic originated in a country irrespective of nationality of the traveler, that is, all travelers seeking to fly out of Britain, be they American or British, would be designated as traffic for British carriers. That would in effect have resulted in a fifty-fifty division of traffic between the two countries. The American counterproposal was that if traffic were to be classified by national origin, then this should not be construed so as to restrict passengers to their own flag carrier, but an American flying out of London, for example, should be free to choose between a British or an American carrier. Rather ominously, Berl's account of this exchange ended with the comment: "The point was not developed in detail."[65] Like a number of other issues, if it had been serious, differences would have become much clearer.

Both agreed in principle about the undesirability of subsidies, but the Americans did not want to rule them out in case it disadvantaged their airlines. They argued for controlling the effects, but the only conclusion they could reach was that subsidies were acceptable for keeping airlines in the air but not for driving them out. The matter was then reserved for future discussion. The case was similar with price-fixing. Both agreed that there should at least be minimum rates, but the British wanted these matters decided by an international authority, which did not accord with American thinking. Berle and Warner suggested that matters might be left to the airlines to decide among themselves and went on to talk rather vaguely of bilateral or multilateral governmental consultations, but when the British reiterated that all that would have to be subject to international control, "the point was reserved."[66] This was followed by an obvious ploy by the British to compensate for their inferior equipment. They suggested that faster planes should not be allowed to charge the same price as slower ones. The American delegation immediately baulked at this and riposted that it would be better to link rates to costs, and while this appeared to be acceptable to both sides, the British again insisted on linking it to approval by the proposed international authority.

What emerges from all this is a series of vague understandings or reserved positions on key issues, but things were about to get worse. It was resonance from the idea of ensuring equitable participation that worried the Americans most, especially when linked with the idea of a strong international regulatory body. In particular they were aroused by the British idea of it imposing quotas that would effectively split the traffic evenly between the United States and Britain. The Americans were totally opposed to a powerful international authority and explained why. The constitution probably did not allow the U.S. government to delegate such regulatory powers to an international authority. The British insistence on creating an authority seemed to derive mainly from security considerations, but these were to be dealt with in separate UN talks. It would be impossible to create an appropriate body to govern in an economic sector that was novel and dynamic and that would develop in unforeseen ways. It would be best to restrict an authority to powers of data collection and consultation and wait to see what developed. Only if developments justified it, might there be a further conference to consider powers for the authority. These arguments prompted the British to comment that "the United States was as backward in its conception of international organizations as the British were in commercial aviation."[67] Even so,

Beaverbrook pressed ahead and presented the Canadian draft Convention as a basis for further talks and possible agreement.[68]

The convention was examined in detail, but Berle's take on it was not encouraging, and he actually said that he thought that it had been put forward with the intent that the United States would have to reject it.

> So far as the United States is concerned this would...subject twenty five years of American development of international aviation, which had been invented, pioneered, developed, and defended by the United States, to the unrestricted rule of an...undetermined international body, upon un-stated standards.[69]

Berle knew that approximately 80 percent of the international passenger market had been carried by U.S. carriers before the war. He also knew that it was impossible to sustain that dominance of the market, but he was damned if he would allow some international body to carve it up and arbitrarily take a substantial part of the market away and distribute it to all and sundry, and especially the British. The Americans reiterated their position. For their part, the British protested again about the security dangers from civil aviation and argued for the need for controls. Impasse prevailed. However, after an adjournment, the British withdrew the Canadian Convention and presented the Balfour Plan, from which the Canadian Draft Convention had actually been developed. Somewhat surprisingly, the Americans said that they could live with it providing that its principles were not interpreted in the same manner as those in the Canadian Convention. They thought that it could provide the basis of a convention that would reflect the American position, that is, an authority with no coercive authority that was purely advisory and consultative and dealt mainly with technical and safety matters. On this basis they acknowledged that it could be used as the basis for future talks.

Both sides knew that it was in their interests to come to some kind of accommodation regarding postwar civil aviation, but any meeting of minds in April 1944 was far more apparent than real. That posed dangers for the future. Furthermore, Berle formed the impression that the British would eventually accommodate to American priorities. While in London, he met with Churchill and Beaverbrook, and from their discussions it was obvious that there were strong political pressures for reaching an understanding that would allow matters to be taken forward. That required compromise.[70] Later, in October 1944, just days before the Chicago conference, Berle's expectations were reinforced in conversation with Michael Wright, first secretary at the British Embassy. Wright explained that the Foreign Office realized a clash was looming at Chicago and that they would need to compromise.

Berle commented that this "conforms to the outline of instructions Prime Minister Churchill gave Beaverbrook in my presence."[71] So, Berle carried away from London expectations of British compromise, and they abided and with good reason, but his expectations were overoptimistically inflated and they would lead to disappointment and anger later that added to the difficulties in Chicago. If one also strips away the fudged agreements and the reserved points and disperses the fog that obscured the divergent views on the Balfour Report, then the auguries for Chicago were indeed inauspicious. In May 1944, an official in London explained to Australian Prime Minister John Curtin that the Canadian Convention was really based on the Balfour Plan and "the plans in principle are almost identical."[72] He offered the opinion that Berle had accepted the latter in the London talks to save face for rejecting the former, but the episode with Churchill suggests that he did so in the expectation that the British would later agree to adjust the Balfour Report substantially. Whatever interpretation one were to put on this, it is clear that the Americans would have to apply a radically different interpretation to the Balfour Report from that of the British if it were to meet their principal requirements. And that is precisely what they insisted on doing. For a short time the British thought that Berle had accepted more than they "might have hoped for," but they were soon disabused, and it became clear that the Americans would not accept anything other than consultative and advisory powers for an international authority.[73] This was further than the British ever intended going. The Americans were interpreting the Balfour Report as a basis for negotiations in a manner that effectively ruled out all that the British wanted.

CHAPTER 9

AMERICAN TRIUMPH, ROOSEVELT'S LOSS, AND THE "BURLESQUE" OF CHICAGO

They [the Americans] further go on and talk about a transition period. This is to me just so much eyewash. I believe that under the guise of provisional arrangements for a transitional period they will establish all their routes all over the world and they will never be removed.

Herbert Symington, President Trans-Canada Airlines[1]

There is something of a logical boner at the bottom of the idea of calling a big international conference to agree to no international supervision.

Samuel Grafton, *New York Post,* November 17, 1944

... I had to sort of play ball because I knew it would fail, but I put forward the transport agreement because that is what Roosevelt commanded us to do.

Welch Pogue, interview with author, August 1, 2000

The International Conference on Civil Aviation has advanced civil flying by at least twenty years.

Adolf Berle 6 December 1944[2]

We have been in travail for a month and have brought forth a mouse.

J. R. Baldwin on the Chicago Conference, November 30, 1944[3]

HIGH-LEVEL POLITICAL PRESSURES, recognition on both sides of the need for an understanding, and oversanguine hopes that the other side would later compromise conjoined to create a false sense of progress in the London talks. Two realities exposed this. The first drove things ineluctably forward and consisted of opportunities for launching civilian air services as the enemy was rolled back. The crucial question was how to proceed when an international conference had not even been called. The only option was bilateralism. Once this was recognized and thoughts applied to the nitty-gritty questions of just how services were to operate, they brought into play American policies that ate away at the illusion of consensus.

Part of the wider problem, however, was the difficulty in getting the American system to deliver a clear aviation policy. Strong differences of opinion within the administration, the snail's progress of deliberations in the Senate Commerce subcommittee, and the warring between Pan American and the seventeen airlines that wanted a slice of the international market prevented the emergence of a clear policy. In the absence of that it was difficult to negotiate an international consensus with foreign governments. So, instead of concerted international movement, the United States moved unilaterally. This made others wary and exacerbated difficulties. Even when the Chicago Conference convened in November 1944, the United States did not have a clear position to present, or at least not one for a uniform and enforceable commercial regime. It did not go unobserved that the United States appeared to have called an international conference to agree that there should be no international regulation, nor that they continued pursuing bilateral agreements at Chicago and beyond.

MOVE-OUT

One concrete result of the London talks was renewal of the Halifax Agreement, which was effected through an exchange of notes drafted at the end of August. Both re-committed not to strike exclusive arrangements and to keep each other informed.[4] This was all achieved rather amicably, but it could not disguise the tensions that now existed as prospects for victory strengthened and civil aviation operations beckoned. Those tensions eventually pushed the United States into a drive for bilateral agreements for routes and rights prior to any international conference, largely, but by no means entirely, in response to fears about what the British were doing. Not all acted solely out of fear of British actions, some Americans thought commercial multilateralism for aviation a pipe dream and threatening to American interests, and for them bilateralism was always their favored option.

On each side, knowledge of maneuverings for a move-out into civilian operations seeped into the public domain heightening controversy, paranoia, and fear of political retribution if steps were not taken to secure national interests. Some accommodations were achieved such as in North Africa, with the Eisenhower-Tedder Agreement allowing BOAC to use spare capacity for civilian passengers, but fears of American dominance in the air continued to stoke up long-smoldering suspicion in London. As soon as Pan American had begun to support the British war effort, talk had arisen of American imperial ambitions. Fears ranged from the possibility of America's dominance in the Western Hemisphere and the Pacific to its penetration of Africa and the Middle East through the Takoradi route, and there were also suspicions American airlines might even take internal routes in Australia at the end of the war as no one else would be equipped to do so.[5] Anxieties on both sides had been set aside or at least downplayed because of overriding war priorities, but with victory looming, even renewing the Halifax Agreement could no longer assuage fears in London or for that matter in Washington.

In February U.S. ambassador John Winant reported from London on British preparations for routes to Spain, Italy, and Portugal. The following month he advised that BOAC was planning routes for liberated Europe and that reactionary elements in London might start an aviation trade war with "discriminatory agreements all over the lot." Four months later the State Department responded by pressing for greater freedom for U.S. airlines to carry civilian passengers. Head of the State Department Aviation Division Stokeley Morgan indicated that this should be openly coordinated with the British, but the most important thing was to achieve freer rein for U.S. airlines. That was not easy because the United States did not have spare transports for civilian use, and any further liberalization of traffic operations would have to be authorized by CAB licensing and that would take time.[6] In July inflammatory articles in the *Chicago Daily Tribune* and the *New York Journal of Commerce* demanded American action to respond to alleged British plans to dominate European aviation, create a commonwealth air bloc, and negotiate exclusionary deals with others.[7] Then British moves ratcheted things up even further: they informed Berle that they wanted to start civilian operations to South America.

> Mr. Berle [stated] that the United States regarded our [British] proposal as being in substance the first major movement for the expansion of commercial air services since the beginning of the war. They were prepared to acquiesce in it, but only on condition that in any given area where BOAC operates, either as a commercial carrier or performing contract services for the RAF Transport Command, duly certified United States air carriers should be allowed to do likewise and that in particular a United States service should be inaugurated as soon as possible from the United States across North Africa to Cairo, which would include the carriage of non-military traffic.[8]

The British thought Berle's response "outrageous" and clearly designed to seize disproportionate advantages for the United States. In the event of winter drawing on and the Boeing flying boats earmarked for the route unable to operate because of weather conditions, the British withdrew. Nevertheless, the episode highlighted much else that was ongoing about jostling for postwar position.

At the head of the drive for a civilian move-out in the United States was Pogue, who accelerated steps to issue new certificates of convenience and necessity and impressed upon both Hull and Berle the importance of ensuring that U.S. airlines could establish international services "at the earliest practicable moment." On May 30 he requested permission from the president to issue new licenses: Roosevelt agreed.[9] On June 12 Morgan sent a note to Berle strongly urging liberalization of the rules forbidding civilian carriage by U.S. overseas operators, and two days later the CAB published a list of desirable postwar routes for U.S. carriers, clearly signaling that America was preparing the ground for a move-out into new international operations.[10] Hearings for awarding the routes were set to start in September 1944. Berle explained the reasoning behind all this to Hull. Although he had always maintained that the British would be able to outgrab the United States in a free-for-all, confronted with what he saw as the reality of a British move-out, he saw no alternative but robustly to follow suit.

> It is now clear that the British propose to throw in their civil aviation as rapidly as the military pressure is lifted; they are already proposing a line from England through Spain and Africa to South America.
>
> Under these circumstances, Mr. Pogue, and Mr. Burden feel, and I agree, that while we should continue to negotiate and press for generalized international agreements, we should also endeavor to push forward on a provisional basis, arrangements, so that our aviation lines can enter the field.[11]

Berle went on to explain that any agreements could be made subject to the overall international agreement "as and when it emerges," but one might note that there was a real danger here that bilateralism would undermine a future international conference. This must have been obvious to Roosevelt, but developments soon dragged him along with bilateralism as well.

During May there was renewed activity from Congress in response to inaccurate newspaper reports about the Berle-Beaverbrook talks in London. The heart of the issue was pique felt by Senators Clark and Bailey over reference to the existence of an "American Plan," of which they had no knowledge. They were reassured that the plan did not exist, but this was followed up in early June with a meeting at the White House. With Berle and Pogue also present, the president wanted to know how far the subcommittee had proceeded with its deliberations. It soon transpired the answer was not far at all though it was clear that several important committee members favored a monopoly for Pan American. Progress had been slow partly because of the lengthy absence of Senator Pat McCarran, who, on his return, had then thrown a spanner in the works by introducing his All American Flag Line Bill in a transparent attempt to secure Pan American's continuing dominance. The president affirmed that he was still strongly wedded to several chosen instruments operating in different areas, and in fact over the following weeks, Pan American's fortunes suffered reversals in Congress and it became clear that an officially sanctioned monopoly was no longer likely.[12] But the monopoly issue was not the president's main concern at the meeting. Force of circumstance was dictating to the president. Not only was he confronted by strong factions in the administration, Congress, and the general public who favored a bilateral and more conservative approach, but actual developments now conspired to promote de facto bilateralism. It was thus an urgent matter to get the Congress on board with the idea of a U.S. move-out, something that would happen before Congress completed even its deliberations on civil aviation policy, never mind ensconcing them in law.

To set the context the president raised the possibility of a German collapse, and Berle elaborated on this by pointing out that civilian opportunities for aviation were already arising in North Africa. Roosevelt explained: "In such case, we should need to have our aviation policy not only fixed but in such shape that we could move out at once....unhappily [he, FDR] might be in the position of not being able to let the matter rock along but would have to move out—depending on the military situation."[13] Clark gave a sort of congressional green light by acknowledging that the president would naturally be obliged to safeguard the national interest.

Now more eager than ever to pursue bilateralism, Pogue made an extraordinary suggestion to Canadian officials in Washington. Pogue was impatient and dreaded the possibility of the British stealing a march on the Americans. An effective preemptive strike would be to accommodate with the Canadians and reach agreement that would provide U.S. airlines transit and stop on the strategically vital routes over Canada to Europe and Asia. If this could be sewn up bilaterally, it would drastically weaken Britain's hand and would be well worth a high price. In most circumstances, predetermining market share was anathema to Pogue and contrary to every statement or intimation given of U.S. policy because it would constrain the expansion of U.S. airlines. But, in some cases, a high price is worth paying. Pogue declared that he had "a strong personal desire that the United States and Canada go ahead and form some International Post-War Civil Air Agreement without waiting for Great Britain, Russia or anybody else." He said he thought that the members of the CAB would unanimously support this and that the U.S. authorities involved "would do everything possible" to arrive at "a full fifty-fifty agreement"—the very thing they had so vehemently denied to the British. What he was proposing, he said, should be regarded as "secret and unofficial."[14] This was not a passing rush of blood to the head. Over the following months various bilateral approaches were made to countries, and again informal proposals were put to the Canadians. They were rejected, because Trans-Canada Airlines, temporarily at least, lacked equipment to compete with U.S. airlines, and equally importantly, the Canadians feared that such negotiations would compromise the chances of success for an international conference.[15] On September 19 Beaverbrook complimented Howe on the "firm stand" he had taken in refusing landing rights to the Americans.[16]

At the end of July Beaverbrook and Richard Law, minister of state at the Foreign Office, came to Washington to discuss postwar oil and civil aviation. On the weekend of July 29-30, Beaverbrook delivered a charm offensive, inviting Berle to New Brunswick along with Law and Clarence Howe. According to Berle, the weekend was "rather fantastic," with rambling walks, river fishing and late dinners accompanied by copious amounts of the finest champagne, Beaverbrook's good humor, and the ever attentiveness of his gentleman's gentleman "Nockles."[17] This was comic opera of the highest order, and one can detect a sneaking admiration of it all in Berle's diary entries, but he was not seduced. Howe sardonically commented on it all: "The time we spent together was devoted largely to fishing which was about as productive as our talks on aviation."[18] The talks may not have been very productive, but they indicated an important line of American policy development and one to which Berle was now fully committed.

He explained to Beaverbrook that they were aware that BOAC was "making every effort to move out and acquire landing rights, and to develop commercial intercourse. This was not the declared policy of the British Government, but the fact was that the BOAC, under the guise of the Army Transport, had been doing just this." Berle observed later that "there was no dissent from this." He went on to say that American airlines disliked the situation under which they were not allowed commercial operations.

> Accordingly I wondered whether the thing to do was not to have an understanding that both sides move out in an orderly fashion, obtaining landing rights along the lines of the routes they wanted, but in no case attempting to exclude the other or prejudice the position of the other.[19]

It should all be done in a friendly way. Berle noted that both Law and Beaverbrook seemed to think that this might not be a bad idea, but he misread the situation: Beaverbrook was later strongly to oppose a move-out. Britain did not have the equipment to do so on any large or competitive scale.

Berle subsequently informed Beaverbrook that under combined pressure of "traffic, public opinion and politics," U.S. airlines would have to move out. They would enter Spain first and then go onwards onto the broad pattern of air routes identified by the CAB as soon as conditions permitted. He argued that the discrepancy between UK and U.S. actions in civil aviation could result in a "real danger of considerable public reaction" if U.S. airlines were not allowed to move forward.[20] The British thought that the Americans were trying to "jump the gun" even though Berle repeatedly tried to reassure them that he was in no way trying to "instigate competitive struggle."[21] All this was accompanied by intense activity in Washington. On August 25, meeting with U.S. policy–makers, Berle identified the two options of an international conference or an orderly move-out. Pogue was totally horrified at the scenario that he feared might emerge. He had long thought that Berle was too timid with the British, and while he did not argue openly with him, he promptly wrote to Hopkins.[22]

> I don't think the British will agree to proceeding in any such manner because of the possibility of buttoning things up themselves behind the curtain if they can get us to wait.
>
> I am convinced...that the American public would be horrified at the idea of our marking time because the British wanted us to or of even agreeing to keeping them informed of everything we are doing in the international field. That just sounds very inept to me politically.
>
> I strongly urge you to stay firmly in this air picture. Rapid progress is absolutely indispensable now; our bargaining position deteriorates day by day.[23]

Beaverbrook did indeed request that the proposed move-out be put on hold and offered to call an international conference in London. He also belatedly tried to readjust Berle's view of BOAC by claiming that while it carried no fare-paying passengers on Atlantic routes, both Pan American and Amex did.[24] Berle was unmoved, and Pogue was energetically pursuing another line of influence to push U.S. airlines ahead. He engaged the help of the pugnacious Texan, Secretary of Commerce Jesse Jones, an old friend and long-standing political ally of the president. Prompted by Pogue, Jones suggested to Roosevelt that he might take up aviation matters directly with Churchill and passed to him a memorandum authored by the CAB chairman.

> Our problem of international negotiation for air transport agreements has been complicated by the British preference for an international authority having power to allocate routes and fix frequencies of service. Up to now, this Government has opposed British policy on this point. Such an arrangement would be unacceptable to American public opinion. It would probably

operate to the disadvantage of this country while benefiting nations with large colonial empires who would be permitted to establish connecting services with their territorial possessions quite independent of the additional routes which might be allocated to them by the international authority. It seems clear that delay in our negotiations with other countries for adequate air rights merely to accommodate the British would be very distasteful to American public opinion.[25]

Pogue wanted both an immediate agreement that would cover the entire commonwealth and India and British support to gain rights elsewhere and "of course, we should reciprocate on any reasonable basis." He continued: "It is believed that it would be highly desirable for the President to discuss the matter with the British Prime Minister with the view of converting British opposition into support for our bilateral negotiation of air transport agreements." If such agreement could be achieved, then Pogue argued that it could be presented to the American people as evidence of world leadership for postwar planning in an area that has "great appeal" to the public who expect "this nation to maintain its pre-eminence in air transport development as an instrument for the preservation of the future peace."[26] Ironically, the British and Canadians viewed U.S. opposition to an international authority to govern postwar civil aviation not only as contrary to their own specific national commercial interests, but also as undermining efforts to construct a broader system to preserve the peace.

It is difficult to assess just how important Pogue's interventions were: Roosevelt did not write to Churchill about this and appears to have been preoccupied with more pressing matters when he talked with the prime minister at the Second Quebec Conference, September 10–17, 1944, but Berle recommended to Roosevelt that the United States call a conference as soon as possible, and like Pogue, he felt anxious and bitter about the British. On September 8 Canadian officials reported that Berle professed that he had never wanted to precipitate a race for postwar advantages and did not wish to do anything to prejudice the success of the forthcoming conference. But he then launched into a tirade against the "wily Britishers," who, he claimed, were taking advantage of the Americans. The Americans, he declared, would not refrain from any bilateral negotiations "they considered necessary and desirable. He was quite emphatic about this."[27] Shortly after, Berle told Beaverbrook that a conference would indeed be called by the president, but in the meantime "it is not possible to enter into agreement suggested by you that United States binds itself not to request landing rights." They had to protect American interests. He rather lamely added that the imminence of the international conference probably made Beaverbrook's request largely redundant anyway.[28]

In preparation for the conference the British issued a government White Paper that reiterated commitment to a strong international regulatory authority with power over the allocation of quotas and frequencies but at least committed to the Four Freedoms.[29] Even so, where, one might ask, was a new liberal regime to be found in all this? What had happened to American multilateralism? How would the bilateral negotiations be reconciled with the multilateralism of an international conference and to what extent might the conference be compromised by them? As one senior Canadian official put it, American policy "is nothing more or less than a return to the unsatisfactory pre-war position."[30] If that were the case, then it was "goodbye" to Franklin Roosevelt's vision of freedom of the air.

BERLE, POGUE, AND ROOSEVELT

Roosevelt compromised in allowing bilateral talks to go ahead, but given the circumstances, it is difficult to see how he might have avoided doing so. His preferred multilateral strategy was coming under intense pressures, and while he approved the move-out, he still preferred to "open designated ports freely to all comers in return for like rights elsewhere," and as Pogue recalled many years later, the president insisted that the United States should shoot for a liberal multilateral agreement at the Chicago Conference.[31] Further evidence of the president's thinking in the months running up to the Chicago Conference is elusive, apart from him repeatedly emphasizing the importance of such a conference. The president was struggling with the onrushing events of the war and broader and higher profile issues of postwar planning, whilst at the same time his health was in serious decline. Even so, what evidence there is indicates that he continued alert to the challenges of civil aviation and that he stuck with the idea of a liberal multilateral exchange of commercial rights and resisted prioritizing military security to the point where it would undermine his vision for civil aviation.

The Pacific was the most security-sensitive security area, and Roosevelt insisted it should be open to all for civil aviation. As Admiral Byrd confirmed, the president knew what this entailed probably better than anyone else.

> My study shows you were right—that you were years ahead of all of us, even those concentrating on the overall aspects of post-war strategy and international air commerce. [It was not] ... until I had made a thorough analysis of the whole problem did I fully comprehend the reasons that brought you to consider this matter of such transcendent importance to the future of this nation.[32]

Roosevelt's keen appreciation of the strategic importance of the Pacific did not lead him to compromise his vision for a liberal aviation regime even in this most sensitive of regions, but that did not mean neglecting security, just striking an appropriate balance. For example, in January he instructed the State Department not to delay negotiations for bases, facilities, and rights for military operations sought by the Joint Chiefs of Staff in deference to civil aviation matters, and securing bases was so important that he would not delegate responsibility for squaring the British with U.S. military needs in the Pacific to anyone other than himself.[33] America had to have its bases in the Pacific for both military and civil aviation. Many would be directly under American control, though for others Roosevelt preferred UN trusteeships. He thought that this would be less provoking to other countries and still provide America with essentially what it needed. However, as 1944 advanced, Roosevelt discovered that compelling specific circumstances obligated compromise on bases, just as they had on civil aviation.

> His enthusiasm for trusteeships reached its peak in the winter and spring of 1944, after which time he began to retreat. His large ideas began to crack on the necessity for precise solutions.[34]

Even so, as far as civil aviation in the Pacific was concerned, the president maintained a consistent liberal line. The Byrd Report demonstrated what Roosevelt already knew, namely, that the transoceanic civil aviation routes would be important to American security. In addition he agreed with analysis prompted by the Byrd Report that claimed: "However tough or merciless foreign competition may be, this nation cannot allow its international airlines to go bankrupt."[35] But he did not see any of these security priorities running counter to the needs of civil aviation. He insisted on opening up the Hawaiian Islands, maybe not with landing rights on Honolulu, but he indicated other possibilities on the island of Hawaii itself.[36] Generally Roosevelt was more tenacious about liberal multilateralism for civil aviation than he was on trusteeships. The Joint Chiefs managed to sideline trusteeships at the Dunbarton Oaks Conference, whereas at the Chicago Conference, multilateralism reached a point at which it looked as though it might succeed. And the most important indicator of all of Roosevelt's abiding determination to create a multilateral commercial aviation regime was the way that he threw himself into the fray that erupted at Chicago and tried to sway Churchill into backing his liberal vision.

Pogue was at odds with the president's views. He never wanted a multilateral agreement on commercial rights. He claimed later that he did as instructed by the president and negotiated for a multilateral agreement at Chicago, but it is clear his heart was not in it, and there is circumstantial evidence that suggests he may have played a more negative role.[37] Prior to Chicago Pogue promoted the American move-out as best he could, though with little success. America had not completed any agreements prior to the conference, but its policy was clear.[38] From mid-1944 onwards the United States pursued a two-pronged approach: bilateralism and multilateralism. At Chicago the Americans were quick to gain agreement to an interim period in which nations could pursue bilateral agreements and promptly took advantage of the assembled delegates to approach as many as they could. Pogue was happy to see the United States vigorously looking after its own interests in this way even if and maybe because it would compromise the chances for multilateral agreement at Chicago. Indeed, with the outcome of Chicago still in the balance, Pogue continued to urge the need for the release of aircraft to increase civilian operations and service what he hoped would be a string of bilateral agreements. Once again the results were not good, and General Arnold explained that the military had no spare capacity to release, but that fact does not detract from what these moves indicate about Pogue's position.[39]

Berle was the most troubled of the three. He felt caught between support for the president's liberal and multilateralist views, which he shared, and the pressures coming from many sources for a more conservative and nationalist bilateralism. All this emphasized his tendency to mood swings and created a degree of uncertainty in his position. Trying to explain to Hull the state of play, he noted that the United States was now promoting bilateral talks for commercial rights with the clear intent of preventing foreign lines competing "with American lines for traffic to and from the United States" even though the president still preferred a more liberal multilateral regime. That preference was supported by many of the airlines, the general public, and a majority in the House of Representatives, "but the influence of the Pan American group has been strong enough to prevent our taking such a position before the Senate Committee."[40] The way forward, Berle stated, was either to move out bilaterally or call an international conference. The United States of course pursued both, but Berle had difficulty in working out what the likely consequences might be that led to contradictions in his analysis. On successive pages of the memorandum, he wrote:

> ...in the crucial parts of the world the British are in a position in one form or another to block our securing landing rights....
> [followed by]
> I do not think many countries are in a position to tell us we are to be excluded.[41]

Berle was not sure how the international environment might respond to American ambitions. The dangers it posed were difficult to assess, and everything was complicated by cross-currents within the U.S. domestic

sphere and within his own mind. He concluded his note to Hull with a summary of the American position largely reflecting what emerged during the
April talks in London, but with added emphasis on the need for "immediate
arrangements for the extension of civil air traffic to the principal centers of
the world on an ad hoc basis," that is, by bilateral agreements. These should
be accomplished through executive agreements and the existing powers
of the CAB so that no new congressional legislation would be required. It
would seem Pogue's sense of urgency had infected Berle as well. After three
years or so, matters might be reviewed to see if another conference were
needed to produce further regulatory rules.[42]

Two weeks later, in a lengthy and ruminative memorandum, Berle
remained ambiguous on a number of matters, including bilateralism and
multilateralism. He knew that the underlying dynamic of the upcoming
conference would be political, not commercial, and he identified the main
problem to overcome as the horizontal alliance between those wanting more
freedom of the air and what he termed the "closed sector theory" consisting
of Pan American, BOAC, British Foreign Office imperialists, and those promoting air cartels. Beaverbrook had confirmed in April that Alfred Critchley
of BOAC and Trippe had reached an understanding to carve up the world
between their two airlines. Although their motives differed, Critchley and
Trippe would end up as kings in their own domains. The net result would be
massive closed air blocks "grinding against each other on the periphery."

> Our real interest in not letting these people have their way is the essential
> interest that no commercial kings or dukes shall achieve a position superior to
> that of the State, and capable of forcing the State, which represents the whole
> public, to bend to their ends.

Here spoke Berle the academic, a leading expert on modern capitalism and
corporations. Roosevelt would have agreed with much of this, but there was
a difference. His commitment to a multilateral solution abided, whereas
Berle was being propelled by developments toward State-led bilateralism,
even so he still conceded:

> The sound solution is undoubtedly the President's, as embodied in the
> memorandum of his conversation with Welch Pogue, Robert Lovett, Edward
> Stetinnius and myself last November; but the problem of approaching it is
> not going to be easy.[43]

Of course it was not, and while practical contingencies pushed Berle toward
bilateralism, others pulled him toward the president's more internationalist
and liberal line. Berle recognized there were dangers in seeking safeguards

in the way that Pogue and others wanted because there would be knock-on effects. Other countries would seek the same, and before one knew it, air blocks would emerge, which he so feared. An acceptable compromise might be reciprocal or *"even general entry"* rights, while conceding some limitation on frequencies. This, for Berle, would be the second best option "if, as appears likely, American interests are so short-sighted as not to see that the doctrine of free air is their plainest road to superiority."[44]

A picture emerges from this of Berle still intellectually wedded in principle to liberal multilateralism, but pragmatically determined to enforce state responsibility over corporate power, ensure the predominance of U.S. civil aviation internationally after the war, and maintain American security. Unfortunately, goals dictated by principle and pragmatism were in conflict and mutually endangering each other. Berle found this hard. By mid-September his expectations were modest.

> My estimate of the situation is that when all is said and done we shall be able to conquer the blocked air theory generally throughout the world except in Soviet Russia. We shall probably have to accept the formula of general or reciprocal access—that is, that countries in which we land have a right to land in our country—which is all to the good; but will have to accept likewise a limitative formula by which the number of landings is held down. Future conferences and struggles will probably revolve around the problem of whether the limitation of landing rights is inherently desirable with the public interest being heavily against such limitation and commercial interests generally plugging for it.[45]

By October, Berle was even less sanguine, and the more he doubted the prospects for a liberal multilateral arrangement, the more emphasis he found himself giving to the necessity of immediately securing air rights as broadly as possible for the United States. That meant stronger and stronger opposition to any international authority with regulatory powers and greater insistence on moving out through bilateral agreements, all of which pushed the British and the Canadians into more defensive positions that in turn seemed to threaten U.S. interests. This was a vicious circle. On October 2 Lester Pearson reported from Washington that in conversations that morning, Berle wavered between multilateralism and bilateralism and only envisaged provisional agreements being arrived at in Chicago. Such agreements should come into effect immediately, in the United States by executive action requiring no congressional authority. Berle thought that rates could be satisfactorily controlled, even though the CAB currently lacked authority to do so, but he was "emphatic that the United States would not at this time agree to setting up of an effective International Air Transport Authority with regulating powers." For the Canadians there seemed to be only one bright spot. Since March they had been struggling to modify their draft convention to meet American objections. This was not easy, but Clarence Howe made one suggestion that Berle seemed to embrace keenly. A key issue for the Americans was that there should be a liberal capacity and frequency regime in order for operations to expand and U.S. airlines to garner maximum market share. Berle had recognized that there would probably have to be some compromise on this, and Howe's proposal fit the bill. It later became known as the escalator clause at Chicago and was a device that allowed market demand to determine things and avoided the imposition of politically predetermined limits of the kind the British favored. In short, if a service was running at 65 percent capacity or above, then this could trigger the introduction of greater capacity and frequency.[46]

However, the overall impression left on Pearson was that Berle was "pessimistic" about Chicago. On October 9 Berle's pessimism was increased when he heard that Lord Swinton would lead the British delegation, replacing Beaverbrook, who had recently resigned the aviation brief. Swinton was widely thought to be anti-American and an old-school imperialist, and despite reassurances to the contrary from Michael Wright from the British Embassy, Berle became troubled and wondered if the British "had now gone in for a closed sky and exclusive arrangements, or whether they were maintaining the general cooperative understanding reached between Churchill and myself."[47] Berle now doubted that agreement on technical matters could be reached never mind on an international authority. He thought that both those clusters of concern would have to be referred to ongoing committees and future conferences. The best that could be hoped for was some kind of agreement on general principles such as equal access and nondiscrimination. This did not augur well and was a rather strange position to take for the senior representative from the leading aviation power on the verge of a conference that his own president had called.

CHICAGO: EVERYTHING BUT ESCALATION AND FIFTH FREEDOMS

The International Civil Aviation Conference convened at the Stevens Hotel Chicago on November 1, 1944. Berle was appointed conference chairman, Pogue led the American delegation, Lord Swinton the British, and Howe the Canadian. Other important figures on the American side were William Burden, Senators Brewster and Bailey, and Fiorella LaGuardia, best known for his time as mayor of New York. On the British team were Sir Arthur Street and George Cribbett, but Swinton was also advised and controlled by a special committee in London chaired by Beaverbrook and including other senior figures such as Stafford Cripps.[48] Key on the Canadian side was Herbert Symington, whose advisers included J. R. Baldwin and Escott Reid.

Opening the conference Berle delivered a message from the president at the heart of which was the hope that

> ...you will not dally with the thought of creating great blocs of closed air, thereby tracing in the sky the conditions of possible future wars.[49]

Some delegates did dally with the idea, but at the end of the day great blocs were avoided. Significantly, there was widespread acceptance of the rights to transit and stop, and these were important achievements. They were a necessary condition for a successful worldwide commercial regime, but they did not speak directly to its functioning character. With regard to that crucial matter the conference was an extraordinary fiasco. The causes were legion: a confluence of lack of preparation, an inappropriate venue that was too much in the public gaze, delegate exhaustion, American and British conflicting priorities, and confusion and divisions within the American camp. Franklin Roosevelt's vision of commercial freedom of the air was not to be realized.[50]

The United States was the key player, but it did not have a full or coherent international plan to present. It had been propelled into the conference by the press of events. There was no consensus between the main players. Britain and the United States struck agreement in April that the Balfour Report could act as the basis for future talks, but they insisted on so many caveats that it was meaningless and that became evident in the first exchanges between Berle and Swinton in Chicago. When Berle said Britain was demanding such rigid controls that it amounted to assigning part of American traffic "to support British aviation," which was as unacceptable now as when it had been broached last spring, Swinton responded, "Did you really think we were going to change our minds?"[51] Those exchanges rudely dispelled any remaining delusions largely formed as a result of what Berle had heard from Churchill in April. The Canadians wanted to be honest brokers and had been amending their Draft Convention since April to make it more amenable to the Americans, but at the heart of it remained a strong regulatory authority and that, as Berle had repeatedly and emphatically explained, was unacceptable to America.[52] To make matters even more difficult for the delegates, the conference opened less than a week away from the U.S. presidential election, and the political problems and sensitivities that presented were compounded by a decision that Berle led the president into making in September. Berle said to Roosevelt that

> ...if he could find it in his heart to have this [the Chicago conference] open to the public and the press from the very beginning I thought we could come in with a proposition which would so powerfully engage public sentiment

that few, if any, countries would care to exclude the United States from its legitimate rights, and that other differences could either be composed in committee or left for later negotiation. The President agreed....[53]

So, added to the mix of difficulties, the delegates would have to play to both the U.S. domestic and the international audience. This would prove deeply problematical for the American delegation caught between nationalist sentiment in Congress and the general public, which was determined that the United States should not "give away" its rightful dominance in civil aviation, and internationalists, who insisted that an equitable solution had to be found not just for the sake of aviation commercialism, but for the sake of future peace. Holding on to any kind of middle ground invited a two-front war.

Berle's expressions of pessimism in the preceding months seem well-founded; however, they had been prompted largely by the adversarial position of the British, whereas equally important for the fate of Roosevelt's vision for commercial multilateralism were deep divisions in the American delegation. The most obvious and widely known problem was posed by Owen Brewster—the senator from "Pan Am," but there was in fact a more important division with others pitched against the idea of any multilateral agreement applying to commercial rights. And, one senses that even Berle was not fully committed to the president's position. He doubted that it could be achieved, and it then became rather like a self-fulfilling prophesy with him overrobustly seeking American national interests that further compromised the chances for commercial multilateralism. What all Americans wanted was immediate scope for their airlines to move out onto foreign routes. That meant reaching agreement on interim arrangements that condoned bilateral agreements and also ideally that there should be multilateral agreement on the rights of transit and stop. But the way this was pursued and prioritized at Chicago by the Americans virtually guaranteed that agreement on a multilateral commercial regime was unlikely.

Out of all the complexity and maneuverings of the conference, it is possible to identify four crucial moves. The first was noncontroversial and involved the steady movement toward agreement on an international authority that would be a consultative clearing house for issues, would collect data, and administer the technical and safety side of international aviation. It emerged as the Provisional International Civil Aviation Organization, later permanently established in Montreal.[54] It was the other three that were controversial.

The first of these was agreement on an interim period in which nations could freely pursue bilateral agreements generally according to standard clauses that stipulated rights of equal access and nondiscrimination but "imposed no restrictions on capacity, rates or fares, or traffic generated and carried between third countries."[55] This was the continuation of Pogue's much-beloved move-out policy, and it was the first matter agreed upon at Chicago. There was a vague understanding that such agreements would have to come in line with whatever was eventually agreed at Chicago, but more likely thereafter in subsequent committee and conference work. The idea of this kind of free-for-all in the interim was anathema to the Canadians, who had consistently insisted on the merits of strong international regulation, among other reasons to prevent U.S. dominance. Symington was initially appalled at these proposals, arguing that the conference had been called to reach multilateral not bilateral agreements. However, he and Howe were preeminently practical men, and they knew better than any that Canada's main interest, namely, access to transatlantic traffic, would be secured through their direct relations with the United States and Britain rather than through any international agreement. In any case, as a contiguous state to the United States, aviation relations would not be automatically embraced by an international agreement. In the light of this and seduced by the idea of the Canadian Draft Convention taking center stage as the basis for continuing talks, the Canadians agreed "to waive parts of their plan which call for strict international regulation of air routes, rates, and frequency of service in the interim period."[56] This was agreed by November 6 and essentially delivered to Pogue and those who favored a robust form of bilateralism what they wanted. For the rest of the conference, while delegates struggled to try to formulate an acceptable multilateral commercial regime, the United States plowed ahead with bilateral talks with a wide range of countries represented in Chicago.

The second was the rights to transit and stop: Freedoms 1 and 2. From the start both Britain and the United States were willing to accept these for the rather compelling reasons that Britain needed rights in Hawaii to cross the Pacific and the United States in Newfoundland to cross the Atlantic.[57] In contrast the Canadians wanted to insist that they should only be granted after a satisfactory commercial regime had been agreed upon, because otherwise they would have prematurely ceded their main bargaining chips. During the conference Freedoms 1 and 2 were dealt with in conjunction with Commercial Rights 3 and 4 and later 5, but when it seemed clear that agreement could not be reached on that basis, both LaGuardia and Symington prompted negotiations that eventually led to a separate agreement. As LaGuardia put it, everyone is against bad weather, but they wanted more than technical agreements and something done for commercial aviation. It was through the Two Freedoms Agreement that was proposed by Britain in the end and widely accepted. For Pogue and others who preferred bilateral negotiations, this was equivalent to a squaring of the circle.[58] They had the best of all possible worlds. Not only could there be a free-for-all that would allow U.S. airlines to expand, but that would be facilitated by the agreement on transit and stop, the sort of multilateralism that Pogue had always favored. This opened the world to U.S. airlines without the tedious bilateral negotiations that would be required to cross countries to get to major commercial gateways. For Pogue, things could not get better than this. In fact, for him and others in the U.S. delegation, signing up to a commercial multilateral agreement had always been seen as a retrograde step. Now it would be tantamount to folly. This at least partly accounts for the failure to reach agreement on a multilateral commercial regime at Chicago.

CHICAGO: THE "BURLESQUE"—ESCALATION AND FIFTH FREEDOMS

Finally, and most controversial of all, at Chicago was the Fifth Freedom. All negotiations between Britain and the United States prior to Chicago were on the basis of an exchange of the Four Freedoms, invented by the Canadians and embodied in their Draft Convention, which became the focus for negotiation. However, at a crucial point in the conference, the Americans insisted on introducing the Fifth Freedom and applying the escalator clause to it. This meant that increased frequencies and capacity would be determined on a route from New York to London and on to Paris not only by increases in load factor from New York, but by increases at London as well. This was the immediate issue that prevented the creation of a multilateral commercial regime at Chicago, but it is important to interrogate the evidence to see if a more important underlying cause prevented agreement.

Opening statements by the British and the Americans clearly showed them to be at loggerheads. Swinton stood by the British White Paper and a powerful regulatory authority, and in response Berle explained:

> ...to the Government of the United States, [this] is the cardinal difficulty— there has not as yet been seriously proposed, let alone generally accepted, any set of rules or principles of law by which these powers could be guided. Thus it is proposed that an international body should allocate routes and divide traffic, but a great silence prevails when it is asked on what basis should routes be allocated or traffic divided; or even, what is "equitable", in these matters.[59]

Barely four days later Berle, even though acknowledging that the "toughest issue" concerning quotas and frequencies remained unresolved, confided to his diary: "The major issues have been met and cracked...the climax has been reached and passed...." On what possible basis did he make these extraordinary claims? While there had been some movement on the toughest issue with the British now prepared to accept the more liberal provisions embodied in the Canadian Draft Convention, one suspects that Berle was so upbeat because developments elsewhere were delivering to the Americans what they wanted. The Canadians had agreed to waive the regulatory powers of the international authority in the interim period clearing the way for bilateral negotiations, and even Swinton was reconciled to this.

> The issue of whether the international organization should have "power" or whether it should be a consultative body: On analysis this issue ceases to be very frightening. Lord Swinton tonight over cocktails agreed with me that for the interim period that authority had to be consultative in any event.[60]

The United States engaged with as many countries as possible and according to Berle they were clamoring for agreements with the United States at Chicago. Swinton saw the writing on the wall, and after saying at the outset that he was not in Chicago to talk routes, now indicated that services would have to start "substantially at once" and that these would be forthcoming after the conference.[61] Furthermore, on other key issues, consensus was emerging: rights to transit and stop were to be exchanged between friendly states and minimum rates at least were to be established. Everything was opening up for U.S. airlines and their main fears of unfair price competition via cutthroat subsidized pricing were being taken care of. The way was clear for Berle to start negotiations looking to bilateral agreements, and he did with Portugal, Spain, Belgium, Iceland, Greece, Turkey, Sweden, Czechoslovakia, Poland, Lebanon, Iraq, and Canada.[62] No wonder he thought that the main issues had been met and cracked. From one perspective they had, at least so far as getting freedom for U.S. airlines to move out immediately in a favorable environment matters could hardly have gone better, but this perspective did not include a multilateral commercial agreement of the kind that Roosevelt wanted. Regarding that the main problem remained—traffic quotas and frequencies.

The British had at least signaled a willingness to move on what they had previously indicated as key issues for them—a powerful international regulatory authority and rigid allocation of capacity and frequencies. And for their part it looked as if the Americans would move toward at least some controls over traffic on the basis of the Canadian escalator clause being applied after initial fifty-fifty quotas were allocated for the start of operations. However, final consummation of all these matters still remained to be accomplished, and in the meantime there were already ructions within the U.S. delegation that augured badly for the idea of compromise.

An article in the *Chicago Daily Tribune* on November 3 ran a front page story reporting that the U.S. delegation were about to give away more than they needed until stopped by "valiant battling" by those opposed.[63] By November 9 Berle's suspicions that Senator Brewster had leaked the information for the story was confirmed. He had used Samuel Pryor of Pan American to feed it to the newspapers.[64] Berle was furious, and while Brewster was not the only one strongly opposed to giving things away to foreigners, he was the only one to make damaging leaks to the press. On November 26 Brewster wrote to Berle explaining that he had to leave Chicago because of prior commitments. He had been a pain for Berle throughout, and it was now unlikely that any multilateral commercial agreement would be made, but Brewster still could not resist a parting shot. He wondered why America could not continue its great civil aviation success story without change: "In the past two decades fifty nations have welcomed American air transports without suggestion of requiring reciprocal rights."[65] At least he made no bones about it. He was the most extreme opponent of any kind of compromise, but others though more closeted in their antireciprocity and antimultilateralism views were very reluctant to give things away as well, and as a consequence it was a real struggle for Berle to determine what American policy should actually be. Years after the event, Pogue, who we should remember led the American delegation at Chicago, echoed Brewster's sentiments: "We had immense advantages that we ought to be taking some credit for and some of these people were throwing it away I thought."[66] Some of those people were presumably Berle and Franklin Roosevelt. Elsewhere Pogue noted that Berle went along with the idea of a multilateral agreement even though he knew that members of the delegation opposed it: it was by no means just Brewster, Pogue in fact was leader of the camp.[67] He thought Roosevelt was too optimistic about a multilateral agreement: "We attempted to comply with his wishes..., but it became clear quite early in the meetings that this Agreement would not be acceptable."[68]

The story of the Fifth Freedom and the escalator clause raises a question about whether or not the U.S. delegation actually wanted a multilateral commercial agreement of the kind the president had instructed them to pursue. Detailed accounts of the story of the Fifth Freedom have been given elsewhere, and there is no need to repeat everything here, for present purposes the key issue is what exactly was the American delegation doing?[69]

The bare bones of what happened are as follows. On November 12 the Americans, Canadians, and the British hived off from the rest of the delegates to try to hammer out a commercial regime. They were in virtual session for two days. According to Berle's account, four main points of agreement, or at least near agreement, emerged. There was a compromise on allocation of traffic. Initial division of traffic by quotas was to be followed by the application of an escalator whenever load factors were 65 percent or above. There were American fears that if they did not go down this route, then they might have to accept even worse conditions in bilateral talks, especially with the British. "Our delegation does not like this, nor do I; but it was recognized in the Delegation discussions that we might be required to accept it."[70] Rather strangely, though, Berle seemed less enthusiastic about the escalator than he had been in previous exchanges about it with the Canadians. Perhaps he was now influenced by and was reflecting the critical attitude toward it as a solution from others in the U.S. delegation who were against any granting of automatic reciprocal traffic rights.

There were two caveats on the traffic allocation agreement. First, its provisions should not affect established business and traffic flows—something that helped the United States where it already dominated markets. Second, to protect states disabled in aviation by the war, there was a "birthright clause" assigning them traffic for a period of three years after which the normal provisions, namely, the escalator, would apply. All this reflected genuine compromise on the part of Britain and the United States. Swinton was as reasonably satisfied with this, as Berle appeared to be.[71] Second, there was movement on agreement about rates with the most likely solution being an operators' conference, recommendations from which would then be submitted for approval by government. Results would be reported to the international authority, but any enforcement would have to be by individual national governments. This very much reflected U.S. views, but was not uncongenial to the British. Third, negotiations had begun on the basis of the Canadian Draft Convention and the Four Freedoms. Berle later explained that the United States had argued for the Five Freedoms and that the British had eventually agreed, only to reverse themselves after further consideration. Berle acknowledged that there was a problem here for the British and that he tried to accommodate them in some way. He suggested for example that the last stop before a transoceanic leg should be exempt from Fifth Freedom traffic. Later this was superseded by the idea of a price differential: a local British service from London to Paris could charge less than Fifth Freedom offerings from a U.S. carrier. This was still an unresolved matter on November 14, and it was not until November 16–19 that attention focused again specifically on the Fifth Freedom. The fourth point concerned strong regulatory power for the international authority. Berle saw this was a touchy matter as both the British and Canadians were strongly wedded to it. However, he pointed out that given agreement on the three preceding points (even though as it transpired the third was in fact far from being resolved), such power became redundant. The authority would have no executive matters with which to deal. According to Berle, the British and the Canadians agreed, and Stokeley Morgan and Cribbett were assigned the task of drafting things for presentation to the rest of the conference.[72]

For the conference and in particular for Roosevelt's vision of a multilateral commercial regime, this was the high water mark. But soon the waters of hope ebbed away as controversy erupted again over the Fifth Freedom, introduced by the Americans in a new draft on November 16. The British had resisted this, but Canadian officials thought that they would probably have to give way in the end.[73] They did, but then the Americans asked for more on the weekend of November 17–19, and it was that which really caused problems. Part of the difficulty was that Swinton had accepted the escalator for Third Freedom traffic on the basis of corrupted instructions from London. The message said "accept the escalator" when, in fact, it should have read "do not accept." Given the sensitivity of the talks, Swinton felt honor bound to keep to his word and escalation therefore should be applied to Third Freedom traffic.[74] That was how things stood on November 17, and it looked as if a compromise had actually been agreed on these most difficult of issues. Then, on November 18, Berle insisted that the escalator should also apply to Fifth Freedom traffic. Initially he had been willing to accept some protection of local traffic by a price differential, which was still hugely difficult for the British, but when the Americans dropped the price differential, the situation became totally unacceptable.[75] It was this issue that prevented agreement on a multilateral commercial agreement.[76]

Berle's account portrays the American line as rational and commonsensible and Swinton and the British as difficult, unbending, and unreasonable, and hence the cause of the impasse. From the Canadian perspective of Herbert Symington, for whom incidentally Berle had nothing but praise for at Chicago, the blame for matters taking such a turn for the worse seemed to come from a rather different source.

> Much progress had been made and was being made when the United States suddenly demanded the addition of the Fifth Freedom.
> … This sudden move… greatly accentuated the difficulties as it introduced the factor of pick-up traffic in various countries flown through on long trunk routes, and correspondingly accentuated the importance and difficulties of the clauses previously drafted relative to the basis of initial allocations and the escalator increase.[77]

Symington added that Berle had an "anti-Anglo prejudice" manifested by "periodic temperamental outbursts." He thought that the United States was "plainly desirous of securing a large measure of domination in the air and is not prepared to surrender her chances by leaving them in the hands of others to approve or deny what it wants."[78]

J. R. Baldwin went even further in both his personal criticisms of Berle and suspicions about American motives. He thought Berle "almost feminine in his trait of having 'on' and 'off' days": maybe this was because he was so shunted about in the positions he found himself obliged to adopt during the conference.[79] Baldwin thought him "much afraid of the reaction of his senatorial advisers," and newspaper reports on November 23 claimed that Berle, after moving toward the British and Canadians on traffic regulation, had retreated again after pressures from his senatorial advisers.[80] On November 21 Baldwin thought that the conference had reached its nadir with Berle beginning to withdraw concessions already agreed upon. He acknowledged that Swinton was pretty unbending, but "justification for this position may be found in the U.S. tactics of raising a new demand every time Canada or the UK gave in on a previous demand."[81] Berle withdrew all reservations supposed to constrain the operation of Fifth Freedoms and was also "inclined to ask for more and more, including the dropping of the 'birthright' article which was intended to protect liberated areas."[82] In a plenary on the November 22 Symington and LaGuardia tried to reenergize things, or, as Berle commented, Symington proceeded "to blow the lid off." He was followed by LaGuardia, who noted that great progress had been made on technical matters, but without addressing issues of freedom of the air: "All the rest is sauce."[83] In fact, progress on commercial rights continued to elude the delegates, but, as already noted, a separate agreement on the Two Freedoms was struck.

Over the following few days the Americans continued to argue for untrammeled Fifth Freedom rights along with the escalator clause being applied to them and withdrew what had been previously agreed on traffic controls, the birthright clause, and the agreement on rates and were not prepared to review the latter until either agreement or a final breach had been made on the escalator clause.[84] The British made one last concession by suggesting unresolved questions such as those surrounding the application of the escalator be referred for adjudication by the new international authority. "By this move the United Kingdom delegation got itself on tenable ground *viz.* impartial decision on a disputed matter by an impartial board, and they clung to that position to the end."[85] At this point Symington approached Pogue to speak to the U.S. delegation in the hope that he could convince them that the British proposals "could well be accepted . . . , but he refused saying it was useless."[86] Things were now largely to do with damage control regarding political and public opinion. Canadian officials thought that Berle had abused his position as chairman of the conference from the start by statements to the press that simply reported American views. Needless to say this ratcheted things upwards and angered the British.[87] All this was part of the price to be paid for making the conference a public circus. Reasons of public and international opinion were largely why London accepted the Two Freedoms Agreement. As Dominions Secretary Amery explained, it would "strengthen our ground for standing firm over the unreasonable demands" of the Americans.[88] For his part Berle, wrote to Roosevelt on November 29 saying that the British wanted a quiet draw down of the conference, but he did not like that. He felt it might leave a wrong impression with the public, in particular that the British were martyrs to the cause of small nations being intimidated into accepting air services from the United States.[89]

Even before these shenanigans and grandstanding, Baldwin thought that the whole thing had degenerated into "Burlesque."

> I must say that I feel that the situation need not have got out of hand if Mr. Berle and the United States delegation had displayed greater generalship. The most charitable explanation is that inexperience and weariness led Mr. Berle to this situation. The most uncharitable explanation is that the conference has been allowed to get out of hand deliberately with the knowledge that any attempt to set up a useful organization will be frustrated by this course.[90]

If Baldwin was correct in his uncharitable interpretation, then Franklin Roosevelt's vision for a multilateral commercial regime was a casualty of American politics and differing views within the American delegation as much as, if not more so than, of the contrary policies of Britain and Canada. It was brought down by opposition to any kind of automatic multilateral exchange of commercial rights that would have destroyed the bilateral route favored crucially by Welch Pogue and others. Interestingly, reflecting on the Chicago conference thirty-five years later, Pogue commented:

> Some members of U.S. delegation ... argued that, for a short term advantage, the United States was being unduly generous in giving away the potentially rich United States air transport market for routes of limited value. To them a process of bilateral bargaining seemed better.
> ... The advocates of the latter position won the day.[91]

One reading of this could be that all he meant was that the United States in fact ended up engaging in bilateral negotiations: alternatively one could see this as a claim that the bilateralists actually won out at Chicago by raising the stakes so high on a multilateral commercial regime that it had to fail with the result that their "position won the day." This interpretation seems at least plausible, but remains tantalizing less than fully confirmed by hard evidence. In contrast there is no doubt about what Roosevelt wanted and intended.

The conference was in real difficulties, and Berle's authority was slipping away. The effects of his erratic, some thought poor, performance at Chicago were later compounded by changes of appointment in the aftermath of the presidential election. Berle lost his post as assistant secretary of state in charge of aviation on December 4. Pogue later saw conspiracy in this and suggested it contributed to the failure to reach a multilateral agreement, but the evidence is weak and circumstantial, and there are errors in some of the things that Pogue claimed. In any case matters were largely determined by the time Berle was told he had lost his job.[92] Berle, on November 21, turned to the president for help, asking him to try to persuade Churchill to intervene and instruct Swinton to accept American proposals.[93] The president sent robust messages, but only to be met with equally robust responses from Churchill and a determination not to budge.

Although the messages were robust, they were largely the work of Hopkins and later Dean Acheson, assistant secretary of state. There is a question as to just how much the president was on the ball. On November 20, after the difficulties of the Chicago conference had been spread across the newspapers repeatedly, he still felt able to write to Senator Bailey: "I feel that it is very important that the world as a whole get a good impression from the Conference. It is new ground, but it will be fine if we can please most of the world on this new subject, even if amendments to the policy are made later."[94] Roosevelt's health was not good. During the period of his correspondence with Churchill about the Chicago conference his blood pressure rose from 210/112 to 260/150. It is not suggested that this was because of the civil aviation controversy, but it is indicative of the stress he was under. He had just come through another presidential election campaign, and there were posts to shuffle and his inauguration to prepare for. The world situation was unbelievably complex and challenging. Greece and Italy, de Gaulle and France were all real headaches. Greece was about to descend into civil war, and on all these matters there were difficulties with the British. There was also the troublesome matter of planning another summit with Stalin as well as the relentless press of the ongoing military battles. On November 27 Roosevelt left for rest and recreation at his retreat in Warm Springs and did not return until after the conference ended. Various eyewitnesses commented on the way his behavior and appearance varied from buoyancy to being very low, frail, and exhausted. Just how much input and how sharp his judgment was about what to do with the difficulties in Chicago is rather a moot point.[95]

Roosevelt's first note was brief but pointed. It was drafted by Hopkins and focused on the picking up of intermediate traffic on long-haul routes as essential to their economic viability. This argument seems to have swayed the president because he stuck to this throughout the exchanges with Churchill. Essentially he argued that the British insistence on limiting Fifth Freedom traffic amounted to "strangulation" by limiting the number of planes irrespective of the traffic offering. The problem was that without the ability to top up with passengers at intermediate points on long-haul routes, planes would gradually fly fewer and fewer passengers as those disembarking were not replaced.[96] After Cabinet discussion of the matter and advice from Beaverbrook, Churchill responded by emphasizing the concessions on both sides and that agreement that had been reached by November 17 involving rates, initial traffic quotas, opening up British bases around the world, Five Freedoms, and escalation for Third Freedom traffic. He explained that the problem arose on the evening of November 18 when Berle demanded untrammeled Fifth Freedom traffic with the escalator applying to it as well. This could not be accepted "since they demand a share of the local traffic between two neighbouring countries by the aircraft of a third country far beyond that which the granting of the right to take up traffic on through service would warrant." Churchill suggested that the compromise reached by November 17 was wise and workable and should be accepted.[97]

Roosevelt's reply was again crafted by Hopkins, and again it was short, but this time barbed with blackmail. "We are doing our best to meet your Lend-Lease needs. We will face Congress on that subject in a few weeks and it will not be in generous mood if it and the people feel that the United Kingdom has not agreed to a generally beneficial air agreement."[98] Churchill was distressed and angered by Roosevelt's letter. Again he consulted the cabinet and Beaverbrook and found himself reiterating to the president the arguments he had previously laid before him but with more emphasis on the facts that Britain had agreed to throw open its bases for air transport around the world and that a wartime agreement between the United States and the UK greatly benefited the United States and disadvantaged the UK as the production of transport aircraft had been concentrated solely in American hands. Those two factors alone would give the United States a "flying start" and, combined with Berle's proposals for Fifth Freedom flights, could mean that Britain and many other countries would be simply "run out of the air" by U.S. airlines. The United States "would not only excel, as they are welcome to do on merits, but dominate and virtually monopolise traffic not only between our country and yours, but between all other foreign countries and British Dominions besides." He could not recommend such an agreement to Parliament: "Nor would I try." Finally, Churchill took the firm ground already adopted by Swinton and his delegation in Chicago and offered to accept arbitration on the outstanding points.[99] Roosevelt did not respond to the suggestion of arbitration, but tried to reassure Churchill of American good intentions, future support, and his country's commitment to fair play, but it was to no avail: the Chicago conference, so far as a multilateral commercial agreement was concerned, was beyond retrieval.[100]

AMERICAN TRIUMPH: ROOSEVELT'S LOSS?

The President... had in mind the body of law brought into existence by Hugo Grotius's famous essay on the freedom of the seas and hoped to transpose that doctrine into the field of air communications.[101]

Roosevelt did not achieve this in terms of a commercial regime, though one must not underestimate the importance of the International Civil Aviation Organization and the Two Freedoms Agreement. Pogue thought of the latter: "That result alone would have justified the holding of the Chicago Conference." Of course, Pogue would because it fitted his split agenda. This was what he wanted—transit and stop multilaterally with the commercial remainder reserved for bilateral negotiations. Over the following fifteen months the Americans moved relentlessly out through bilateral agreements culminating in the greatest prize of all an agreement with Britain in February 1946. This was indeed a triumph for the expansion of American airlines abroad, but this was not liberal multilateralism.

The president had throughout striven for a multilateral commercial regime with all Five Freedoms. He had never essentially wavered from this. However, if one were to argue that forces in the U.S. delegation, including Pogue, kept raising the bar so that a multilateral agreement would not be achievable, then was the president not complicit in this given the robustness with which he supported the American hard-line with Churchill? In short, did Roosevelt not realize that his demands to Churchill could not be met and thus the multi-lateral commercial regime would fall? This would be a perverse reading of Roosevelt given his previous consistency. His motive in robustly promoting Fifths and the escalator was not to derail multilateralism, but to try to salvage it. It seems clear that he was persuaded by his advisers that without Fifth Freedom escalator rights, international aviation really would be overrestricted and U.S. long-haul operations unviable without subsidies. Perhaps, if his health had been better things might have been different. Perhaps, if he had not been so tired he might have been more critical of the messages drafted by Hopkins and Acheson. And if he had not been so oppressed by other more critical war issues, he might have perceived the danger of the collapse of the proposals for a commercial regime and been willing to compromise more with Churchill. But all this is speculative: what happened, happened. Roosevelt acted in good faith to try to salvage a workable multilateral commercial regime. He failed, and his vision was not realized, but it abided for decades as an ideal to be pursued: a liberal multilateral regime of freedom of the air where airlines operated largely according to the market place and were freed from political regulation imposed by doctrine or national security imperatives.

ROOSEVELT'S LEGACY

...the objectives are rather simple...that we will have a free air...[1]
Franklin Roosevelt, October 1, 1943

LEGACY: SHORT TERM

Roosevelt did not live to see the resolution of Anglo-American civil aviation problems, but he had the consolation of seeing the American hand strengthen. The United States tried to get "as many gateways to Europe as possible and with no limitations on frequencies," and in January 1945 was on the verge of an agreement with Eire, which included Fifth Freedom rights that raised the specter for Britain of being bypassed by U.S. airlines refuelling and topping up their passenger numbers in Eire on their way to Europe.[2] When Churchill learnt of this, he was furious, writing to Roosevelt on January 27: "I cannot feel sure that this affair has been brought to your notice...."[3] There was no reply, but Roosevelt hesitated. When Churchill's message arrived, acting Secretary of State Joseph Grew was about to sign the agreement with Eire. Now Roosevelt asked him to justify that course of action. Grew explained that they had already signed similar agreements with Spain, Iceland, Denmark, and Sweden.

> All our people here including Civil Aeronautics Board feel signature of this agreement with Ireland is not only necessary as act of good faith but very much in best interests of United States. We feel in addition to the objections voiced by the Prime Minister there may be British aviation considerations behind his message. In any event, we feel we have gone so far in this matter we simply could not now turn back. Domestic consequences of refusing to sign might have repercussions out of all proportion to importance of civil aviation question.[4]

Roosevelt held Grew from signing until February 3, but that was all.[5] When the agreement was finalized, Churchill wrote again asking the president to "take the necessary steps to have the agreement annulled." Predictably, Roosevelt said there was no question of that: "I am sorry but there it is."[6] There followed a tense period in which both sides tried to establish routes and limit the other.

Jockeying for position continued after both Roosevelt and Churchill had departed from office to be succeeded by Harry Truman and Clement Attlee, respectively. But the British situation became dire with the atom bomb's sudden ending of the war. The hoped-for economic transition period for Britain with the continuing help of lend-lease was abruptly curtailed. Britain became a supplicant in Washington for financial help. With industry shattered, export markets depleted, and its currency fragile because of enormous debts, it was difficult to see how Britain would survive without U.S. financial assistance. That assistance was sought by Lord Keynes on behalf of the British government in the closing months of 1945. Succor from those talks came in the form of the Anglo-American Loan Agreement of 1945–46 providing a line of credit amounting to $3.75 billion, but in early 1946, it still required approval of the U.S. Congress.

British diplomats had tried to persuade other countries not to grant Fifth Freedom Rights to the United States, but that was difficult when they "had no incentives to offer."[7] Britain was prostrate economically, and everything depended on receiving help from the United States. It was in those circumstances at the end of January 1946 that British and American officials came together on the island of Bermuda to seek a settlement of their troubled aviation relations. There was hard bargaining, but the outcome was a forlorn conclusion. Civil Aviation Minister Lord Winster put his finger on Britain's vulnerability when toward the end of the proceedings, he wrote:

> ...if the Cabinet felt that the signing of the agreement was of vital importance from the point of view of our general relations with the United States and the consideration of the loan agreement by Congress, he was willing that our delegation should be authorised to sign.[8]

By this time not only was Britain dependent on the United States for financial help but the early signs of the Cold War also made it imperative for it to maintain good relations with Washington for security reasons. The British signed.

The United States achieved what it had always wanted on capacity and frequency: effectively airlines could mount whatever capacity and frequency they liked with only vague provisions for ex post facto adjustments if the operations of one side were substantially damaging the interests of the other, or alternatively there was the extreme measure of unilaterally denouncing the agreement. With these provisions agreed, the two sides exchanged the Five Freedoms for their airlines, which were to be substantially owned and controlled by their respective nationals. There was to be "fair and equal opportunity" for both sides.[9] In addition a pricing regime was agreed. The International Air Transport Association formed in the aftermath of Chicago would convene rate conferences to fix prices that would then have to be approved by government. Pogue, who attended Bermuda, argued strongly for this and for the necessary authority for the CAB to approve such prices: he succeeded. The Americans represented the acceptance of this price regime as a concession to the British, but this was simply not true. The Americans had always wanted price controls.

What emerged from all this was a postwar aviation regime that embodied some, but by no means all, of Roosevelt's liberal multilateral vision. The establishment of the United Nations International Civil Aviation Organization and the wide acceptance of the Two Freedoms Agreement were major achievements and fully in accord with what the president had sought. However, the commercial regime that was established fell far short of what he had hoped for. The rate conferences of the International Air Transport Association working in conjunction with processes of government approval provided order for pricing and avoided the dangers of cutthroat competition and the worst effects of subsidies, and again this was in harmony with what Roosevelt had sought. But elsewhere there were what he would have seen as serious shortcomings, which ran directly contrary to the principles of multilateralism that both he and Secretary of State Cordell Hull had done so much to promote and that the United States advocated in trade and monetary relations generally for the new postwar economic order. Instead of multilateralism, there was a lack of uniformity and the economic playing field for aviation remained very uneven. The Americans held Bermuda up as a model for the future for all other countries to follow: this provided some harmonization for the international regime, and it was the closest they could get to a common international agreement. Whether others would actually follow the model, however, was another matter. In fact they did not, and agreements and practices grew up that restricted commercial freedom and penalized the traveling public.

What had been achieved was certainly more liberal and internationalist than had existed in the interwar period. The regime operated in a way that allowed international aviation to expand and U.S. airlines to thrive, and that was what Roosevelt had sought. While his vision was not fully realized, he had been instrumental in crafting an agenda that delivered results in

1946 and that could be used for further liberation from both nationalist and market-hostile regulation in the future.

LEGACY: THE LONG TERM

Much has happened since 1946, and as one moves away from Roosevelt's time, the harder it becomes to talk meaningfully about legacy. Nevertheless, it is possible to detect resonance from Roosevelt's ideas in six key developments since the Bermuda Agreement. These are the aftermath of Bermuda; U.S. deregulation; Bermuda 2; the creation of the Single European Aviation Market; U.S. "open-skies" policy; and the attempt to create a transatlantic Open Aviation Area.

After Bermuda a two-tier system developed. When the United States was party to a bilateral, it embodied the liberal provisions of Bermuda; if it was not, a more regulatory outcome was common. According to one highly experienced official, bilateralism always has a tendency toward commercial conservatism: "Airlines and governments sat down and said whatever this agreement [Bermuda] meant to say we aren't going to let you do more than we want to do."[10] The result in Europe was a pattern of government and industry collaboration and collusion. Airlines operated in an environment devoid of competition, full of government-favored instruments in dominant positions and under regulations that carved up the market and stunted development.[11] This was very different from what Roosevelt had envisaged, but little of this affected the United States directly and nothing happened to change things until the mid-1970s. Then things began to happen. A second postwar phase developed, partly prompted by a growing unease among the Europeans that Bermuda-style bilaterals gave away too much market share to U.S. airlines on the lucrative transatlantic routes, but more so by the emergence of economic and political ideas in the United States that advocated deregulation.

In his first message to Congress on March 4, 1977, President Carter urged "Congress to reduce Federal regulation of the domestic commercial airline industry."[12] Subsequently, the 1978 Airline Regulatory Reform Bill initiated rapid moves to a free untrammeled domestic airline system. It also set in motion forces that dispelled the conventional wisdom that economies of scale did not apply to the airline industry.[13]

What was discovered were economies of scale..., i.e. you organized your system in such a way that you were able to consolidate large amounts of traffic at a point and then redistribute that traffic. For each unit...that you flew, if you had...higher load factors on that piece of equipment in effect you had a more productive piece of equipment—a more productive unit of production.[14]

This was the hub-and-spoke configuration of routes. Well-positioned through their domestic interconnected hubs and their vast number of feeder spokes to assemble large numbers of passengers, domestic U.S. operators now used their dominance over that market, approximately 40 percent of the entire world's, to thrust out their spokes into the international sphere. They did so in the context of two other moves by the Carter administration: the first was a challenge mounted by Chairman of the CAB Alfred Kahn to International Air Transport Association price-fixing, which gradually but ineluctably led to price competition; and second, the pursuit of even more liberal air service agreements than Bermuda, promoted—though not as much as Carter would have liked—by the International Air Transportation Competition Act, 1979.[15]

This U.S. surge toward making international aviation more of a straightforward commercial affair ran into its most serious difficulties with the British. The result was a conference replay of 1946 resulting in Bermuda 2. In 1976, the British were so disgruntled with the market share held by U.S. carriers that they took the nuclear option and denounced Bermuda 1. The United States and Britain then had under the terms of that agreement twelve months in which to negotiate an alternative. The outcome was to be rued by the Americans for the next thirty years. They were simply outnegotiated and outmaneuvered. The net result, as one senior U.S. official put it, was that

> every city pair market is restricted in terms of entry. Every city pair market is restricted in terms of capacity. Every city pair market is restricted in terms of the fares the airlines may charge the passengers. There is no aspect of the market that is not being regulated pursuant to UK insistence.[16]

Even worse, in follow-up talks in 1980, the Americans fell into more difficulties. The British entwined them in their traffic distribution policy for London airports such that only Pan American and TWA or their corporate successors were allowed to fly into Heathrow. This turned out to be the ace in the hole for the British over the following twenty-five years. When the Americans subsequently argued for a more liberal air service agreement, and most importantly for freer access to Heathrow—the busiest international hub in the world—the British response was always: "Why should competition stop at the water's edge? We'll open up Heathrow and our cabotage if you'll open U.S. cabotage and/or change airline ownership and control rules." Either change would have allowed British airlines to arrange better feeder and distribution services for their transatlantic flights in the United States by setting up operations within the U.S. domestic market. The British argued that without such services they could not compete on an even playing field with their U.S. counterparts and that reserving 40 percent of the world's entire airline market as U.S. cabotage was simply too protectionist. The British and the Americans never resolved this impasse, at least not by themselves.[17]

While Britain seemed unrelentingly regulatory to Americans, its behavior in Europe was very different. There it took the lead and worked closely with the European Commission toward creating a competitive free aviation market for the European Community that reflected many of the New Deal's values of responsibly controlled private enterprise. In a series of three packages of reform between 1987 and 1992, the Single European Aviation Market gradually came into being: it reached internal completion in 1997.[18] The market was subjected, at least in operations within the European Community, to common rules. Competitive pricing and liberal licensing rules were adopted and pooling arrangements outlawed, new routes were opened, capacity and frequency controls were removed, and cabotage was abolished and the concept of community airlines adopted, which meant any airline from within the European Union could operate anywhere within the union. For all intents and purposes, airlines ceased to be national corporations and became European. That was fine internally, but it would eventually cause immense problems externally as all existing bilaterals with other countries, including the United States, had national, not community, ownership and control clauses, as such they were now illegal.

As the Single European Aviation Market came into being, the United States became even more aggressive in its overseas aviation policy. Among other things, there were nagging fears about the European Union becoming an economic fortress, leading to curbs on commercial rights for U.S. airlines. The United States began to pursue what it called "open-skies" agreements that embodied free pricing, and unrestricted Third, Fourth, and Fifth Freedoms. They also offered a tempting incentive: antitrust immunity for alliances between U.S. and foreign airlines. This would allow airlines of those countries that entered "open-skies" agreements with the United States to moderate the problem of getting U.S. feeder and distribution services, something that Britain had so often complained about. They could benefit from their U.S. alliance partner's feeder and distribution services to and from international gateways in the United States. The first "open-skies" agreement to be consummated in Europe was with the Netherlands in 1992. Over the years many more followed. Britain alone of the main aviation nations in Europe resisted. Then everything was tipped into turmoil by the European Court of Justice in November 2002. It ruled that bilateral air service agreements between the United States and Member States of the European Union were illegal because they contained nationality clauses and did not recognize the concept of community air carriers. It was in the interests of both sides to remove this legal anomaly, but to the astonishment of many, the Europeans came up with the most radical of solutions.[19]

As a matter of urgency the European Council of Ministers granted authority to the European Commission to negotiate a new community-wide agreement with the United States. Full-scale talks began with the commission delegation led by Michael Ayral and the U.S. side led by Richard Byerly, deputy assistant secretary of state for transportation affairs. The United States had its standard "open-skies" agenda, including the offer of antitrust immunity for alliances and unlimited Fifths within and beyond the European Union: from the European perspective, Fifths within the European Union now amounted to cabotage rights. The European agenda was more radical. The Europeans wanted to create an Open Aviation Area that would merge European and U.S. cabotage and that would permit 100 percent ownership and control of U.S. airlines by Europeans and vice versa, and a harmonization of competition and safety regulations.

The negotiations were long drawn out, partly because the European Council of Ministers rejected a draft agreement in 2005 on the grounds that it did not go far enough on the crucial issue of ownership and control. The U.S. Department of Transportation now tried to circumvent congressional hostility to changes in ownership and control by an executive reinterpretation of existing rules to make them more liberal, but the political outcry was such that they had to abandon this tactic, and talks with the Europeans ground to a halt in the second half of 2006. Then, in early February 2007, the Transport Council president, Wolfgang Tiefensee, and the commissioner for transport, Jacques Barrot, went to Washington to see if they could revive things. They succeeded, and two rounds of negotiations followed, which resulted in agreement in March, subject to ratification by the European Union Transport Council.

U.S. law on control and cabotage remained unchanged. Europeans were allowed to buy more of an American airline's nonvoting stock, but the limitation on ownership of 25 percent of the controlling voting stock remained. The Americans made concessions elsewhere, but did not depart very substantially from traditional U.S. "open-skies" agreements, except very importantly for recognition of the concept of EU Community carriers. Furthermore, the one thing that might have persuaded the U.S. to embark upon a more radical path appeared to have been given away because the Americans were granted open access to Heathrow. When the agreement came before the European Transport Council, the decision was unanimous in favor of acceptance, but the British managed to persuade Jacques Barrot to make clear that if there were no movement on U.S. ownership and control by 2010 in the follow-on stages of negotiations, then the EU would have the option of withdrawing from the agreement. There have been subsequent talks, but little advance has been made on what was agreed in 2007.

*   *   *

Where would Roosevelt have stood on all of this and to what extent do these developments naturally flow from the regime that he promoted in the Second World War?

Roosevelt's use of the term "free air" is not all that far removed from the idea of "open-skies," particularly when one also recalls his admonitions to colleagues in November 1943 that they must aim for a "very free interchange" that would allow airlines to take on and discharge passengers in other states. He wanted international agreement on the liberal operation of the Five Freedoms. In many ways, at least prior to the Open Aviation Area, he was still ahead of developments in his talk of multilateral agreements automatically granting freedoms that would allow international commercial aviation to flourish without restrictive controls on capacity and frequencies.

Regarding his notions on competition and pricing, the picture is more ambiguous. Roosevelt had opposed Pan American's monopoly, but conceived of U.S. airlines being allocated regions within which to operate and compete against foreign airlines. Head-to-head competition by U.S. airlines on the same routes was beyond his vision in 1943 and 1944. Also, on pricing, although the Americans ducked and weaved on this with the British and tried to give the impression that they were granting a concession on price-fixing at Bermuda in 1946, in fact they always favored price regulation and became even more strongly so after trouble with Pan American and what amounted to predatory pricing in 1945 that threatened other American airlines as much if not more so than foreign. There had always been concern about the danger of cutthroat competition, but during the Chicago conference, Roosevelt argued with Churchill: "It has been a cardinal point in [U.S.] policy throughout that the ultimate judge should be the passenger and the shipper."[20] In other words, let the market decide wherever possible. If one were to imagine him remaining steadfast to that principle as aviation developed over the following decades, it does not seem too fanciful to imagine that Roosevelt would have found little difficulty with head-to-head competition between U.S. airlines and competitive pricing. Indeed, one might imagine him championing such developments.

Finally, cabotage and ownership and control: these two areas are the ones in which the Europeans, after trailing for so long on U.S. liberal coattails—coattails that Roosevelt did much to design—have taken the lead. The European Union's demand for common cabotage and ownership and control rules were not acceptable to the United States. This is partly to do with the protectionism of labor, the pilots, and some members of Congress, but also hinges on widespread concern about defense and security, in particular regarding the Civil Reserve Air Fleet and the importance of keeping it under direct American control. During the war, internationalist proposals for the free operation of airlines were dubbed "globaloney," but such "globaloney" rarely went so far as to consider the idea of opening cabotage and abolishing national ownership and control regulations. In that sense they were beyond the ken of most policy-makers at that time, including Roosevelt. So, it might be stretching things to suggest that Roosevelt ever seriously entertained such radical proposals. And yet during the war he argued for liberal access for all nations' airlines to islands in the Pacific, an extremely sensitive strategic area for the United States. If strategic concerns in the Pacific did not trump commercial needs for Roosevelt in 1944, is it beyond the bounds of credibility that similar strategic concerns would have failed to override the temptation to open U.S. cabotage and change U.S. ownership and control rules in 2007? After all, these changes would have created a truly open and free transatlantic commercial aviation market, which would chime harmoniously with Roosevelt's general and many of his specific views on civil aviation and freedom.

This book has tried to make it clear what Roosevelt thought about civil aviation, what policies he favored and tried to nurture, how he struggled with forces at home and abroad, and what emerged from all this at the war's end. It has also tried to identify Roosevelt's legacy in later developments. The commercial civil aviation regime that we now have seems, from some perspectives at least, to owe much to Roosevelt and his vision for postwar civil aviation. Roosevelt strove for a multilateral commercial regime in 1944 and failed. Sixty-three years later the United States struck what was effectively a multilateral agreement with the European Union to enable U.S. airlines to enjoy the Fifth Freedom with every member state of the European Union. Is it really too fanciful to claim that here is justification and consummation of Roosevelt's liberal multilateralist vision? It might not be globally embracing, but there are those who have ambitions to roll it out beyond the United States and the European Union.[21]

There is a discernible thread that runs through, albeit with various snags along the way, from Roosevelt's ideas in the 1930s and 1940s to the present. What one makes of those snags will largely determine views of the extent to which Roosevelt bequeathed a legacy to the industry and how much of his vision was lost or changed in the political battles of what have been termed elsewhere as "peaceful air warfare."[22]

NOTES

PREFACE

1. Cabotage is, thanks to author Alan Dobson, my new word for the day. His description is full and precise; mine is less restrained—and imbued with traditional American liberalism (economic version): Cabotage is that inane and sometimes insane combining of nationalism and the search for money that restrains trade while preventing thee and me to travel inside our own country on any but airlines owned by our own nationals. One effect is micronations or nations with microeconomies leasing (rarely can they buy) aircraft, painting them over with the national colors, hiring foreign pilots, and losing money. Go figure! Even a major nation like Great Britain seems to have cut off its nose to spite its face by insisting on "cabotage." Why would a nation with so much invested in tourism do anything to slow the flow? Dreams of (a lost) empire? National pride? Apparently both played a role, but I leave that story to Alan Dobson.
2. *Churchill & Roosevelt: The Complete Correspondence*, W. F. Kimball, ed. (3 vols; Princeton, NJ: Princeton University Press, 1984), III, 421.

CHAPTER 1   INTRODUCTION: TWO
CHALLENGES—ROOSEVELT AND CIVIL AVIATION

1. F. Handley Page, "The Future of the Skyways," *Foreign Affairs* 22, no. 3 (1944): 404–12, at 404.
2. Henry Luce, owner of the *Time-Life* publishing empire, popularized the idea of "the American Century."
3. Boaz Moselle et al., The Brattle Group, "The Economic Impact of an EU--U.S. Open Aviation Area" (2002), report for European Commission DG TREN, 2002, available at www.brattle.com/_documents/Publications/ArticleReport2198.pdf.
4. Warren F. Kimball, *Churchill and Roosevelt: The Complete Correspondence, 3 volumes* (London: Collins, 1984), for example, see volume 3, 402–7.
5. John Rawls, *A Theory of Justice* (Cambridge, MA: Harvard University Press, 1971), and Ronald Dworkin, *Taking Rights Seriously* (London: Duckworth, 1977). Both argue that *the* key trait of humanity is the individual's ability to exercise will and revise one's goals.

6. *Author interview with Welch Pogue*, August 1, 2000, Cosmos Club, Washington, DC.
7. For Roosevelt scholarship see: Robert E. Sherwood, *The White House Papers of Harry L. Hopkins: An Intimate History, 2 volumes* (London: Eyre and Spottiswoode, 1949); James McGregor Burns, *Roosevelt: The Lion and the Fox 1882–1940* and *Roosevelt: The Soldier of Freedom* (New York: Harcourt Brace and Jovanovic/World, Harvest editions, 1956 and 1970, respectively); Robert Dalleck, *Franklin D. Roosevelt and American Foreign Policy 1932–1945* (New York: Oxford University Press, 1979); Frank Freidel, *Franklin D. Roosevelt: A Rendezvous with Destiny* (New York and Boston: Little Brown and Company, 1990); Warren F. Kimball, *The Juggler: Franklin Roosevelt as Wartime Statesman* (Princeton, NJ.: Princeton University Press, 1991); and Jean Edward Smith, *FDR* (New York: Random House, 2008).
8. Joseph P. Lash, *Roosevelt and Churchill 1939–1941: The Partnership That Saved the West* (London: Andre Deutsch, 1977), 36–37; A. T. Mahan, *The Influence of Sea Power Upon History 1660–1783* (New York: Dover, 1987).
9. *Franklin D. Roosevelt Library* (hereinafter *Roosevelt Library*), Berle Papers, Box 169, Articles and Book Reviews 1964–67, folder Articles and Book Reviews 1965, "The International Civil Aviation Treaties Twenty Years later," Columbia University, March 1965.
10. Sherwood, *White House Papers of Hopkins,* volume 2, 705.
11. Alan K. Henrikson, "FDR and the 'World-Wide Arena,'" in *FDR's World: War, Peace, and Legacies,* eds. David B. Woolner et al (New York: Palgrave, 2008), 35–63, at 42.
12. For Roosevelt's modus operandi, see Kimball, *Juggler.*
13. See Burns, *Lion and the Fox,* .
14. Stuart Banner, *Who Owns the Sky? The Struggle to Control Airspace from the Wright Brothers On* (Cambridge, MA, and London: Harvard University Press, 2008), 7.
15. *United States v. Causby,* 328 U.S. 256 (1946).
16. "Convention Relating to International Air Transport," *Command. 266, 1919.*
17. See Alan P. Dobson, *Peaceful Air Warfare: The United States, Britain, and the Politics of International Aviation* (Oxford: Clarendon Press, 1991), *Flying in the Face of Competition: The Policies and Diplomacy of Airline Regulatory Reform in Britain, the USA and the European Community 1968–94* (Aldershot, UK: Avebury, 1995), and *Globalization and a Regional Response: The Origins, Development and Impact of the Single European Aviation Market* (London: Routledge, 2007).
18. Carl Solberg, *Conquest of the Skies: A History of Commercial Aviation in America* (Boston: Little Brown, 1979), 17 and 56.
19. Ibid., 63.
20. Dik Alan Daso, *Hap Arnold and the Evolution of American Air Power* (Washington, DC, and London,: Smithsonian Institute Press, 2000), 87.
21. Ibid., 101.

22. Anthony Sampson, *Empires of the Sky: The Politics, Contests and Cartels of World Airlines* (London: Hodder and Staughton, 1984), 40.

23. Solberg, *Conquest of the Skies*, 74; *Roosevelt Library*, Official File (hereafter *FDR OF*) 249, box 1, Folder: Aeronautics, March-April 1934, Air Transport Facts Published by Aeronautical Chamber of Commerce of America.

CHAPTER 2   ROOSEVELT'S INHERITANCE

1. Quoted in Marylin Bender and Selig Altschul, *The Chosen Instrument: Pan Am, Juan Trippe—The Rise and Fall of an American Entrepreneur* (New York: Simon and Schuster, 1982), 67–68.

2. For Hoover as secretary of commerce, see Joseph Brandes, *Herbert Hoover and Economic Diplomacy* (Pittsburgh, PA: University of Pittsburgh Press, 1962).

3. See R. E. G. Davies, *Airlines of the United States since 1914* (London: Putnam, 1982).

4. Carl Solberg, *Conquest of the Skies: A History of Commercial Aviation in America* (Boston: Little Brown, 1979), 64.

5. Along with M. Josephson, *Empire of the Air: Juan Trippe and the Struggle for World Airways* (New York: Arno Press, 1972) and R. Daley, *An American Saga: Juan Trippe and His Pan American Empire* (New York: Random House, 1980), Bender and Altschul, *Chosen Instrument*, provides a wealth of biographical detail about Trippe.

6. The five contract winners were National and Air Transport and Varney Airlines, which later became important components of United Airlines; Western Air Express, later absorbed into TWA; Colonial, which fed into Eastern Airlines; and Robertson Aircraft Company, which later became part of American Airlines.

7. *The Smithsonian National Aeronautical and Space Museum Archives*, Trippe Papers, box 8, folder: 1956, Newspapers and Magazines, draft chapter by Vern Haugland; *New York Times*, May 12, 1968, "Last of Aviation Pioneers Retires"; A. A. Arnold, *Global Mission* (Blue Ridge Summit, PA: Military Classics Series Tab Books, 1989), 115–16; and Daley, *American Saga*, 33.

8. Davies, *Airlines of the United States*, 114.

9. *Public Papers of Herbert Hoover 1929* (Washington, DC: Government Printing Office, 1974), 326, News Conference, October 15, 1929.

10. HR 11704, McNary-Watres Act, April 19, 1930.

11. W. S. Myers and W. H. Newton, *The Hoover Administration: A Documented Narrative* (New York: Scribner's, 1936), 430; Davies, *Airlines of the United States*, chapter 5.

12. Brandes, *Hoover*, 15–22.

13. R. K. Murray, *The Harding Era: Warren G. Harding and His Administration* (Minneapolis: Minnesota University Press, 1969), 410–11; R. L. Wilbur and H. M. Hyde, *The Hoover Policies* (New York, Scribner's, 1937), 215–16.

14. *FDR OF* 2955, box 2, CAB 1938–42, folder: CAB 1938, Clinton Hester radio speech, July 18, 1938.

15. *Report of The President's Aircraft Board* (Morrow Board), November 30, 1926 (Washington, DC: Government Printing Office, 1926).

16. Department of Commerce, Statement of Secretary Hoover on Commercial Aviation, Press Release, September 24, 1925 and Wilbur and Hyde, *Hoover Policies*, 215–18.

17. Ibid.

18. *Morrow Board Report.*

19. Dick Alan Daso, *Hap Arnold and the Evolution of American Air Power* (Washington, DC, and London: Smithsonian Institute Press, 2000), 114.

20. *National Archives*, Washington, DC (hereinafter *NA*), State Department decimal files, 841.796/288, Atherton to Secretary of State, March 21, 1930; *Public Papers of Herbert Hoover 1929*, "State of the Union Message to Congress," December 3, 1929, 419–20. These figures were so impressive they were reported in the British Cabinet: *British National Archives (BNA)*, CAB 24/201, CP(29)4, 14 January 1929, "Air Estimates."

21. Stuart Banner, *Who Owns the Sky? The Struggle to Control Airspace from the Wright Brothers On* (Cambridge, MA, and London: Harvard University Press, 2008), 200.

22. *United States v. Causby*, 328 U.S. 256 (1946).

23. John W. R. Taylor et al., eds., *The Guinness Book of Air Facts and Feats* (London: Book Club Associates, 1977), 107.

24. Solberg, *Conquest of the Skies*, 63.

25. For strategic importance of the Panama Canal, see David Haglund, "De-lousing Scadta: The Role of Pan American Airways in U.S. Aviation Diplomacy in Colombia, 1939–1940," *Aerospace Historian* 30 (1983): 177–90.

26. Arnold, *Global Mission*, 114–15.

27. Solberg, *Conquest of the Skies*, 90.

28. Andre Priest was appointed by Trippe as Pan American's chief engineer, and he developed early radio navigation aides: see Daley, *American Saga*, 36–55.

29. Paris Convention 1919, article 1. In Europe, George Holt Thomas, head of Air Transport and Travel, launched cross-channel services in 1919 and established the International Air Traffic Association of airline companies for the purposes of exchanging statistical information and cooperating in the fields of timetabling, safety standards, and fares. It was the issue of fares that was later to become an important matter for discussion by the United States at the 1944 Chicago International Civil Aviation Conference and immediately afterwards when the original IATA was reincarnated as the International Air Transport Association in 1945.

30. Shortly after the United States signed the Havana Convention, it was invited to attend an extraordinary meeting of the International Commission for Air Navigation in Paris. President Hoover's secretary of state, Henry Stimson, accepted and sent William McCracken in the hope that it might

be possible to agree to a reconciliation of the differences between the Paris and the Havana Convention. Unfortunately the talks dragged on, and U.S. Isolationism turned opinion against an agreement. Eventually, in 1934, President Roosevelt ended any further consideration of matters. See Alan P. Dobson, *Peaceful Air Warfare: The United States, Britain, and the Politics of International Aviation* (Oxford: Clarendon Press, 1991), 27–29.

31. Josephson, *Empire of the Air,* 52–53.
32. See Haglund, *De-lousing Scadta.*
33. *Foreign Relations of the United States* (hereinafter *FRUS*), 1929, volume 1, U.S. Government Printing Office: Washington, DC, 542–44, White to undersecretary of state and secretary of state to White, July 6 and 12, 1929; Wilbur and Hyde, *Hoover Policies,* 222.
34. Daley, *American Saga,* 86.
35. Josephson, *Empire of the Air,* 52–53.
36. *Roosevelt Library,* OF 2955, box 1 CAB 1936–1937, folder: CAB July–December 1937, Grover Loening, aeronautical adviser, to chair Maritime Commission, July 20, 1937.
37. Frank Freidel, *Franklin D. Roosevelt: A Rendezvous with Destiny* (New York and Boston: Little Brown and Company, 1990), 73; Jean Edward Smith, *FDR* (New York: Random House, 2008), 275–76; and Burns, *Lion and the Fox,* 139.

CHAPTER 3 AN UNEASY START: CIVIL AVIATION 1933–37

1. *Roosevelt Library,* Samuel I. Rosenman Papers, box 33, folder: aviation. Statement of the Administration's Attitude Towards Aviation, undated.
2. Frank Freidel, *Franklin D. Roosevelt: A Rendezvous with Destiny* (New York and Boston: Little Brown and Company, 1990), 85–105; James McGregor Burns, *The Lion and the Fox 1882–1940* (New York: Harcourt Brace and Jovanovic, 1956), 161–68; Elgin Groseclose, *Fifty Years of Managed Money: The Story of the Federal Reserve* (New York: Macmillan, 1966), 189–90. See also William E. Leuchtenburg, *Franklin D. Roosevelt and the New Deal, 1932–1940* (New York: Harper and Row, 1963).
3. Burns, *Lion and the Fox,* 170–71.
4. William E. Leuchtenburg, "The Roosevelt Reconstruction: Retrospect," in *Twentieth Century America: Recent Interpretations,* ed. Barton J. Bernstein and Allen J. Matusow, 2nd edition (New York: Harcourt Brace, Jovanovich, 1969), 224.
5. *The Brownlow Report: President's Committee on Administrative Management, Report with Special Studies* (Washington, DC: Government Printing Office), 1937.
6. George McJimsey, ed., *Documentary History of the Franklin D. Roosevelt Presidency, Volume 21: Executive Reorganization 1937–1939* (New York: Lexis Nexis, Reed Elsevier, 2004), 734–64.
7. Robert J. Serling, *When the Airlines Went to War* (New York: Kensington Books, 1997), 11.

8. Charles S. Rhyne, *Civil Aeronautics Act: Annotated with the Legislative History Which Produced It and the Precedents Upon Which It Is Based* (Washington, DC: National Law Book Company, 1939), 25.

9. Dick Alan Daso, *Hap Arnold and the Evolution of American Air Power* (Washington, DC, and London: Smithsonian Institute Press, 2000), quoting Arnold to his wife, Eleanor, April 9, 1934, source Robert Arnold Collection, Sonoma, California.

10. Samuel I. Rosenman, *Public Papers and Addresses of Franklin D. Roosevelt, 13 volumes* (New York: Random House, 1938–50), 141–42, 1934, FDR to secretary of war and note.

11. A. A. Arnold, *Global Mission* (Blue Ridge Summit, PA: Military Classics Series Tab Books, 1989), 148, 165; Daso, *Hap Arnold*, 133; Serling, *When the Airlines Went to War*, 9.

12. *FDR OF* 2955, box 2, folder: Aeronautics 1935, correspondence various.

13. *Roosevelt Library* FDR Personal File (hereafter *FDR PF*), 1820 speech material, box 8, folder: Speech Material Aviation, February–April 1934, statement by Ernest R. Breech, president, North American Aviation, March 7, 1934.

14. Burns, *Lion and the Fox*, 431.

15. Rosenman, *Public Papers and Addresses,* 138–40, at 138, 1934, Roosevelt to McKellar March 7, 1934.

16. Ibid., 140.

17. Ibid., 139.

18. Air Mail Act 1934, June 12, Public Law 308.

19. Serling, *When the Airlines Went to War*, 11.

20. *Roosevelt Library*, Papers of James Roosevelt, Secretary to the President 1937–38, box 3, folder: Aviation, January 17– 31, 1938, quoted in Grover Loening, "Bermuda Air Mail Proposal," January 1938.

21. Rosenman, *Public Papers and Addresses,* 147, and note 142, 1934; Marylin Bender and Selig Altschul, *The Chosen Instrument: Pan Am, Juan Trippe— The Rise and Fall of an American Entrepreneur* (New York: Simon and Schuster, 1982), 242.

22. Carl Solberg, *Conquest of the Skies: A History of Commercial Aviation in America* (Boston: Little Brown and Co., 1979).

23. Ibid.

24. *Report of the Federal Aviation Commission 1935, Summary of Recommendations* (Washington, DC: U.S. Government Printing Office, 1935), paragraph 19.

25. Ibid., paragraphs 1 and 21.

26. Ibid., paragraph 23.

27. Ibid., paragraph 22.

28. Ibid., paragraph 29.

29. *FDR OF* 2955, box 1, folder: CAB 1936–37, Comparison of Report of the President's Aviation Commission and HR 7273, at p.12 (25), sent to FDR by Lea July 23, 1937.

30. *Report of the Federal Aviation Commission Summary*, paragraph 4.

31. *FDR OF* 2955, box 1, CAB 1936–37, folder: Civil Aeronautics Board, 1936–June 1937, excerpts from Federal Aviation Commission Report.

32. *Report of the Federal Aviation Commission Summary*, paragraph 17.

33. Ibid., paragraphs 9 and 13.

34. Ibid., paragraph 25.

35. Ibid., paragraph 26.

36. Rosenman, *Public Papers and Addresses*, 68–70, 1935, A Message to the Congress on Air Transportation, January 31, 1935.

37. *Roosevelt Library*, FDR Speech Files (hereafter *FDR SF*) 763–79, box 21, folder: FDR Draft of Aviation Commission, January 31, 1935, Message to Congress.

38. This may seem a little ironic to those readers well versed in the chaotic manner of FDR's administrative style, but it was important to him that he could wield effective power when he needed to do so. This became ever more apparent with the "obstructionism" of the Supreme Court to aspects of New Deal legislation and the massive expansion of the role of government.

39. *Roosevelt Library, FDR SF* 763–79, box 21, folder: FDR Draft of Aviation Commission, January 31, 1935, Message to Congress.

40. *FDR OF* 2955, box 2, CAB 1938–42, folder: CAB, 1938, Clinton Hester speech on radio, July 18, 1938.

41. *Roosevelt Library*, Papers of James R. Rowe, box 6, folder: Civil Aeronautics Authority, address by Edgar S Gorrell, Civil Aeronautics Act of 1938 and Reorganization of 1940, National Aviation Forum, May 28, 1940. The ATA was formed in 1936 in the aftermath of the airmail cancellation fiasco to provide a more united voice for the airline industry: Gorrell was its first president.

42. Ibid.

43. *Schechter Poultry Company v. US* 1935, 295 US 495, Supreme Court.

44. *James Roosevelt Papers*, secretary to the president, 1937–38, box 3, folder: Aviation, December 1937, cited in Hester memorandum for James Roosevelt December 10, 1937.

45. Burns, *Lion and the Fox*, 345.

46. *Roosevelt Library*, Papers of R. Walton Moore, Aviation: Civil Aeronautics Authority: International Civil [1935–37] box 2, file, Aviation International Civil 1935, Air Transport Act of 1935, Mr. Truman Committee on Interstate Commerce subcommittee following report to accompany S. 3420, July 29, 1935.

47. *FDR OF* 2955, box 1, CAB 1936–37, folder: CAB 1936–37, Branch to McIntyre, May 27, 1937.

48. Ibid., Comment of the Post Office Department Upon the McCarran-Lea Bills, July 26, 1937, forwarded to FDR at his request by Harllee Branch, July 26, 1937..

49. Ibid., folder: CAB July–December 1937, Pending Aviation Legislation, Maritime Commission, July 1937.

50. Ibid., folder: CAB 1936–37, Lea to Rayburn, May 26, 1937.

51. On Kennedy's departure to take his new post as ambassador to Britain, Rear Admiral Emory S. Land became chairman of the Maritime Commission in February 1938.

52. *FDR OF* 2955, box 1, CAB 1936–37, folder: CAB July–December 1937, Report to chairman, Maritime Commission, from Grover Loening, aeronautical adviser, "The Pan American Foreign Air Monopoly," July 20, 1937.

53. *Complete Presidential Press Conferences of Franklin Delano Roosevelt, 25 volumes* (New York: Da Capo Press, 1972), 11, 59–60, no. 423, January 7, 1938.

54. Bender and Altschul, *Chosen Instrument,* 279–80. Authors in fact claim that Trippe used Friendly to feed drafts to Gorrell.

55. *Rowe Papers* box 6, folder: Civil Aeronautics Authority, "Government and Private Management in Air Transportation," Gorrell speech, February 5, 1940, Engineering and Maintenance Conference, Air Transport Association of America, Kansas City, Missouri.

56. Bender and Altschul, *Chosen Instrument,* tend to see most outcomes in civil aviation policy at this time as directly attributable to Trippe, but this is clearly influenced by overreliance on sources such as Trippe himself and his admirers. For Gorrell's role in engaging the airlines in the war effort, see Serling, *When the Airlines Went to War.*

57. Ibid., 278.

58. *FDR OF* 2955 box 1, folder: July–December 1937, Trippe to Commissioner Eastman, July 20, 1937.

59. Ibid., folder: CAB, July–December 1937, Secretary of Commerce Roper to FDR, July 26, 1937.

60. Ibid., folder: CAB, 1936–37, "Comparison of Report of the President's Aviation Commission and HR 7273" sent to FDR by Lea July 23, 1937.

61. *James Roosevelt Papers,* box 3, file: Aviation, October–November 1937, Secretary of Commerce Roper to Johnson Assistant Secretary of Commerce, October 22, 1937.

62. *FDR OF* 2955, box 1, CAB, 1936–37, folder: CAB, July–December 1937, FDR to McIntyre, May 31, 1937.

63. Beatrice Bishop Berle and Travis Beal Jacobs, *Navigating the Rapids 1918–1971: From the Papers of Adolf A. Berle* (New York: Harcourt, Brace, Jovanovich, 1973), 178, diary entry June 16, 1938.

64. *FDR OF* 2955, box 1, CAB, 1936–37, folder: CAB, 1936–June 1937, Lea to FDR February 8, 1937; Truman to FDR June 1, 1937.

65. Rhyne, *Civil Aeronautics Act,* 50.

66. *FDR OF* 2955, box 1, CAB, 1936–37, folder: CAB, July–December 1937, Lea to Rayburn and Rayburn to FDR May 26, 1937.

67. Ibid., FDR to McIntyre, May 31, 1937; and folder: CAB, 1936–June 1937, Lea to FDR and FDR to Lea (dictated by James Roosevelt), respectively, June 2 and 3, 1937.

68. Ibid., folder: CAB, July–December 1937, Lea to FDR July 30, 1937.

69. Ibid., Branch to McIntyre, July 27, 1937.

70. Ibid., folder: CAB, 1936–June 1937, FDR to Branch, July 31, 1937.

71. Ibid., Secretary of Commerce to McIntyre, September 15, 1937.

CHAPTER 4   THE PASSAGE OF THE 1938
CIVIL AERONAUTICS ACT

1. Two "autobiographies" of James Roosevelt shed little but anecdotal light on his work in the White House, and civil aviation is not mentioned. James Roosevelt with Bill Libby, *My Parents: A Different View* (Chicago: Playboy Press, 1976) and James Roosevelt and Sidney Shalett, *Affectionately F.D.R.: A Son's Story of a Lonely Man* (Harcourt Brace and Company, 1959): 233–50 and 290–311, respectively, cover his time in the White House.

2. Charles S. Rhyne, *Civil Aeronautics Act: Annotated with the Legislative History Which Produced It and the Precedents Upon Which It is Based* (Washington, DC: National Law Book Company, 1939), 52; Civil Aeronautics Act 1938, PL No. 706, seventy-fifth Congress, third Session, 23 June 1938.

3. James McGregor Burns, *The Lion and the Fox 1882–1940* (New York: Harcourt Brace and Jovanovic, 1956), 155.

4. See Samuel I. Rosenman, *Working with Roosevelt*, (London: Rupert Hart-Davis, 1952) passim; Frank Freidel, *Franklin D. Roosevelt: A Rendezvous with Destiny* (New York and Boston: Little Brown, 1990), 65–66.

5. Acknowledgments go to Charlie Whitham, who provided much of this information.

6. Bernard M. Baruch, *The Public Years* (London: Odhams, 1961), 14, 228, and 240.

7. Quoted from Warren F. Kimball, *The Juggler: Franklin Roosevelt as Wartime Statesman* (Princeton, NJ: Princeton University, 1991), 7.

8. Burns, *Lion and the Fox*, 155.

9. John Edward Smith, *FDR* (New York, Random House, 2008), 239, citing *New York Times,* July 5, 1929.

10. Baruch, *Public Years*, 237.

11. Ibid., 238, Baruch to J. Leonard Replogle, in 1937.

12. *James Roosevelt Papers*, box 3, folder: Aviation, January 17–31, 1937, Hester to James Roosevelt.

13. Ibid., folder: Aviation, October–November 1937, "Report by the Air Commerce Planning Committee of the Business Advisory Council for the Department of Commerce Supplement to Report of 30 June 1937," dated October 20 and approved Executive Committee November 5, 1937. Chairman of the committee was Robert G. Elbert, with members Henry I Harriman, Sidney J. Weinberg, Samuel P. Weatherill, Robert E. Wood, and William E. Woodward.

14. Ibid.

15. Ibid.

16. Ibid.

17. Ibid.

18. Ibid.

19. Ibid.

20. *Complete Press Conferences*, volume 11, 59–60, no. 423, January 7, 1938.

21. Ibid., and *FDR OF* 2955, box 1, CAB 1936–37, folder: CAB July–December 1937, secretary of commerce memorandum to McIntyre, September 15, 1937; *Rowe Papers* box 6, folder: Civil Aeronautics Authority, address by Edgar S Gorrell, "Civil Aeronautics Act of 1938 and Reorganization of 1940," National Aviation Forum, May 28, 1940. In his address Gorrell names September 27 as the date the Interdepartmental Committee on Civil Aviation Legislation (IDCCAL) was formed.

22. *James Roosevelt Papers*, box 3, folder: Aviation, October–November 1937, Secretary of Commerce Roper to Johnson, assistant secretary of commerce, October 22, 1937.

23. Ibid., Hester to James Roosevelt November 15, 1937, and Johnson to James Roosevelt, November 26, 1937.

24. Ibid., Johnson to James Roosevelt, November 26, 1937.

25. Ibid., folder: Aviation, December 1937, Hester to J. Roosevelt, December 30, 1937, with comparison attached. In fact it is no longer attached and does not appear until the next folder, see below in following note.

26. Ibid., folder: Aviation, January 1–16, 1938, "Major Differences in Policy between HR 7273 and the Subcommittee Print of the Civil Aviation Bill," undated. Authorship is unclear, but almost certainly Clinton Hester.

27. *Rowe Papers*, box 2, folder: Address by James Roosevelt, January 20, 1938, New York City Town Hall.

28. *New York Herald Tribune*, "Fight Brewing Over Proposed Aviation Board," February 5, 1938; *Airline Pilot*, "Pending Air Legislation Threatens to Become Factor in Federal Reorganization Plan," February 1938.

29. Beatrice Bishop Berle and Travis Beal Jacobs, *Navigating the Rapids 1918–1971: From the Papers of Adolf A. Berle* (New York: Harcourt, Brace, Jovanovich, 1973) , 178, entry June 16, 1938.

30. *James Roosevelt Papers*, box 3, folder: Aviation, January 1–16, 1938, "Major Differences in Policy between HR 7273 and the Subcommittee Print of the Civil Aviation Bill," undated.

31. Ibid.

32. Ibid.

33. Ibid., folder: Aviation, December 1937, Memorandum, Confidential to the secretary to the president [James Roosevelt], subject: Proposed Bill for Civil Aviation, December 1, 1937, no author indicated, but almost certainly from Grover Loening, Maritime Commission.

34. Ibid., Hester memorandum for James Roosevelt reporting on the President's Committee on Administrative Management views on the IDCCAL bill December 10, 1937, and Hester to James Roosevelt December 13, 1937, indicating the president's intention of speaking with McCarran and Lea.

35. *Roosevelt Library, Pare Lorenz Chronology*, meeting of McCarran with FDR, 12–12.15 P.M., January 4, 1938; Rhyne, *Civil Aeronautics Act*, 52.

36. Edward G. Hamilton, "Pending Air Legislation Threatens to Become Factor in Federal Reorganization Program," *Airline Pilot*, February 1938.

37. Rhyne, *Civil Aeronautics Act*, 52, citing McCarran Hearings on S. 3659, seventy-fifth Congress, third session.

38. Quoted from Michael J. Ybarra, *Washington Gone Crazy: Senator Pat McCarran and the Great American Communist Hunt* (Hanover, NH: Steerforth, 2004), 161.

39. *James Roosevelt Papers*, box 3, folder: Aviation, January 1–16, 1938, Hester to James Roosevelt. January 7, 1938.

40. Ibid., folder: Aviation, January 17–31, 1938, Hester to James Roosevelt, January 18, 1938.

41. Ibid.

42. Ibid., Hester to James Roosevelt, January 18, 1938, and "Section by Section Analysis of House Interstate Commerce Subcommittee Print of Civil Aviation Bill," undated. The differences included the IDCCAL's preference to favor Post Office authority over terminals, stops and airmail schedules, whereas McCarran and Lea favored vesting such authority in the CAA; the administration's wish to impose a legal maximum on mail rates; presidential authority over the CAA concerning the approval or disapproval of existing overseas operating rights; whether or not to rewrite the 1926 Air Commerce Act of 1926; over labor provisions; over proposals that the Maritime Commission should have the right to make loans for the construction of aircraft; over the administration's wish to prohibit ownership by an airline in any other aspect of aeronautics; over nomenclature of operating certificates—the IDCCAL preferred airline route certificates for domestic operations and airline operation approval certificates for foreign operations, whereas McCarran and Lea favored the blanket term certificates of convenience and necessity. Finally, while there was agreement on the regulation of domestic fares, there was not on international rates.

43. *James Roosevelt Papers*, box 3, folder: Aviation, January 1–16, 1938, memorandum for Senator Barkley from James Roosevelt, undated. On January 7 the president was asked in a press conference if he favored a three-man CAB: *Complete Press Conferences volume 11*, 59–60, no. 423, January 7, 1938.

44. *James Roosevelt Papers*, box 3, folder: Aviation, January 17–31, 1938, Hester to James Roosevelt January 18, 1938.

45. Ibid., Hester to James Roosevelt, January 23, 1938.

46. Ibid., Hester to James Roosevelt, January 26, 1938.

47. Ibid., Monroe Johnson to Hester, January 26, 1938, and Hester to James Roosevelt, January 25, 1938.

48. *James Roosevelt Papers*, box 3, folder: Aviation, March 1938, Memorandum for James Rowe from Hester, March 3, 1938.

49. Ibid., folder: Aviation, January 1–16, 1938, Hester to Senator Barkley, undated.

50. Hamilton, "Pending Air Legislation," ; see also *New York Herald Tribune*, February 5, 1938, "Fight Brewing Over Proposed Aviation Board."

51. *James Roosevelt Papers*, box 3, folder: Aviation, February 1938, memorandum Hester to Rowe, February 28, 1938.
52. Ibid., folder: Aviation, March 1938, memorandum for James Rowe, March 3, 1938, author not indicated, but almost certainly Hester.
53. Ibid.
54. Ibid., McCarran to James Roosevelt and separately to Lea, March 3, 1938.
55. Ibid., box 4, folder: Aviation, March 1938, memorandum for James Roosevelt, March 8, 1938.
56. Ibid., memorandum for James Roosevelt.
57. HR 9738, seventy-fifth Congress.
58. *James Roosevelt Papers*, box 3, folder: Aviation, December 1937, Hester to James Roosevelt, December 13, 1937; *Rowe Papers*, box 6, folder: Civil aeronautics, Edgar S. Gorrell, "The Civil Aeronautics Act of 1938 and Reorganization of 1940," address to the National Aviation Forum, Washington, DC, May 28, 1940.
59. Ibid., address by Gorrell.
60. Alonzo L. Hamby, *Man of the People: A Life of Harry S. Truman* (New York: Oxford University Press, 1998), 218.
61. Rhyne, *Civil Aeronautics Act*, 53.
62. *Rowe Papers*, box 6, folder: Civil Aeronautics Authority, much of the detail of the congressional fortunes of aviation legislation is taken from Edgar S. Gorrell, "The Civil Aeronautics Act of 1938 and Reorganization of 1940," address to the National Aviation Forum, Washington, DC, May 28, 1940.
63. *Civil Aeronautics Act 1938*, Title 1, Declaration of Policy.
64. Ibid., Title IV.
65. Ibid., Title X.
66. *Ibid.*, Title IV, section 414.
67. Ibid., Title I.
68. *James Roosevelt Papers*, box 3, file: Aviation, October–November 1937, "Report by the Air Commerce Planning Committee of the Business Advisory Council for the Department of Commerce Supplement to Report of 30 June 1937," dated October 20 and approved Executive Committee November 5, 1937.
69. Samuel I. Rosenman, *Public Papers and Addresses of Franklin D. Roosevelt, 13 volumes* (New York: Random House, 1935–50), 101–2, "A Greeting to the National Aviation Forum," January 24, 1939.

CHAPTER 5   THE CHALLENGES OF INTERNATIONAL AVIATION 1933–39

1. Samuel I. Rosenman, *Public Papers and Addresses of Franklin D. Roosevelt, 13 volumes* (New York: Random House, 1938–50), 101–2, "A Greeting to the National Aviation Forum," January 24, 1939.
2. Stanley Baldwin, in the House of Commons, as reported by *Times*, November 11, 1932.
3. RFC HQ memorandum, September 22, 1916, quoted from M. J. Armitage and R. A. Mason, *Air Power in the Nuclear Age, 1954–84: Theory and Practice* (Basingstoke, UK: Macmillan, 1985), 4.

4. Ibid., 2.

5. Giulio Douhet, *The Command of the Air* (New York: Arno Press, 1942).

6. Ibid., 6.

7. A. A. Arnold, *Global Mission* (Blue Ridge Summit, PA: Military Classics Series Tab Books, 1989), 265.

8. Air Corps Tactical School, Air Force Part 1, "Air Warfare," March 1, 1936, quoted in Armitage and Mason, *Air Power*, 5.

9. Ramsay McDonald, speech to the delegates at Geneva Disarmament Conference, March 16, 1933, text from J. W. Wheeler-Bennett, *The Disarmament Deadlock* (London: Routledge, Kegan and Paul, 1934), appendix 2, 267–92.

10. *Roosevelt Library*, Papers of R. Walton Moore, Aviation: Civil Aeronautics Authority, International Civil (1935–37) box 2, folder: Aviation Civil, 1935, Hull to FDR, June 27, 1935, in response to FDR's June 20, 1935, letter; William Phillips, acting secretary of state to chiefs of division, August 2, 1935.

11. Ibid., folder: Aviation, International Civil, 1937, Moore to FDR, February 2, 1937.

12. For conflict between Commerce Department and Pan American, see David Haglund, "De-Lousing Scadta: The Role of Pan American Airways in U.S. Aviation Diplomacy in Colombia, 1939–1940," *Aerospace Historian* 30 (1983).

13. For the long-running civil aviation tussle between the United States and Britain, see A. P. Dobson, *Peaceful Air Warfare: The United States, Britain, and the Politics of International Aviation* (Oxford: Clarendon Press, 1991).

14. *Trippe Papers*, box 20, "History of Transatlantic Air Service,", 17–18; *British National Archives* (hereinafter BNA) FO 371/19635, ICIAC minutes, June 19, 1935; *FRUS*, 1935, volume 1, 510–19, Hull to Ambassador Bingham, April 24, 1935, and minutes of meeting, Moore, Trippe et al., May 6, 1935.

15. *BNA*, CAB 24/257, CP(35)222, joint memorandum by Chancellor of the Exchequer Chamberlain and Secretary of State for Air Cunliffe-Lister (later Lord Swinton), December 2, 1935, which includes summary of report on "Proposed Commonwealth Agreement for an Atlantic Air Service."

16. *Moore Papers*, Aviation: Civil Aeronautics Authority, International Civil (1935–37) box 2, folder: Aviation International Civil 1935, Agenda for the Interdepartmental Committee on Civil International Aviation (ICCIA), July 15, 1935.

17. Ibid., ICCIA meeting, December 2, 1935.

18. Ibid.

19. Ibid.

20. Ibid.

21. *BNA*, CAB 24/259, CP(36)14, "The Report of the UK Air Mission to North America November to December 1935," Donald Banks and F. C. Shelmerdine to Sir Warren Fisher, chairman of Interdepartmental Committee on International Air Communications, December, 30, 1935. The idea of a joint operating company, albeit dominated by Imperial Airways, actually continued, but eventually faded away during the war, among other

reasons because the Canadians actively opposed it as they looked to develop their own independent service.

22. *Moore Papers,* box 2, folder: Aviation International Civil, 1935, December 5 meeting with British, Irish and Canadian delegations.

23. The second meeting of the ICCIA attended by Trippe shows how reliant the committee was on him for what was going on; see *Moore Papers,* box 2, folder: Aviation Civil, 1935, ICCIA meeting, July 22, 1935.

24. Ibid., December 12 meeting with British, Irish and Canadian delegations; press release by Moore, December 12, 1935; *USNA* 811.79640/120, statement by Moore, December 12, 1935.

25. *Moore Papers,* box 2, folder: Aviation Civil, 1936, Moore to Armour, U.S. Legation, Ottawa, March 10, 1936.

26. *BNA,* CAB 24/259, CP(36)14, "The Report of the UK Air Mission to North America November to December 1935," Donald Banks and F. C. Shelmerdine to Sir Warren Fisher, chairman of Interdepartmental Committee on International Air Communications, December 30, 1935.

27. Dobson, *Peaceful Air Warfare,* 119; R. Daley, *An American Saga: Juan Trippe and His Pan American Empire* (New York: Random House, 1980), 208–9.

28. *Moore Papers,* box 2, folder: Aviation Civil, 1936, Banks to Moore, January 22, 1936.

29. *British House of Commons Reports, Hansard,* July 30, 1936, volume 315, column 1,733.

30. *Moore Papers,* box 2, folder: Aviation Civil, 1936, Branch to Moore, April 13, 1936.

31. Ibid., H. J. Seymour Foreign Office to Washington, June 29, 1936; Hull to Foreign Office July 9 and 17, 1936; and Eden to Washington December 26, 1936.

32. *James Roosevelt Papers,* box 3, folder: Aviation, January 17–31, 1938, Harllee Branch, memorandum on "Air Navigation Bill: Carrying Mails of Foreign Countries," January 27, 1938.

33. Ibid.

34. *Moore Papers,* box 2, folder: Aviation Civil, 1936, H. J. Seymour, Foreign Office, to Washington June 29, 1936

35. Ibid., folder: Aviation Civil 1937, Moore to Hull, February 10, 1937.

36. Ibid.

37. David MacKenzie, *Canada and International Civil Aviation 1932–48* (Toronto: Toronto University Press, 1989), 53, citing source Canadian National Archives (hereinafter CNA) RG25 G1, vol. 1,766, file 72-M pt. 3, Canadian high commissioner, UK, to secretary, External Affairs, November 27, 1936.

38. *FDR* OF 2955, box 2, folder: Aeronautics 1937, *New York Times,* April 8, statement by Assistant Secretary of Commerce Johnson.

39. *Ibid.,* box 1, folder: CAB, July–December 1937, "The Pan American Foreign Air Monopoly," July 20, 1937, Report for Chairman of the Maritime Commission by Grover Loening; and *James Roosevelt Papers,* box 3,

folder: Aviation, January17–31, 1938, Loening to James Roosevelt, "Bermuda Air Mail Proposal," which was passed on to FDR on January 26, 1938.

40. Daley, *American Saga*, 222.

41. Ibid., 229.

42. See *Moore Papers*, box 2, folder: Civil Aeronautical Authority 1938 and 1939. It should be noted that by 1938 it was the Germans who were best equipped and prepared to mount transatlantic operations between the United States and Europe, but the U.S. Government was not prepared to move forward with them.

43. *USNA*, 841.796/415 and /421, US Consul Southampton to State Department, October 5, 1938, and Johnson to Hull, January 24, 1939, enclosing clippings from *Daily Mail*, January 21, 1939.

44. *Hansard*, February 1, 1939, volume 343, column 187, Balfour.

45. *Moore Papers*, box 2, folder: Aviation, Civil Aeronautics Authority 1938 and 1939, undated draft for Moore to Pan American.

46. *FDR* PSF box 115, folder: American Export Lines, Trippe to CAA, February 9, 1939.

47. Carl Solberg, *Conquest of the Skies: A History of Commercial Aviation in America* (Boston: Little Brown, 1979), 237–38.

48. *FDR OF* 2955 CAB1938-1942, box 2, folder: CAB 1939, Chairman Hinckley to FDR, May 18, 1939.

49. Daley, *American Saga*, 228–29.

50. *FDR OF* 2955, box 1, folder: CAB, July–December 1937, "The Pan American Foreign Air Monopoly," July 20, 1937, Report for Chairman of the Maritime Commission by Grover Loening.

51. Daley, *American Saga*, 271.

52. *Moore Papers*, box 2, folder: Aviation International Civil, 1935, ICCIA, August 19, 1935, includes July 17 note on July 16 conference with War and Navy Departments.

53. Ibid., folder: Aviation International Civil, 1935, Agenda for the ICCIA, July 15, 1935.

54. Ibid., folder: Aviation International Civil, 1936, ICCIA, June 4, 1936.

55. *USNA* 811.0141, Phoenix Group/79.5, memorandum by Moffat of discussions between FDR, Leahy, and Gruening, April 18, 1938.

56. Solberg, *Conquest of the Skies*, 299.

57. Quoted from Daley, *American Saga*, 170, source, *San Francisco Chronicle, Examiner and News*, November 23, 1935.

58. Anthony Sampson, *Empires of the Sky: The Politics, Contests and Cartels of World Airlines* (Hodder and Staughton, 1984), 59.

59. Hawaii was a crucial landing base for the British. They tried to bargain landing rights in Fiji for Pan American's route to Australia in return for rights into Hawaii, but again the Americans refused, and Pan American developed a staging post at Pago Pago in the American Samoan Islands: see Sampson, *Empires of the Sky*, 59.

60. *Trippe Papers*, box 1, Trippe address to Foreign Service Association, February 24, 1966; Daley, *American Saga*, 182.

61. M. R. Megaw, "The Scramble for the Pacific: Anglo-American Rivalry in the 1930s," *Historical Studies* 17 (1977): 458–73, at 458–59.

62. *Trippe Papers*, box 1, Gatty to Trippe, October 7, 1936; and M. R. Megaw, *The Scramble for the Pacific*: Anglo-American Rivalry in the 1930s," *Historical Studies* 17 (1977): 465–70.

63. Quoted from Daley, *American Saga*, 200.

64. *Moore Papers*, box 2, folder: Aviation International Civil 1936, Captain W. D. Puleston, U.S. Navy, Director Naval Intelligence, March 3, 1936.

65. Ibid.

66. Ibid.

67. *FDR OF*, box 1, folder: CAB, 1936–37, FDR to Louis Johnson and Charles Edison enclosing report for them to read and return, E. J. Noble to FDR, October 31, 1938, presenting "Review of German and Italian Aeronautical Exports to Latin America," signed G. Grant Mason.

68. Ibid., 3760, folder: Special Interdepartmental Committee on the Development of Aviation in the Western Hemisphere, memorandum by James Rowe, "Plan for Aeronautical Development in the Western Hemisphere," August 4, 1939; also to be found in *Rowe Papers*, box 6, folder: CAA.

69. Ibid.

70. Arnold, *Global Mission*, 201–2.

71. *USNA*, 821.796, Sca 2/409, Office of Naval Intelligence report, March 1, 1939.

72. See David Haglund, "De-lousing Scadta: The Role of Pan American Airways in US Aviation Diplomacy in Colombia 1939–40," and Spruille Braden, *Diplomats and Demagogues: The Memoirs of Spruille Braden* (New York: Arlington House, 1971), 235–36.

73. *Berle Papers*, box 211, Diary, May 10, 1940.

74. *FDR OF* 2955, box 1, folder: CAB, July–December 1937, "The Pan American Foreign Air Monopoly," July 20, 1937, Report for Chairman of the Maritime Commission by Grover Loening.

75. Daley, *American Saga*, 221, citing author interviews with Trippe as the source.

76. *James Roosevelt Papers*, box 3, folder: Aviation, January 17–31, 1938, Loening to James Roosevelt, "Bermuda Air Mail Proposal," which was passed on to FDR on January 26, 1938.

77. Ibid.

78. *FDR OF* 2955, box 1, folder: CAB, July–December 1937, "The Pan American Foreign Air Monopoly," July 20, 1937, Report for Chairman of the Maritime Commission by Grover Loening.

CHAPTER 6   THE COMING OF WAR: POLICIES, PREPARATIONS, AND MORE REORGANIZATION 1939–41

1. Samuel I. Rosenman, Public Papers and Addresses of Franklin D. Roosevelt, 13 volumes (New York: Random House 1938–1950), 1939, 460–64.

2. See John McVickar Haight, *American Aid to France* (New York: Atheneum, 1970).

3. *Rowe Papers*, box 6, folder: Civil Aeronautics Authority, cutting from *American Aviation Daily*, July 25, 1940.

4. George McJimsey, ed, *Documentary History of the Franklin D. Roosevelt Presidency, vol. 21, Executive Reorganization, 1937–39* (New York: Lexis Nexis Elsevier, 2004), 764.

5. *Rowe Papers*, box 6, folder: AAP CAB Letters, Rowe memorandum for Budget director, August 19, 1940.

6. *Moore Papers,* box 2, folder: Civil Aeronautical Authority, 1938 and 1939, Johnson to Roper, August 13, 1939, Roper to Moore, August 15, 1939, and Moore to Johnson, August 16, 1939.

7. Ibid., Farley to Moore acknowledging Moore's letter of October 22, indicating the demise of the ICCIA; *FDR OF* 2955 box 2, folder: CAB, 1938, Moore to Noble, October 3, and FDR to Moore October 18, 1938.

8. *Rowe Papers*, box 6, folder: Civil Aeronautics Authority, Rowe memorandum for General Watson, March 16, 1939.

9. *The Congressional Record*, Senate, March 22, 1939, 4364.

10. *Rowe Papers*, box 6, folder: Civil Aeronautics Authority, Rowe memorandum for General Watson, March 25, 1939.

11. *FDR OF* 2955, box 2, folder: CAB, 1938–42, M. A. Harlan from the CAA to Edward M. Watson, secretary to the president, August 22, 1939.

12. Ibid., Staff Memorandum, undated, "Summary of Civil Aeronautics Study" by Division of Administrative Management. Other matters to be assigned to the administrator were aircraft registration and a limited area of safety regulation, requirements for notices as to hazards to air commerce, and control over appointments and over expenses necessary to the performance of the administrator's duties.

13. Ibid., address by Edgar S Gorrell, "Civil Aeronautics Act of 1938 and Reorganization of 1940," National Aviation Forum, May 28, 1940.

14. Ibid.

15. Ibid.

16. *Rowe Papers*, box 6, folder: Civil Aeronautics Authority, Press Release by the President, April 30, 1940.

17. Ibid.

18. *FDR OF* 2955, box 2, CAB, folder: CAB, July–December 40, FDR to secretary of commerce and director, Bureau of the Budget, July 8, 1940.

19. *Third and Fourth Plans on Government Reorganization*, House Documents, Nos. 681 and 692, seventy-sixth Congress, 1940.

20. *FDR OF* 2955, box 2, folder: CAB 1938–42 address by Edgar S. Gorrell, "Civil Aeronautics Act of 1938 and Reorganization of 1940," National Aviation Forum, May 28, 1940, 17.

21. A. A. Arnold, *Global Mission* (Blue Ridge Summit, PA: Military Classics Series Tab Books, 1989), 177.

22. Ibid., 177–78 and 207.

23. John Morton Blum, *Roosevelt and Morgenthau: A Revised and Condensation of From the Morgenthau Diaries* (Boston: Houghton Mifflin, 1970), 273.

24. John Edgar Smith, *FDR* (New York, Random House 2008), 429, suggests that the president was "jawboning" for effect and that he cut back the military supplemental budget from $1.8 billion to $525 million.

25. General Lucius Clay, in charge of overall procurement policy, sought to set priorities. He then communicated them to Hopkins, who then saw to it that FDR's publicly announced targets were quietly modified. For FDR, figures were a matter of politics and morale. Understandably this often infuriated the service chiefs. For example, in his State of the Union Message in January 1942, FDR pulled the figure of 60,000 aircraft a year out of his hat, or rather from Lord Beaverbrook. Calculations were made by multiplying by fifteen what Beaverbrook thought Canada was capable of producing. To some this was just plain irresponsible, but in the end, U.S. production far outdistanced even Beaverbrook's somewhat fancifully arrived at figure. See Smith, *FDR*, 548–49, citing source from *Roosevelt Library*, memorandum, Beaverbrook to FDR, December 29, 1941.

26. Blum, *Roosevelt and Morgenthau*, 274–84; Robert Dallek, *Franklin D. Roosevelt And American Foreign Policy* (New York: Oxford University Press, 1979), 171–75.

27. *FDR OF* 2955, box 2, folder: CAB 1938, "Proposed Program for Vocational Training in Aviation," undated.

28. Dallek, Franklin D. Roosevelt And American Foreign Policy, Parts 2 and 3; Robert A. Divine, *Second Chance: The Triumph of Internationalism in America during World War Two* (New York: Atheneum, 1971). passim.

29. *Complete Press Conferences*, volume 12, 284–285, December 6, 1938.

30. See Donald M. Pisano, *To Fill the Skies with Pilots: The Civilian Pilot Training Program 1939–1949* (Urbana: University of Illinois Press, 1993).

31. *Rowe Papers*, box 6, folder: Civil Aeronautics Authority, Farley address, North Beach Airport, October 15, 1939.

32. Ibid., box 84, Folder: Department of Commerce Civil Aeronautics, Administration Board Addresses, Speeches. Speeches by Robert H. Hinckley, assistant aecretary of commerce, Winston-Salem, North Carolina, February 18, 1941, and at U.S. Conference of Mayors, Jefferson Hotel, St. Louis, Missouri, February 21, 1941.

33. *FDR OF* 2955, box 2, folder CAB 1941, "Staff Handbook CAA: CAA for Defense," published by Department of Commerce, Washington, DC, September 1, 1941.

34. *Pare-Lorenz Chronology*, Trippe met with FDR for 15 minutes on June 14, 1940.

35. *Rowe Papers*, box 6, folder: Civil Aeronautics Authority, memorandum of "Proposed Plan," undated but circa early July 1940.

36. Robert J. Serling, *When Airlines Went to War* (New York: Kensington Books, 1997), 34.

37. *Rowe Papers*, box 6, folder: Civil Aeronautics Authority, Confidential Memorandum for Mr. Forrestal, July 16, 1940: authorship unclear but

presumably Rowe. Most of the note concerned the political wisdom of keeping the proposal brief and trying quietly to navigate the financial appropriations especially as the acting comptroller general in the General Accounting Office was a "narrow man...engaged almost wholly in playing petty and partisan party politics."

38. *FDR OF* 2955, box 2, CAB, 1938–1942, folder: CAB, July–December 1940, Welles, undersecretary of state to FDR, July 8, 1940.

39. Ibid., box 4, CAB, folder: CAB, Rowe to FDR, July 30, 1940.

40. Ibid., box 2, folder CAB 1941, Branch, chairman CAB, to FDR, September 2, 1941.

41. Deborah Wing Ray, "The Takoradi Route: Roosevelt's Prewar venture beyond the Western Hemisphere," *Journal of American History* 62, no. 2 (1975): 340–58.

42. *FDR OF* 2955, box 2, CAB 1938–42, folder: CAB, July–December 1940, "Hemisphere Aspects of U.S. Policy in International Air Transport," December 30, 1940.

43. Ibid.

44. Carl Solberg, Conquest of the Skies: *A History of Commercial Aviation in America* (Boston: Little Brown, 1979), 240.

45. *Rowe Papers*, box 6, folder: Civil Aeronautics Authority, Rowe memorandum for FDR, September 27, 1940.

46. Ibid.

47. Ibid., FDR memorandum for Rowe, September 28, 1940.

48. *FDR OF* 2955, box 2, CAB, 1938–42, folder: CAB, July–December 1940, "Hemisphere Aspects of U.S. Policy in International Air Transport," December 30, 1940.

49. W. A. Burden, *The Struggle for Latin American Airways* (New York: Council on Foreign Relations, 1943), 145–46.

50. *FDR OF,* box 92, folder: Subject File American Export Line, Hull to FDR, January 17, 1941.

51. *Rowe Papers*, box 6, folder: Civil Aeronautics Authority, Rowe memorandum for FDR, January 31, 1941.

52. Ibid.

53. *FDR PSF,* box 92, folder: Subject File American Export Line, FDR to Congressman Taylor, February 6, 1941.

54. Ibid., Rowe memorandum for the president, March 1, 1941.

55. The CAB actually found against Pan American's takeover of AOA, but it was overruled by President Harry S. Truman.

56. *Rowe Papers*, box 6, folder: Civil Aeronautics Authority, Rowe to FDR, memoranda, April 23 and July 26, 1941.

57. *Ibid.*, Pogue to Rowe, July 19, 1941.

58. *FDR OF*, 2955, box 2, folder: CAB, 1941, FDR to Whitney, April 25, 1941, letter drafted by Postmaster General Frank Walker in response to president's request, April 18, 1941. Walker responded April 24, 1941.

59. Ibid., memorandum for acting secretary of state, postmaster general, and chairman of the CAB, July 31, 1941.

60. Serling, *When Airlines Go to War,* 16–19.
61. Ibid., 19.
62. Ibid.
63. Ibid., 39.
64. *Rowe Papers,* box 6, folder: Civil Aeronautics Authority, memorandum for Harry Hopkins, "Northwest Airlines," March 14, 1941, authorship unclear, but presumably Rowe.

CHAPTER 7 FORMING U.S. INTERNATIONAL AVIATION POLICY—DECEMBER 1941–MAY 1943

1. *Roosevelt Library,* Papers of Harry Hopkins, box 132, folder: Aviation, Grover Loening to Hopkins, May 22, 1942.
2. *FDR OF,* 2955, box 3, CAB, 1943–45, folder: CAB, January–March 1943, Bailey to McIntyre January 16, 1942, enclosing letter from Pogue effecting grandfathering of domestic airline routes. Approved and returned February 1, 1942; *USNA* RG40, Department of Commerce box 95, folder: 102517 (4) presidential executive order placing all civil aviation in hands of secretary of commerce subject to direction by secretary of state for war, December 19, 1941.
3. *Pogue Interview.*
4. Ibid.
5. *Berle Papers,* box 59, folder: International Civil Aviation Conference, Chicago, November 1944, business correspondence, notes, appointment diaries, Berle to Stimson, undated but circa October 16–18, 1944.
6. *CNA,* Papers of W. L. Mackenzie King, MG26 J4, reel C4266, Imperial Conference Records C126051–C126203, Committee on Civil Air Communications, Subcommittee on the Trans-Tasman and Trans-Pacific Services, first meeting, June 3, 1937.
7. Ibid., reel C4253, C108376–8 and C110872-79, respectively, "Proposed Civil Aviation Agreements with U.S." June 17, 1938; "Proposed Exchange of Notes to Conclude a Reciprocal Arrangement Relating to Air Transport services as agreed by Canadian-United States Civil Aviation Conference Ottawa 9–11 August 1939." The exchange of notes did not take place until 1940.
8. *CNA,* RG25 volume 2107, folder: AR 405/2 Part 1, memorandum of conversation Pearson with Berle on postwar aviation questions, February 16, 1943.
9. Beatrice Bishop Berle and Travis B. Jacobs, *Navigating the Rapids 1918–71: From the Papers of Adolf A. Berle* (New York: Harcourt, Brace, Jovanovich, 1973), 481; Berle to Hull, September 9, 1942.
10. *Berle Papers,* box 54, folder: Aviation International January–May 1943, Pogue to Berle March 2, 1943, "Report of the Interdepartmental Sub-Committee on International Civil Aviation" in response to assignment given on January 29, 1943.

11. *CNA*, RG 25, volume 2713, folder: 72-HA-40, ICICA "Interim Report," June 17, 1943, see also "Interim Report to War Cabinet Committee," dated July 1943 at *King Papers* Reel H1473, C158823-834; and *CNA*, RG 25, volume 2713, folder: 72-HA-1-40, vol. I, First Draft: "Recommendations to the War Committee on International Air Transport After the War," May 10, 1943.

12. Alan P. Dobson, *US Wartime Aid to Britain* (London: Croom Helm, 1986), and *The Politics of the Anglo-American Economic Special Relationship* (Brighton and New York: Harvester Wheatsheaf and St. Martin's, 1988); Randall Bennett Woods, *Changing the Guard: Anglo-American Relations 1941–1945* (Chapel Hill: University of North Carolina Press, 1990).

13. *BNA*, CAB 87/2, RP(42)28 and RP(42)48, the Shelmerdine and Finlay Reports, respectively, April 28 and December 15, 1942; CAB 66 WP(43)259, Balfour Report June 22, 1943.

14. Ibid., CAB 87/2, RP(A) (43)8, March 3, 1943, memorandum by Leo Amery, secretary of state for India.

15. Ibid., CAB 87/2, RP(42)48, "Internationalisation of Civil Aviation After the War," the Finlay Report, December 15, 1942.

16. Ibid., CAB 66, WP(43)257, June 22, 1943, "Post-War Civil Aviation," note by Prime Minister and Minister of Defence Winston C. Churchill.

17. This was something that developed over time and involved various individual agreements. See, for example, Survey by British Minister of Production, September 3, 1942, *BNA* WP(42)393 CAB 66(28)23, and CAB 65/28 WM140(42)1, October 13, 1942; *US Library of Congress*, Leahy Papers, box 5, memorandum November 5, 1942; and Alec Cairncross, ed., *Sir Richard Clarke, Anglo-American Collaboration in Peace and War 1942–49* (Oxford: Clarendon Press 1982), chapter 1.

18. A. W. Tedder, *With Prejudice: The War Memoirs of Marshal of the Royal Air Force Lord Tedder* (London: Cassell, 1966), 219, recording conversation with Gledhill of Pan American, February 1, 1941.

19. *FRUS*, 1942, volume 4, 23, Eden to Hull, July 28, 1942, the Halifax Agreement.

20. Marylin Bender and Selig Altschul, *Chosen Instrument: Pan Am, Juan Trippe—The Rise and Fall of an American Entrepreneur* (New York: Simon and Schuster, 1982), 365.

21. *USNA*, RG 40, Department of Commerce, box 95, folder: 102517 (4), Hinckley to Myron C. Taylor, December 22, 1941.

22. Hopkins to Edward Stettinius, December 31, 1941, quoted from Bender and Altschul, *Chosen Instrument*, 361, citing source Office of Lend-Lease Administration, U.S. National Archives.

23. *FDR OF*, 2955, box 2, folder January to June 1942, January 23, 1942, FDR approves TWA route to Cairo and Amex's to Foynes in Ireland.

24. *FDR OF* 2955, box 4, CAB, folder: CAB, Rowe to FDR, December 19, 1941.

25. Ibid., Early to FDR, December 5, 1941, and Hopkins to FDR, December 13, 1941.

26. Ibid., FDR memorandum for Latta, December 29, 1941.

27. *Berle Papers*, box 54, folder: Aviation International, June 1942, January to May 1943, L. Welch Pogue, "National Sovereignty of Air Space: Freedom of the Air," June 22, 1942.

28. L. Welch Pogue, "Aviation as a Law Molding Force," *Nebraska Law Review* 21 (1942): 53–74 at 73.

29. *Hopkins Papers*, box 336, folder: book 9, Air Conference Postwar Aviation, Welch Pogue Aviation Day Speech, Minneapolis, St. Paul, April 9, 1943, "Common Sense in Aviation Thinking."

30. L. Welch Pogue, "Some Contributions of Significant Public Service of Enduring Value to Aviation in the United States," June 15, 1999, copy courtesy of author.

31. *CNA* RG25 volume 2713, folder: AR 405/2 Part 1, Massey (London) to External Affairs Department, Ottawa, January 9, 1943, regarding recent telegram from UK ambassador in Washington, DC, Halifax, to Foreign Office, London.

32. *Berle Papers*, box 54, folder: Aviation International, June 1942, January to May 1943, L. Welch Pogue, "National Sovereignty of Air Space: Freedom of the Air," June 22, 1942.

33. Berle, *Navigating the Rapids*, 482; Berle, January 2, 1943.

34. *USNA* 841.796/463, Hull to Winant, January 9, 1943.

35. *Roosevelt Library*, Papers of Sumner Welles, box 164, folder: 12, memorandum "Civil Aviation," March 11, 1943; *King Papers* reel 1472, C158779–81, Reid to MacKenzie King, April 5, 1943.

36. *Berle Papers*, box 54, folder: Aviation International, 1942–43, Berle to H. D. Smith, director bureau of the Budget, February 2, 1943; *FDR OF* 2955 box 3, folder: January–March 1942, Berle to FDR, 12 March 1943, FDR to Bureau of the Budget and reply, March 19 and 27 and FDR to Hull, March 29, 1943. The subcommittee composition was Pogue, Thomas Burke, Robert G. Hooker, Livingston Satterthwaite, and Stephen Latchford, all from the State Department; William Burden, Commerce Department; William Brinkerhoff and Charles McVeagh from the Board of Economic Warfare; Quincy Wright from the Office of Lend-Lease Administration; Colonel Harold Harris, War Department; and Commander Malcolm Aldrich from the Navy. Other representatives from the War and Navy Departments attended sporadically. Attendance at meetings was voluntary and positions taken were personal and not official views of or binding on departments. Much work was also done in smaller working groups.

37. *Rowe Papers*, box 34, folder: AAG CAB, Rowe memorandum for FDR, September 8, 1942.

38. *Berle Papers*, box 54, folder: Aviation International, June 1942–January–May 1943, Hull to Stettinius, January 27, 1943; Berle to FDR, March 12, 1943.

39. *USNA*, RG 40, Department of Commerce, box 95, folder: 102517 (4), Pogue to Wayne C. Taylor, undersecretary of commerce, January 7, 1943.

40. *Berle Papers*, box 54, folder Aviation International, June 1942–January–May 1943, Matthews, London Embassy to secretary of state, February 12, 1943, reporting on House of Lords debate, February 10, 1943.

41. John Morton Blum, ed., *The Price of Vision: The Diary of Henry A. Wallace, 1942–1946* (Boston: Houghton Mifflin, 1973), 182; Wallace to Roosevelt, February 5, 1943.

42. Henry Wallace, "What We Will get Out of the War," *American Magazine*, March 1943.

43. *Berle Papers*, box 54, folder: Aviation International, June 1942–January–May 1943, Berle to Stettinius, January 17, 1943, acknowledging importance of seeking agreements for postwar use of U.S. air bases built abroad with lend-lease funds. In July 1943 five senators led by Richard Russell embarked on a sixty-five-day tour of inspection of U.S. military bases and installations overseas. This was initially prompted by concerns over waste and corruption, but it was all part and parcel of growing concerns about how the United States was expending its resources and what it received in return, and this had major implications for reconstruction and postwar planning.

44. Henry Wallace, "Freedom of the Air—A Momentous Issue," *New York Times*, June 27, 1943.; see also J. S. Walker, *Henry A. Wallace and American Foreign Policy* (Westport, CT: Greenwood Press, 1976).

45. *New York Times,* February 10, 1943.

46. Bender and Altschul, *Chosen Instrument*, 377–78

47. *Leahy Papers*, Diary, July 1, 1943.

48. *Berle Papers*, box 214, January–March 1943, folder: Diary, memorandum, February 18, 1943, and undated memorandum "Implications of Right of Innocent Voyage," both authored by Berle.

49. Ibid.

50. *CNA* RG 25, volume 2713, folder: 72-HA-40, note of Berle's statement in Congressional Hearings. *Berle Papers*, box 54, State Department Subject File, 1938–45, folder Atlantic Charter, Extension of Lend-Lease Act Hearings before House Committee on Foreign Affairs, February 15, 1943.

51. Ibid., folder: Aviation International, June 1942–January–May 1943, Pogue to Berle, March 2, 1943, covering letter and enclosing "Interdepartmental Subcommittee of International Aviation: Preliminary Report as Adopted March 1, 1943." Pogue disliked the term "rights" and instead usually used the word "privilege."

52. Ibid., 19.

53. Ibid., 23.

54. Ibid., box 54, folder: Aviation International, 1942–43, Berle memorandum to FDR, March 12, 1943.

55. *Ibid.,* folder: Aviation International, June 1942–January–May 1943, Minutes of ICIA, March 11 dated March 13, 1943.

56. Bender and Altschul, *Chosen Instrument*, 367.

57. *Berle Papers*, box 54, folder: Aviation International June 1942–January–May 1943, Berle to Hooker and memorandum by Berle "Aviation Policy," both dated March 24, 1943.

58. Ibid.
59. *CNA* RG 25 volume 2713, folder: AR 405/2 Part 1, memoranda of conversation Pearson with Berle and Reid with Berle, February 16 and March 24, 1943, respectively.
60. *Berle Papers*, box 54, folder: Aviation International, June 1942–January–May 1943, Berle memorandum for Hull, April 30, 1943.
61. Ibid.
62. Ibid.
63. Ibid.
64. Ibid., folder: Aviation International June 1942–January–May 1943, memorandum to be included with the minutes of the Aviation Committee, May 26, 1943: Hull, Welles, Norman Davis, Pogue and Berle.
65. Ibid.
66. Ibid., folder: Aviation International, June 1942, January to May 1943, Welch Pogue, "National Sovereignty of Air Space: Freedom of the Air," June 22, 1942.

CHAPTER 8   OF SUBORDINATES AND THE PRESIDENT

1. *CNA* Papers of C.D. Howe, MG27 111 B20, box 100, folder: Post-War Civil Aviation, Government Policy, Undersecretary of State for External Affairs Norman Robertson to Vincent Massey, Canadian high commissioner to the UK, January 18, 1944.
2. Many of the "domestic" airlines were now, of course, operating abroad under the auspices of the Air Transport Command, but they did not have international routes as such for commercial operations.
3. *Berle Papers*, box 55, folder: Aviation International, June–July 1943, Trippe to CAB, May 31, 1943.
4. Ibid., box 54, folder: Aviation International, 1942–43, R. G. Hooker to Berle, June 15, 1943.
5. Ibid., box 55, folder: Aviation, June–July 1943, "Reply to Statement of Important Aviation Questions, 18 May 1943"; and "Reply to Statement of Important Civil Aviation Questions by Manufacturers: Post-war Development Committee of the Aeronautical Chamber of Commerce," companies agreeing with the statement included Bell, MacDonald Douglas, General Electric, and Lockheed (undated); *FDR OF*, 2955 box 3, CAB 1943–45, folder: CAB, April–December 1943, "Supplementary Reply to Statement of Important Civil Aviation Questions and Notice of Intention of Signatory Airlines to File Applications for Certificates of Convenience and Necessity for Certain Routes in Foreign Air Transportation," July 15, 1943.
6. *Time* magazine, July 26, 1943; Marylin Bender and Selig Altschul, *Chosen Instrument: Pan Am, Juan Trippe—The Rise and Fall of an American Entrepreneur* (New York: Simon and Schuster, 1982), 379–80.
7. *Berle Papers*, box 55, folder: Aviation, June–July 1943, "Reply to Statement of Important Aviation Questions" (undated).

8. *New York Times,* July 16, 1943.

9. *Berle Papers,* box 55, folders: Aviation, January–May and June–July 1943; in conversation with Welles in May, Berle suggested the fraught issue of Pan American's monopoly should be left to Congress to sort out, memorandum of conversation, Berle and Welles, May 16, 1943; later comments by Burke from Pogue's subcommittee on the issue of monopoly prompted Berle again to suggest that the State Department steer clear of the issue and leave it to Congress: Berle memorandum, June 23, 1943.

10. Ibid., folder: Aviation, June–July 1943, Berle "Main Heads of Aviation Policy," June 19, 1943.

11. Jennet Conant, *The Irregulars: Roald Dahl and the British Spy Ring in Wartime Washington* (New York: Simon and Schuster, 2008), 132–33; A. A. Arnold, *Global Mission* (Blue Ridge Summit, PA: Military Classics Series Tab Books, 1989), 550.

12. *Hopkins Papers,* box 336, folder: Book 9 Air Conference Post-War Aviation, William A. Burden, Aviation Assistant to Secretary of Commerce, "Notes on Present British Opinion on Post-War Transport Policy," June 5, 1943.

13. *Berle Papers,* box 55, folder: Aviation, June–July 1943, Berle "Aviation" memorandum to Hull, July 9, 1943.

14. Ibid.

15. Ibid., "Proposals for consideration by Principal Committee and Minority Report," June 19, 1943.

16. Ibid., P. T. David to Berle, presenting draft proposals, August 17, 1943.

17. *FDR PSF,* box 92, folder: Subject File Aviation, 1943, Berle, Taylor, Lovett, Gates, and Pogue to Hull, August 31, the response to FDR's request for proposals, March 29, 1943. Memorandum on International Aviation, August 31, 1943, as revised and adopted August 26 by the ICIA: "Major Recommendations."

18. *Berle Papers,* box 55, folder: Aviation, August–December 1943, Berle to Hull memorandum, "Quebec Trip: Aviation," August 18, 1943. Much of this brief was based on work done by P. T. David, see ibid., David to Berle, August 17, 1943. Berle also advised that any Pan American-BOAC cartel arrangement should be rejected, and if the question of transport supplies were raised, Hull could point out that the British had already received over 400 transports to date. What he did not mention was that they were recallable at will once wartime lend-lease ended.

19. *USNA,* 800.796/450, memorandum of conversation, Berle and Pearson, September 28, 1943.

20. Lester Pearson, *Memoirs 1897–1948: Through Diplomacy to Politics* (London: Victor Gallanz, 1973), 231–32; *Howe Papers,* box 101, folder: civil aviation (25), Civil Air Transport British Commonwealth Conversations ATL (43), October 1943; *CNA,* RG 25, volume 2,107, folder: AR 405/2 Part III, minutes of Interdepartmental Committee on Air Transport Policy, meeting, September 8, 1943.

21. *New York Herald Tribune*, October 1, 1943.

22. *Complete Press Conferences*, October 1, 21–22, 1943.

23. *Hopkins Papers*, box 336, folder: Book 9 Air Conference Post-War Aviation, Beaverbrook to Hopkins and his reply October 18 and 27, 1943.

24. Text of seminar by Pogue, "International Civil Air Transport—Transition Following World War Two," *MIT Flight Transportation Library Report FTL-R79-6*, June 1979, copy courtesy of the author.

25. *Berle Papers* box 70, folder: Stettinius Memoranda, October 1943–44, Berle to Stettinius, October 16, 1944.

26. *Hopkins Papers*, box 336, folder: Book 9 Air Conference Post War Aviation 2, FDR to Stettinius, October 20, 1943.

27. Ibid., series of memoranda prepared for Berle by P. T. David, "Rights to Engage in Air Commerce," "Rights of Transit and Technical Stop," "Prevention of Cutthroat Competition," "Allocation of Transport Planes," "Need for a United Nations Conference," all dated early September 1943. The committee was later rejigged but no longer played a major part in policy development.

28. *Pogue Interview.*

29. *Hopkins Papers*, box 336, folder: Book 9 Air Conference Post War Aviation, Pogue to Hopkins, September 22, 1943, "Recommendations on Two Overriding Issues in the International Civil Aviation Field." Not everyone shared this optimistic view of growth for the airlines. Churchill, for example, thought claims about growth were overexaggerated as possibly did Patterson, head of United Airlines.

30. Ibid., Pogue to "Harry," October 28, 1943, enclosing draft memorandum.

31. Ibid.

32. Ibid., Lovett to Hopkins, November 3, 1943, enclosing memorandum "Post-War Civil Aviation," November 3, 1943.

33. *Ibid.*, folder: Air Conference II, Hopkins to FDR, November 10, 1943.

34. *USNA*, 800.796/495 memorandum of conversation by Assistant Secretary of State Adolf Berle, November 11, 1943. The president later approved this record of the conversation, see file memorandum, December 27, 1943; FDR requested Grace Tully to telephone Berle saying the record was OK, *FDR PSF*, box 93, folder: Aviation, Subject File 1943 Legislation.

35. *USNA*, 800.796/495 memorandum of conversation by Assistant Secretary of State Adolf Berle, November 11, 1943; Bender and Altschul, *Chosen Instrument*, 9–10, citing Bender and Altschul interviews with Pogue December 15, 1976, and January 19, 1979..

36. *USNA*, 800.796/495 memorandum of conversation by Assistant Secretary of State Adolf Berle, November 11, 1943

37. *Hopkins Papers*, box 336, folder: Book 9 Air Conference Post War Aviation, Pogue to Hopkins, November 10, 1943, enclosing draft speech to New York Herald Tribune Forum to be delivered November 16, 1943.

38. Ibid.

39. Ibid.

40. *Berle Papers*, box 55, folder: Aviation International, August–December 1943, Berle to Hull and Stettinius, November 26, 1943.

41. *Hopkins Papers*, box 336, folder: Book 9, Air Conference Post War Aviation, Pogue to Hopkins, November 21, 1943.

42. Ibid., Pogue to Hopkins, November 25, 1943.

43. *Howe Papers*, box 100: folder Civil Aviation (21), Robertson to Howe, November 21, 1943, reporting on conversations with Ray Atherton, U.S. ambassador in Ottawa, and Howe to Beaverbrook, December 4, 1943.

44. *Berle Papers*, box 55, folder: Aviation International, August–December 1943, Berle to Hull, December 20, 1943. "The Problem of Reciprocal Landing Rights" was one of a series of problem papers on aviation that Berle sent to Hull during December, and they were largely based on work prepared for Berle by P. T. David, the secretary of Pogue's subcommittee.

45. Ibid.

46. *FDR PSF*, box 93, folder Aviation Subject File Aviation 1944, Berle to Hull, December 31, 1944, "Freedom of Passage."

47. *Hopkins Papers*, box 336, folder: Book 9, Air Conference Post War Aviation, Arnold to Hopkins, July 18, 1944, enclosing April 3, 1944, "Army Air Force's Policy in Regard to Post War International Civil Aviation." This was approved by Secretary of War Stimson on April 20, though he was subsequently to forget that, see correspondence in *FDR PSF*, box 93, folder Aviation, Subject File Aviation, 1944.

48. *Hopkins Papers*, box 336, folder: Book 9 Air Conference Post War Aviation, Arnold to Hopkins, July 18, 1944, enclosing April 3, 1944, "Army Air Force's Policy in Regard to Post War International Civil Aviation" and *FDR PSF*, box 93, folder Aviation, Subject File Aviation, 1944, Arnold to FDR, March 26, 1944, memorandum for the president, "Policy of the United States Army Air Force in Regard to International Commercial Aviation."

49. Ibid., "International Transport Policy: Special report of the CAB," April 12, 1944.

50. Ibid.

51. Samuel I. Rosenman, *Working with Roosevelt* (London: Rupert Hart-Davis, 1952), 361–62.

52. *Roosevelt Library*, Map Room (hereinafter *FDR MR*) box 162, folder 5 sect. A4-2-Air Routes, Knox to King, August 17, 1943: "What the President particularly desires is an investigation of the islands from the standpoint of post war commercial air routes.... "

53. *FDR MR*, box 162, folder: 5 sect. A4-2-Air Routes, memorandum for the files, Admiral Wilson Brown, Naval Air to the president, August 27, 1943; for the Knox FDR exchanges, see ibid., Knox to FDR and his reply, March 10 and 12, 1943. For much more detail on the issue of American bases in the Pacific, see William Roger Louis, *Imperialism at Bay: The United States and the Decolonization of the British Empire, 1941–1945* (Oxford: Oxford University Press, 1977). Louis argues that Roosevelt favored UN mandates over the Japanese Islands in the Pacific, whereas the Navy wanted outright annexation. Interestingly, Berle shared the Navy position.

54. *Howe Papers*, box 100, folder: Post-War Civil Aviation Government Policy (21), secretary of state for dominion affairs to secretary of state or external affairs, Canada, January 18, 1944.

55. *Ibid.,* folder: Post War Civil Aviation Government Policy (22), secretary of state for dominion affairs to secretary of state for external affairs, Canada, December 31, 1943.

56. *Berle Papers,* box 55, folder: Aviation 1944, Berle to Hull, February 3, 1944. A day later Berle recorded a conversation with Sir Ronald Campbell from the UK Embassy in Washington in which he confessed that the deal FDR had agreed to at Casablanca to grant operating rights to BOAC in Liberia was against his, Berle's, better judgment: box 214, folder: Diary, January–March 1944, February 4 entry 1944.

57. *FDR PSF,* box 93, folder: Aviation, 1944, Berle to FDR and his reply February 12 and 141944, respectively, and Pogue to FDR February 16, 1944.

58. Ibid., Hull to FDR memorandum "Aviation Conversations," March 11, 1944.

59. Alan P. Dobson, "Canadian Civil Aviation 1935–1945: Flying between the USA and Great Britain," currently unpublished conference paper delivered to British Association for Canadian Studies annual conference, July 18, 2010, London: publication imminent, 2012.

60. *Howe Papers,* box 100, folder: Post-War Civil Aviation Government Policy (21), Baldwin memorandum, March 27, 1944, "Air Transport-U.S. Statement of Views."

61. Ibid., box 101, folder: Trans Canada Airlines (26), Symington to Howe, March 31, 1944.

62. Ibid.

63. *Berle Papers,* box 63, folder: London Air Conversations, "Report on Air Conversations," April 19, 1944.

64. This was one of the matters that occasioned subsequent controversy. Beaverbrook made the commitment public, and this embarrassed Berle politically once back in Washington. By May 1944 the British recognized there was a problem, and after reports of Hull giving assurances to the U.S. Senate that Berle had made no such commitment, they were obliged to revert to the understanding that supply of such aircraft was dependent on a satisfactory civil aviation agreement. *USNA,* 841.70/7-2144 and 841.796/637, U.S. Ambassador Winant to secretary of state, two notes, May 31, 1944.

65. *Berle Papers,* box 63, folder: London Air Conversations, "Report on Air Conversations," April 19, 1944.

66. Ibid.

67. *USNA, 841.796/6-0345,* "Summary of Developments," June 3, 1945.

68. *CAN,* RG 25 volume 2713, folder: 72-HA-40 volume 2, Interdepartmental Committee on Air Transport Policy Document 22, Report to War Cabinet Committee submitting "Draft Air Transport Convention" based on Balfour Report and a report on security at the October 1943 Commonwealth Talks in London.

69. *British House of Lords Record Office,* Papers of Max Beaverbrook, box D/238, April 6, 1944, Civil Air Transport Committee Minutes; *Berle Papers,* box

63, folder: London Air Conversations, "Report on Air Conversations," April 19, 1944.

70. Beatrice Bishop Berle and Travis Beal Jacobs, *Navigating the Rapids 1918–1971: From the Papers of Adolf A. Berle* (New York: Harcourt, Brace, Jovanovich 1973), 486.

71. *Berle Papers*, box 216, folder: Diary, entry October 21, 1944, memorandum of conversation, Wright and Berle.

72. *Howe Papers*, box 99, folder: Air Agreements (17), D. McEvey to prime minister of commonwealth of Australia, May 15, 1944.

73. *Beaverbrook Papers*, box D/238, P. G.M. Masefield memorandum on Berle's April 18 telegram to Beaverbrook and Berle to Beaverbrook, April 21, 1944.

CHAPTER 9   AMERICAN TRIUMPH, ROOSEVELT'S LOSS, AND THE "BURLESQUE" OF CHICAGO

1. *Howe Papers*, box 99, folder: Conference Post-War Civil Aviation (20), Symington to Howe, September 15, 1944.

2. *Berle Papers*, box 59, folder: ICAC 1944, Berle, Summary, December 6, 1944.

3. *Howe Papers* box 99, folder: Conferences Post-War Civil Aviation (19), Baldwin to Howe, November 30, 1944.

4. *FRUS*, 1944 volume III, 162–67.

5. *Howe Papers*, box 100, folder: Post-War Civil Aviation Government Policy (23), Canadian high commissioner in Australia to secretary of state for external affairs, Canada, April 15, 1943, and Robertson to Howe September 1, 1943, forwarding telegram for T. C. Davies from High Commissioner's Office, Canberra.

6. *USNA*, 841.79652/10; 841.796/598; 841.796/633; 841.79652/13: Winant to secretary of state, February 19 and March 14, 1944, Morgan to Berle, June 12, 1944, and Lovett to Berle, May 24, 1944; *Berle Papers*, box 55 folder: Aviation International, 1944, Berle reporting Winant's views to Hull, March 10, 1944.

7. *Chicago Daily Tribune* and *New York Journal of Commerce,* respectively, July 24 and 26, 1944.

8. *Howe Papers*, box 100, folder: Post-War Civil Aviation Government Policy (21), secretary of state for dominion affairs to secretary of state for external affairs, July 31, 1944.

9. *FDR PSF*, box 93, Subject File Aviation, 1944, Pogue to Hull and Berle, May 5 and 16, respectively, and Pogue to FDR and his reply, May 30, 1944.

10. *USNA, 841.79652/13,* Morgan to Berle, June 12, 1944.

11. *Berle Papers,* box 59, State Department Subject File 1938-45, Berle to Hull, May 30, 1944.

12. On June 23 Berle noted Trippe was in trouble because of counteraction in Congress by other airlines. Trippe was also concerned about route hearings scheduled September 16 to February 1945. By August Pogue suspected

Trippe might offer to sell Pan American to the government, but without actually ceding control. He advised that such an offer should be accepted. It would solve the problem of dislodging Pan American from its embedded position, and he suspected that government would eventually be able to capture full control of the company. Trippe's offer never came, except in the form of the All American Flag Line Company. At the end of August 1944, the Pan American monopoly was still an issue, but the administration was standing firm. In a note to Senators Clark and Bailey, drafted by Pogue for FDR, they were told: "I see no occasion to change... policy [of 1938 Aeronautics Act requiring competition] in the foreign field." Finally in February 1945 the Senate Committee came out in favor of a degree of competition, which finally put paid to Trippe's hopes for favored instrument status. Crucially Senator Bailey switched from favoring to opposing Pan American. See *Berle Papers,* box 216, folder: Diary May–August 1944, entry June 23, 1944; *FDR OF* 2955, box 4, folder: CAB, Daniels to FDR memorandum, August 18, 1944; *Hopkins Papers,* box 336, folder: book 9 Air Conference Post War Aviation 2, Pogue's proposed reply to Bailey and Clark to FDR, August 19, 1944, dated August 31; and Marylin Bender and Selig Altschul, *Chosen Instrument: Pan Am, Juan Trippe—The Rise and Fall of an American Entrepreneur* (New York: Simon and Schuster, 1982), 403–8.

13. *Berle Papers*, box 216, folder Diary, May–August 1944, FDR, Berle, Pogue, and senators Bailey and Clark "Aviation Policy" meeting, June 10, 1944. As unlikely as a German collapse might have seemed in June, the progress of the war was so favorable for the allies that at the Second Quebec Conference in September a Combined Chiefs of Staff intelligence report suggested a possible German collapse in December 1944: sadly it never happened, see Mark A. Stoler, *Allies in War: Britain and America against the Axis Powers 1940–1945* (London: Hodder Arnold, 2005), 168.

14. *CNA.*, RG25 volume 2,713, folder: 72-HA-2-40 volume 2, Leighton McCarthy, Canadian ambassador to Washington to secretary of state for external affairs, June 20, 1944.

15. *CNA* RG25 volume 2,713, folder: 72-HA-1-40 volume 2, J. R. Baldwin, Air Transport Committee Document 37, "Canada-U.S. Air Services," July 22, 1944.

16. *Howe Papers* 100, folder: Civil Aviation (24), Beaverbrook to Howe, September 19, 1944.

17. Beatrice Bishop Berle and Travis Beal Jacobs, *Navigating the Rapids 1918–1971: From the Papers of Adolf A. Berle* (New York: Harcourt, Brace, Jovanovich 1973), 492, diary entry, July 29–30, 1944.

18. *Howe Papers*, box 100, folder: Post-War Civil Aviation Government Policy (21), Howe to Robertson, August 24, 1944.

19. Berle and Jacobs, *Navigating the Rapids*, 495, memorandum, July 30, 1944.

20. *Howe Papers*, box 100, folder: Post-War Civil Aviation Government Policy (21), secretary of state for the dominions to secretary of state for external

affairs, August 22 and 29 (twice) and September 13, 1944 and *Beaverbrook Papers*, box D/289, Berle to Beaverbrook, August 23, 1944.

21. Ibid., Peter Masefield memorandum, August 23, 1944; *Howe Papers*, box 100, folder: Post-War Civil Aviation Government Policy (21), secretary of state for the dominions to secretary of state for external affairs, August 22, 1944.

22. *Pogue Interview.*

23. *Hopkins Papers*, box 335, folder; Air Conference 2, Pogue to Hopkins, August 26, 1944.

24. *Berle Papers*, box 55, folder Aviation International, 1944, Beaverbrook to Berle, August 29 and September 1, 1944.

25. *FDR MR,*box 162, folder: 5 sect. A4-2-Air Routes, Jesse Jones to FDR, September 7, 1944, enclosing memorandum by Pogue.

26. Ibid.

27. *Howe Papers*, box 100, folder: Post-War Civil Aviation Government Policy (21), Canadian chargé d'affaires, Washington, to secretary of state for external affairs, September 8, 1944.

28. *Berle Papers,* box 55, folder: Aviation International, 1944, Berle to Wright for Beaverbrook, September 9, 1944.

29. *British Government White Paper,* "International Air Transport," Command Paper 6561, 1944.

30. *CNA* RG25 volume 2,713, folder: 72-HA-1-40, volume 2, Baldwin memorandum on Commonwealth Discussions of Air Transport, September 22, 1944.

31. *Berle Papers,* box 55, folder: Aviation 1944, Berle to Hull, August 31, 1944, and *Pogue Interview.*

32. *FDR MR,*box 162, folder: section A4-2-Air Routes, Byrd to FDR, April 14, 1944.

33. Ibid., Roosevelt to Hull, January 7, 1944, and see ibid. in Chapter 8, Knox to FDR and his reply, March 10 and 12, 1943.

34. William Roger Louis, *Imperialism at Bay: The United States and the Decolonization of the British Empire, 1941–1945* (Oxford: Oxford University Press, 1977), 356.

35. *FDR MR,* box 207, Book IV Senior Members' Review of "Byrd Report," undated, but 1944.

36. *Berle Papers,* box 216, folder Diary, May–August 1944, FDR, Berle, Pogue, and Senators Bailey and Clark "Aviation Policy" meeting, June 10, 1944.

37. *Pogue Interview.*

38. *Howe Papers,* box 100, folder: Post War Civil Aviation (24), Howe to Beaverbrook, October 4, 1944.

39. *FDR OF,* box 8, folder Aeronautics "Official" 1943–45, Roosevelt to Arnold and his reply November 20 and 24, 1944.

40. *Berle Papers,* box 55, folder: Aviation 1944, Berle to Hull, August 31, 1944, memorandum, "International Air Matters: State of Negotiations to Date."

41. Ibid.

42. Ibid.
43. *Berle Papers*, box 59, folder: International Civil Aviation Conference, November 1944, Business Correspondence, Notes, Appointments, Diaries, memorandum by Berle, International Civil Aviation Conference, September 16, 1944.
44. Ibid.
45. Ibid.
46. Howe Papers MG27 III B20, box 100, folder: Post-War Civil Aviation Government Policy (21), Pearson to Robertson, October 2, 1944.
47. Ibid., box 216, folder: Diary entry, October 9, 1944, memorandum of conversation between Berle and Wright.
48. *BNA CAB 65/44* 148(44)3, November 8, 1944, prime minister confirmed that a Cabinet Committee chaired by Lord Privy Seal Beaverbrook had been established to advise Swinton at Chicago, terms of reference at WP(44)621.
49. *FDR OF* 5584b Office of War Mobilization and Reconversion, OF 5585-5610, Berle to FDR, undated draft message of welcome to International Civil Aviation Conference. The message was delivered by Berle on behalf of FDR on November 1, *Berle Papers,* box 60, folder: International Civil Aviation Conference 1944, Speeches.
50. Even the hotel had serious shortcomings, lifts were slow, telephoning took time, rooms were small and noisy: it was all rather second rate. See David MacKenzie, *Canada and International Civil Aviation 1932–1948* (Toronto: Toronto University Press, 1989), 179–80.
51. *FDR PSF,* box 93, folder: Subject File Aviation, 1944, Berle to FDR, December 7, 1944, "International Civil Aviation Conference [Report]"; and *Berle Papers,* box 216, folder: Diary November–December 1944, memorandum for undersecretary of state and interested offices and divisions, November 1, 1944.
52. Berle, *Navigating the Rapids*, 499, entry November 2, 1944, on opening statements.
53. *FDR PSF* box 93, folder: Subject File Aviation, 1944, memorandum of conversation Berle and FDR, September 9, 1944.
54. See David MacKenzie, *ICAO: A History of the International Civil Aviation Organization* (Toronto: University of Toronto Press, 2010).
55. L. Welch Pogue, "Personal Recollections From the Chicago Conference: ICAO Then, Now, and in the Future," *Annals of Air Space and Law*, volume XX 1995, Part I, pp. 35–48; and *British White Paper* "International Civil Aviation Conference," Command 6614, December 7, 1944.
56. *Chicago Tribune,* November 7, 1944. The Canadians were desperate for recognition of their international status and achieving this prominent role helped to deliver that.
57. *FDR PSF,* box 93, folder: Subject File Aviation, 1944, Berle to FDR, December 7, 1944, "International Civil Aviation Conference [Report]," note, p. 21.
58. Swinton reserved the position of Newfoundland until Canada had signed the Two Freedom Agreement. That caused the Americans some anxiety thinking Swinton had pulled a fast one, but it all went ahead as planned.

Beaverbrook Papers, box D/248, Dominions Office to Newfoundland, January 17, 1945, and extract from Swinton's speech in the House of Lords, January 16, 1945. A month later the UK indicated that its signature of Two Freedoms Agreement should now also be taken to include Newfoundland, see ibid. Foreign Office to Washington, February 5, 1945.

59. *Howe Papers,* box 100, folder: Civil Aviation (24), statement for the press, Berle, November 1, 1944, for release, November 2.

60. Berle, *Navigating the Rapids,* 501, entry November 6, 1944.

61. Ibid.

62. *FDR PSF,* box 93, folder: Subject File Aviation, 1944, Berle to FDR, December 7, 1944, "International Civil Aviation Conference [Report]," 22.

63. *Chicago Daily Tribune,* November 3, 1944.

64. Berle, *Navigating the Rapids,* 500–501, entries, November 4 and 9, 1944.

65. *Berle Papers,* box 59, folder: International Civil Aviation Conference, Chicago, November 1944, Business Correspondence, Notes, Appointment Diaries, Brewster to Berle, November 26, 1944.

66. *Pogue Interview.*

67. Pogue, International Civil Air Transport—Transition Following World War Two," MIT Flight Transportation Library Report FTL-R79-6, June 1979, copy courtesy of the author.

68. Ibid.

69. Dobson, *Peaceful Air Warfare: The United States, Britain, and the Politics of International Aviation* (Oxford: Clarendon Press, 1991), 162–72; MacKenzie, *Canada and International Civil Aviation,* 172–200.

70. *Berle Papers,* box 216, folder: Diary November–December 1944, memorandum for undersecretary of state and interested offices and divisions, November 14, 1944.

71. *Beaverbrook Papers,* box D/249, Swinton to Bridges, November 13, 1944.

72. Ibid.

73. *CNA RG2* 18 volume 18, folder: A-15-1 (W), September–December 1944, telephone transcript of conversation between Heeney and Baldwin, November 16, 1944.

74. *Berle Papers,* box 216, Berle to undersecretary of state and interested offices and divisions, November 26, 1944; *Howe Papers,* box 99, folder: Conferences Post-war Civil Aviation (19), Baldwin to Howe, November 25, 1944, explains discovery of the error; *BNA* CAB 66/56 WP(44)680, memorandum by Cripps refers to escalator clause "inserted (against our desires) to provide a means of increasing the share of frequencies...."

75. *BNA* CAB 65/44 153(44)2, November 22, 1944; and *Howe Papers,* box 99, folder Conferences-Post-War Civil Aviation (19), Baldwin to Howe, November 21, 1944.

76. *Berle Papers,* box 216, Berle to undersecretary of state and interested offices and divisions, November 14 and 26, 1944.

77. *CNA RG70* volume 23, Air Canada, folder: TCA 3-3-4 volume 2, Symington to Howe, December 29, 1944, enclosing report on the Chicago conference.

78. Ibid.

79. *Howe Papers*, box 99, folder: Post War Civil Aviation (19), Baldwin to Howe, December 1, 1944.

80. *Washington Times Herald* and *Chicago Daily Tribune*, November 23, 1944.

81. *Howe Papers*, box 99, folder: Post War Civil Aviation (19), Baldwin to Howe, November 2, 1944.

82. Ibid.

83. *Berle Papers*, box 60, State Department Subject File 1938–1945, International Civil Aviation Conference Annex I–VIII—Latin American Republics General, folder: International Civil Aviation Conference, 1944: Speeches, Verbatim Minutes Joint Plenary Meeting of Committees I, II, and III, November 22, 1944, Symington and LaGuardia; and *Berle Papers*, box 216, folder; Diary, November–December 1944, memorandum for undersecretary of state and interested offices and divisions, November 26, 1944.

84. Ibid., Joint Subcommittee of Committees I, II, and IV, November 24, 1944.

85. *RG70* volume 23, Air Canada, folder: TCA 3-3-4 volume 2, Symington to Howe, December 29, 1944, enclosing report on the Chicago conference.

86. Ibid.

87. Ibid., Reid to Symington, December 15, 1944, enclosing December 14 memorandum completing his report on the Chicago conference.

88. Ibid., secretary of state for dominion affairs to secretary of state for external affairs, Canada, November 27, 1944.

89. *FDR MR*, box 32, folder: Air Conferences (1) Chicago Air Conference, Berle to FDR, November 29, 1944.

90. *Howe Papers*, box 99, folder: Conferences-Post-War Civil Aviation (19), Baldwin to Howe, November 25, 1944.

91. Pogue, "International Civil Air Transport."

92. Pogue, "International Civil Air Transport"; Irwin F. Gelman, *Secret Affairs: FDR, Cordell Hull and Sumner Welles* (New York: Enigma Books, 2002), 361; and *FDR PSF*, box 93, folder: Subject File Aviation 1944, Berle to FDR, December 7, 1944 "International Civil Aviation Conference [Report]," 22. Pogue recalls meeting on December 4 at which Berle told him he had just received a telegram from the president accepting his resignation, which was strange as he had not resigned. In fact Berle had heard from the president on November 29, two days after the resignation of Cordell Hull as secretary of state offering him the embassy in Rio de Janeiro, so he knew that things were afoot even then. Hull had actually sent his resignation letter to FDR on November 21. Pogue records that Berle thought powerful airline interests opposed to multilateralism and working through "someone in a position of power" had engineered his dismissal. If that were so, then it was very odd as a multilateral solution was already dead in the water by November 27. Furthermore, Pogue comments: "The President yielded [to pressure for Berle's dismissal] although theretofore he had been very supportive of Berle and his ideas." But this is an even stranger thing to say. A multilateral commercial regime was FDR's idea and championed by him and not so much by Berle, so for the president to yield to those forces who wanted to get rid of Berle

because he was supposedly a champion of a multilateral solution would have been strange indeed, especially as FDR was about to correspond in the very strongest terms with Churchill to try to salvage commercial multilateralism.

93. *FDR MR,* box 32, folder Air Conferences (1) Chicago Air Conference, memorandum Grace Tully for Stettinius indicating Berle had telephoned Hopkins asking for FDR's intervention, November 21, 1944.

94. *FDR OF,* boxes 5584b/5585–OF5610, folder: OF 5594 International Civil Aviation Conference, 1944.

95. Jim Bishop, *FDR's Last Year* (London: Hart-Davis MacGibbon, 1974), 185–220.

96. Kimball, *Correspondence volume III,* pp. 402–3, FDR to Churchill, November 21, 1944.

97. Ibid., pp. 404–5, Churchill to FDR, November 22, 1944.

98. *Ibid.,* pp. 407–8, FDR to Churchill, November 24, 1944.

99. *Ibid.,* pp. 419–21, Churchill to FDR, November 28, 1944.

100. *Ibid.,* pp. 424–25 and 427, FDR to Churchill, November 30 and his reply, December 1, 1944.

101. *Berle Papers,* box 169, Articles and Book Reviews, 1964–67, folder: Articles and Book Reviews, 1965, "The International Civil Aviation Treaties Twenty Years Later," Columbia University, 1965.

CHAPTER 10   ROOSEVELT'S LEGACY

1. *Complete Press Conferences,* volume 21–22, October 1, 1943.

2. *USNA,* 811.79641D/1-2945, Grew to U.S. Legation, Dublin, January 29, 1945.

3. Kimball, *Correspondence vol. 3,* 519–20, Churchill to Roosevelt, January 27, 1945.

4. *FDR MR,* box 32, folder: Air Conference (1) Chicago Air Conference, Grew to FDR, January 30, 1945.

5. Ibid., FDR to Grew, January 31 and February 2, 1945.

6. Kimball, *Correspondence vol. 3,* 566–67, Churchill to Roosevelt, March 6 and FDR's reply, March 15, 1945.

7. *BNA,* CAB128/5 11(46)8, February 4, 1946, Ernest Bevin, foreign secretary, considering memos. CP37(46) by Aviation Minister Lord Winster and CP(40) by Hugh Dalton, chancellor of the exchequer.

8. Ibid.

9. *British White Paper,* "U.S., UK, Civil Air Services Agreement Bermuda," Command 6747, 1946.

10. *Interview with Robert Ebdon,* Head of Government Affairs, British Airways, conducted by the author August 5, 1991.

11. *The Treaty of Rome,* 1957, Article 3, Title 4 Transport Articles 74–84, and Rules on Competition Articles 85–102.

12. *Jimmy Carter Library,* Staff Offices, Domestic Policy Staff, Eizenstat box 148, folder: Aviation Airline Regulatory Reform, Message to Congress, March 4, 1977, attached to Eizenstat to Carter, February 22, 1977.

13. For the story of deregulation, see Alan P. Dobson, *Flying in the Face of Competition: The Policies and Diplomacy of Airline Regulatory Reform in Britain, the USA and the European Community 1968–94* (Aldershot, UK: Avebury, 1995).

14. *Interview with Cyril Murphy,* Vice President for International Affairs, United Airlines, conducted by the author, July 1, 1991.

15. An important coda needs to be added here. None of this would have been possible without a quantum leap forward in the technology of computers. Ensuring that passengers fed in through multiple spokes for a common destination and then speedily fed out on the relevant spoke to that destination could not have been done without computers. By the mid 1980s the major computer reservation systems could "juggle one hundred million fares at a single time." B. S. Peterson, *Bluestreak: Inside Jetblue, the Upstart that Rocked the Industry* (New York, Portfolio, 2004), 101.

16. *Interview with Jeffery Shane,* assistant secretary for policy and international affairs, U.S. Department of Transportation, conducted by the author, April 5, 1991.

17. For various aspects of the troubled U.S.–UK aviation relations in this period, see Alan P. Dobson "Regulation or Competition? Negotiating the Anglo-American Air Service Agreement of 1977," *Journal of Transport History* 15, no. 2 (1994): 144–65; "Aspects of Anglo-American Aviation Diplomacy 1976–93," *Diplomacy and Statecraft* 4, no. 2 (1993): 235–57; and "The USA, Hegemony and Airline Market Access to Britain and Western Europe, 1945–96," *Diplomacy and Statecraft* 9, no. 2 (1998): 129–59.

18. For the story of reform in Europe, see Alan P. Dobson, *Globalization and a Regional Response: The Origins, Development and Impact of the Single European Aviation Market* (London, Routledge, 2007).

19. See *COM(2002)649*, Final, "Communication from the Commission on the consequences of the Court judgments of 5 November for the European air transport policy," November 19, 2002.

20. Kimball, *Correspondence, vol. 3*, 402–3, Roosevelt to Churchill, November 21, 1944.

21. Alan P. Dobson and Joseph A. McKinney, "Sovereignty, Politics and U.S. International Airline Policy," *Journal of Air Law and Commerce*, 74, no. 3 (2009): 527–52.

22. Alan P. Dobson, *Peaceful Air Warfare: The United States, Britain, and the Politics of International Aviation* (Oxford: Clarendon Press, 1991).

Bibliography

Books

Armitage, M. J. and Mason, R. A. *Air Power in the Nuclear Age, 1954–84: Theory and Practice* (Basingstoke, UK: Macmillan 1985).

Arnold, A. A. *Global Mission* (Blue Ridge Summit, PA: Military Classics Series Tab Books, 1989).

Banner, Stuart. *Who Owns the Sky? The Struggle to Control Airspace from the Wright Brothers On* (Cambridge, MA, and London: Harvard University Press, 2008).

Baruch, Bernard M. *The Public Years* (London: Odhams, 1961).

Bender, Marylin. and Selig Altschul. *The Chosen Instrument: Pan Am, Juan Trippe—The Rise and Fall of an American Entrepreneur* (New York: Simon and Schuster, 1982).

Berle, Beatrice Bishop, and Travis Beal Jacobs. *Navigating the Rapids 1918–1971: From the Papers of Adolf A. Berle* (New York: Harcourt, Brace, Jovanovich, 1973).

Bishop, James Alonzo. *FDR's Last Year* (London: Hart-Davis MacGibbon, 1974).

Blum, John Morton. *The Price of Vision: The Diary of Henry A. Wallace, 1942–1946* (Boston: Houghton Mifflin, 1973).

———. *Roosevelt and Morgenthau: A Revised and Condensation of From the Morgenthau Diaries* (Boston: Houghton Mifflin, 1970).

Braden, Spruille. *Diplomats and Demagogues: The Memoirs of Spruille Braden* (New York: Arlington House, 1971).

Brandes, Joseph. *Herbert Hoover and Economic Diplomacy* (Pittsburgh, PA: University of Pittsburgh Press, 1962).

Burden, William A.M. *The Struggle for Latin American Airways* (New York: Council on Foreign Relations, 1943).

Burns, James McGregor. *Roosevelt: The Lion and the Fox 1882–1940* (New York: Harcourt Brace and Jovanovic, 1956).

———. *Roosevelt: The Soldier of Freedom* (New York: World, Harvest, 1970).

Cairncross, Alec, ed. *Sir Richard Clarke, Anglo-American Collaboration in Peace and War 1942–49* (Oxford: Clarendon, 1982).

Conant, Jennet *The Irregulars: Roald Dahl and the British Spy Ring in Wartime Washington* (New York: Simon and Schuster, 2008).

Daley, Robert. *An American Saga: Juan Trippe and His Pan American Empire* (New York: Random House, 1980).

Dalleck, Robert. *Franklin D. Roosevelt and American Foreign Policy 1932–1945* (New York: Oxford University Press, 1979).

Daso, Dick Alan. *Hap Arnold and the Evolution of American Air Power* (Washington, DC, and London: Smithsonian Institute Press, 2000).

Davies, Ronald Edward George. *Airlines of the United States since 1914* (London, Putnam, 1982).

Divine, Robert A. *Second Chance: The Triumph of Internationalism in America during World War Two* (New York: Atheneum, 1971).

Dobson, Alan P. *Flying in the Face of Competition: The Policies and Diplomacy of Airline Regulatory Reform in Britain, the USA and the European Community 1968–94* (Aldershot, UK: Avebury, 1995).

———. *Globalization and a Regional Response: The Origins, Development and Impact of the Single European Aviation Market* (London: Routledge, 2007).

———. *Peaceful Air Warfare: The United States, Britain, and the Politics of International Aviation* (Oxford: Clarendon Press, 1991).

———. *The Politics of the Anglo-American Economic Special Relationship* (Brighton, UK, and New York: Harvester Wheatsheaf and St. Martin's, 1988).

———. *U.S. Wartime Aid to Britain* (London: Croom Helm, 1986).

Douhet, Giulio. *The Command of the Air* (New York: Arno Press 1942).

Dworkin, Ronald. *Taking Rights Seriously* (London: Duckworth, 1977).

Freidel, Frank. *Franklin D. Roosevelt: A Rendezvous with Destiny* (New York and Boston: Little Brown, 1990).

Gelman, Irwin F. *Secret Affairs: FDR, Cordell Hull and Sumner Welles* (New York: Enigma Books, 2002).

Groseclose, Elgin. *Fifty Years of Managed Money: The Story of the Federal Reserve* (New York: Macmillan, 1966).

Haight, John McVickar. *American Aid to France* (New York: Atheneum, 1970).

Hamby, Alonzo L. *Man of the People: A Life of Harry S. Truman* (New York: Oxford University Press, 1998).

Josephson, Matthew. *Empire of the Air: Juan Trippe and the Struggle for World Airways* (New York: Arno Press, 1972).

Kimball, Warren F. *Churchill and Roosevelt: The Complete Correspondence, 3 volumes* (London: Collins, 1984).

———. *The Juggler: Franklin Roosevelt as Wartime Statesman* (Princeton, NJ: Princeton University Press, 1991).

Lash, Joseph P. *Roosevelt and Churchill 1939–1941: The Partnership That Saved the West* (London: Andre Deutsch, 1977).

Leuchtenburg, William E. *Franklin D. Roosevelt and the New Deal, 1932–1940* (New York: Harper and Row, 1963).

———. "The Roosevelt Reconstruction: Retrospect," in *Twentieth Century America: Recent Interpretations*, 2nd ed., ed. Barton J. Bernstein and Allen J. Matusow (New York: Harcourt Brace, Jovanovich, 1969).

Louis, William Roger. *Imperialism at Bay: The United States and the Decolonization of the British Empire, 1941–1945* (Oxford: Oxford University Press, 1977).

MacKenzie, David. *Canada and International Civil Aviation 1932–1948* (Toronto: Toronto University Press, 1989).

————. *ICAO: A History of the International Civil Aviation Organization* (Toronto: University of Toronto Press, 2010).

Mahan, Alfred Thayer. *The Influence of Sea Power upon History 1660–1783* (New York: Dover Publications, 1987).

McJimsey, George, ed. *Documentary History of the Franklin D. Roosevelt Presidency, Volume 21: Executive Reorganization 1937–1939* (New York: Lexis Nexis, Reed Elsevier, 2004).

Murray, Robert K. *The Harding Era: Warren G. Harding and His Administration* (Minneapolis: Minnesota University Press, 1969).

Myers, William S., and Walter H. Newton. *The Hoover Administration: A Documented Narrative* (New York: Scribner's, 1936).

Pearson, Lester. *Memoirs 1897–1948: Through Diplomacy to Politics* (London, Victor Gallanz, 1973).

Peterson, Barbara S. *Bluestreak: Inside Jetblue, the Upstart that Rocked the Industry* (New York, Portfolio, 2004).

Pisano, Donald M. *To Fill the Skies with Pilots: The Civilian Pilot Training Program 1939–1949* (Urbana: University of Illinois Press, 1993).

Rawls, John. *A Theory of Justice* (Cambridge, MA: Harvard University Press, 1971).

Rhyne, Charles S. *Civil Aeronautics Act: Annotated with the Legislative History Which Produced It and the Precedents upon Which It Is Based* (Washington, DC: National Law Book Company, 1939).

Roosevelt, James, with Bill Libby. *My Parents: A Different View* (Chicago: Playboy Press, 1976).

Roosevelt, James, with Sidney Shalett. *Affectionately F.D.R.: A Son's Story of a Lonely Man* (Harcourt Brace, 1959).

Rosenman, Samuel I. *Public Papers and Addresses of Franklin D. Roosevelt, 13 volumes* (New York: Random House, 1938–1950).

————. *Working with Roosevelt* (London: Rupert Hart-Davis, 1952).

Sampson, Anthony. *Empires of the Sky: The Politics, Contests and Cartels of World Airlines* (London: Hodder and Staughton, 1984).

Serling, Robert J. *When the Airlines Went to War* (New York: Kensington Books, 1997).

Sherwood, Robert E. *The White House Papers of Harry L. Hopkins: An Intimate History, 2 volumes* (London: Eyre and Spottiswoode, 1949).

Solberg, Carl. *Conquest of the Skies: A History of Commercial Aviation in America* (Boston: Little Brown, 1979).

Smith, John Edward. *FDR* (New York: Random House, 2008).

Stoler, Mark A. *Allies in War: Britain and America against the Axis Powers 1940–1945* (London: Hodder Arnold, 2005).

Taylor, John W. R. et al., eds. *The Guinness Book of Air facts and Feats* (London: Book Club Associates, 1977).

Tedder, A. W. *With Prejudice: The War Memoirs of Marshal of the Royal Air Force Lord Tedder* (London: Cassell, 1966).

Walker, J. Samuel. *Henry A. Wallace and American Foreign Policy* (Westport, CT: Greenwood Press, 1976).

Wheeler-Bennett, J. W. *The Disarmament Deadlock* (London: Routledge, Kegan and Paul, 1934).

Wilbur, R. L. and H. M. Hyde. *The Hoover Policies* (New York, Scribner's, 1937).

Woods, Randall Bennett. *Changing the Guard: Anglo-American Relations 1941–1945* (Chapel Hill: University of North Carolina Press, 1990).

Ybarra, Michael J. *Washington Gone Crazy: Senator Pat McCarran and the Great American Communist Hunt* (Hanover, NH: Steerforth, 2004).

ARTICLES AND CHAPTERS

Dobson, A. P. "Aspects of Anglo-American Aviation Diplomacy 1976–93," *Diplomacy and Statecraft* 4, no. 2 (1993): 235–57.

———. "Regulation or Competition? Negotiating the Anglo-American Air Service Agreement of 1977," *Journal of Transport History* 15, no. 2 (1994): 144–65.

———. "The USA, Hegemony and Airline Market Access to Britain and Western Europe, 1945-96," *Diplomacy and Statecraft* 9, no. 2 (1998): 129–59.

Dobson, A. P., with J. A. McKinney. "Sovereignty, Politics and U.S. International Airline Policy," *Journal of Air Law and Commerce* 74, no. 3 (2009): 527–52.

Haglund, David. "De-lousing Scadta: The Role of Pan American Airways in U.S. Aviation Diplomacy in Colombia, 1939–1940," *Aerospace Historian* 30 (1983): 177–90.

Henrikson, Alan K. "FDR and the 'World-Wide Arena,'" in *FDR's World: War, Peace, and Legacies,* eds. David B. Woolner, Warren F. Kimball, and David Reynolds. (New York: Palgrave, 2008), 35–63.

Megaw, M. R. "The Scramble for the Pacific: Anglo-American Rivalry in the 1930s," *Historical Studies*, 17 (1977): 458–73.

Page, F. Handley. "The Future of the Skyways," *Foreign Affairs*, 22, no. 3 (1944): 404–12.

Pogue, L. Welch. "Aviation as a Law Molding Force," *Nebraska Law Review* 21 (1942): 53–74.

———. "International Civil Air Transport—Transition Following World War Two," MIT Flight Transportation Library Report FTL-R79-6, June 1979, copy courtesy of the author.

———."Personal Recollections from the Chicago Conference: ICAO Then, Now, and in the Future," *Annals of Air Space and Law*, volume XX, 1995, Part I, pp. 35–48.

———. "Some Contributions of Significant Public Service of Enduring Value to Aviation in the United States," June 15, 1999, unpublished article, copy courtesy of the author.

Ray, Deborah Wing. "The Takoradi Routs: Roosevelt's Prewar venture beyond the Western Hemisphere," *Journal of American History* 62, no. 2 (1975): 340–58.

ARCHIVAL SOURCES

UNITED STATES NATIONAL ARCHIVES, WASHINGTON, DC

State Department decimal files
Department of Commerce RG40

FRANKLIN D. ROOSEVELT LIBRARY

FDR Map Room Files
FDR Official Files
FDR Personal Files
FDR President's Secretary Files
FDR Speeches Files
Papers of Adolf A. Berle
Papers of Harry L. Hopkins
Papers of R. Walton Moore
Papers of James Roosevelt
Papers of Samuel I. Rosenman
Papers of James R. Rowe
Papers of Sumner Welles
Pare Lorenz Chronology

JAMES E. CARTER LIBRARY

Files: Staff Offices, Domestic Policy Staff

UNITED STATES LIBRARY OF CONGRESS

Papers of Admiral W. D. Leahy

THE SMITHSONIAN NATIONAL AERONAUTICAL AND SPACE MUSEUM ARCHIVES, WASHINGTON DC

Papers of Juan T. Trippe

BRITISH NATIONAL ARCHIVES

Cabinet Papers
Foreign Office General Correspondence FO 371

BRITISH HOUSE OF LORDS RECORD OFFICE

Papers of Lord Beaverbrook

CANADIAN NATIONAL ARCHIVES

Privy Council Office RG 2
Department of External Affairs RG25
Papers of W. L. Mackenzie King MG26 J
Papers of C.D. Howe MG27 111 B20

WEB SITE SOURCES

www.brattle.com/_documents/Publications/ArticleReport2198.pdf.

GOVERNMENT AND OTHER PRIMARY SOURCE PUBLICATIONS

BRITISH COMMAND PAPERS

"Convention Relating to International Air Transport," *Command. 266,* 1919.
"International Air Transport," *Command Paper 6561,* 1944.
"International Civil Aviation Conference," *Command 6614,* 1944.
"U.S., UK, Civil Air Services Agreement Bermuda," *Command 6747,* 1946.

BRITISH PARLIAMENTARY REPORTS: HANSARD

Complete Presidential Press Conferences of Franklin Delano Roosevelt, 25 volumes (New York: Da Capo Press, 1972).
Foreign Relations of the United States volumes various and published from time to time (U.S. Government Printing Office: Washington, DC).
Public Papers of Herbert Hoover 1929 (Washington, DC: Government Printing Office, 1974).
Report of the Federal Aviation Commission 1935, Summary of Recommendations (Washington, DC: U.S. Government Printing Office, 1935).
Report of the President's Aircraft Board (Morrow Board), November 30, 1926 (Washington, DC: Government Printing Office, 1926).
The Brownlow Report: President's Committee on Administrative Management, Report with Special Studies (Washington, DC: Government Printing Office).

THE CONGRESSIONAL RECORD

Third and Fourth Plans on Government Reorganization, House Documents, Nos. 681 and 692, Seventy-sixth Congress 1940.

EUROPEAN COMMUNITY/UNION DOCUMENTS

COM(2002)649, Final, "Communication from the Commission on the consequences of the Court judgments of 5 November for the European air transport policy," November 19, 2002.

INTERVIEWS BY THE AUTHOR

Welch Pogue, CAB chairman 1942–46, August 1, 2000.
Robert Ebdon, head of government affairs, British Airways, August 15, 1991.
Cyril Murphy, vice president for international affairs, United Airlines, July 1, 1991.

Jeffery Shane, assistant secretary for policy and international affairs, U.S. Department of Transportation, April 5, 1991.

NEWSPAPERS AND EPHEMERA

American Aviation Daily
Chicago Daily Tribune
New York Herald Tribune
New York Journal of Commerce
New York Times
San Francisco Chronicle, Examiner and News
The Airline Pilot
The American Magazine
The Times
Washington Times Herald

INDEX